Behind the Smile:
Orphaned by Hitler's Madness

(Memoir)

Peter R.K. Brenner

Library of Congress Control Number: 2011917196
ISBN: Hardcover   978 - 1 - 4653 - 6819 - 5
                    Softcover   978 - 1 - 4653 - 6818 - 8
                    Ebook   978 - 1 - 4653 - 6820 - 1

This book was printed in the United States of America.

To order additional copies of this book, contact:
Xlibris Corporation
1 - 888 - 795 - 4274
www.Xlibris.com
Orders@Xlibris.com
104020

Contents

ACKNOWLEDGMENTS

My life's journey would never have found its way onto these pages if it had not been for the loving support and ongoing encouragement of Bonnie, my loving wife of forty years, and our two sons - Erik and Tim.

Next, I would like to thank my close friends Liz and Bob Engstrom for editing my drafts - whenever called upon.

Particular thanks go to Dr. Wayne Rollins and Donnalou Rollins for providing insight, guidance and thoughtful suggestions.

Nor will I forget the faithful colleagues of our "Wednesday Night Writer's Group" started by Connie Muther and championed by Rita Reali and George Lillenstein. Throughout the process they diligently guided me through a series of dark moments and enlightened awareness.

A special thanks to Ruth Ennis, who translated German tapes and critical documents to help me stay on course at critical junctures of my journey.

PROLOGUE

I was born Norwegian and orphaned on the war - torn soil of Germany during the winter of 1944. However, for me, life began at the age of five. The world prior to 1949 was a dark hole to be avoided.

But I didn't care . . . or so I believed.

I learned that life's continuum is not always a straight line or smooth. Events, like speed bumps in a parking lot, unexpectedly interrupt a person's journey. This story is about persistent pressures pushing and pulling at lost memories. Eventually, slivers of buried history poked to the surface and into the mainstream of my thinking.

I realized that my mind never completely wiped clean the experiences from my first five years. Rather, like chalk on a blackboard, its residue would repeatedly alarm me. Etched in my memory banks were secrets that would hobble forth from the forgotten region of pain, fear, shame and ridicule. They spoke to me while I slept: nightmares shocking my senses with sounds exploding all around me; images filling my thoughts and challenging my curiosity to examine their meaning; revealed clues guiding my footsteps over soiled history strewn with crying babies and empty faces.

THE DREAM

The car weaved precariously down the narrow mountain road. At every bend, only two wheels managed to hug the curve before smacking down on all fours for the brief straightaway. The young driver pressed down on the accelerator forcing the bulky, green Hudson to speed forward into the night.

"Slow down," the young lady implored. "You're driving too fast."

"I know," was the curt reply.

"Then slow down before you drive this heap into a tree."

"No!" The tone was unwavering in its resolve. The driver snapped his head to the right.

The woman was still there. Her fine features were taut with fear; white knuckles indicated her fingers were pressed firmly into the dashboard; the color drained from her cheeks left a pasty white hue surrounding her hazel eyes, round as marbles; dark waves framed the sides of her face accentuating her wide-eyed look. Her laser stare seared into him, as though it could will him to stay on course.

The car surged toward the oncoming bend in the road.

A sense of urgency highlighted her plea. "Peter, stop this madness. You are going to kill us if you continue driving this way." Then she vanished.

"Peder, keep your eyes on the road! Slow down," the new girl, a teenager, pleaded. "You're frightening me."

The driver blinked and then rubbed his eyes. He gasped in disbelief unable to force his gaze away from the face of the Norwegian girl. Her smooth, silky, light-brown hair spilled generously over her shoulders, complementing her high cheekbones and ruddy complexion. Her hazel eyes mesmerized him. His heart skipped an extra beat every time the two images switched back and forth, like a revolving door.

CHAPTER I

American Bound

"I have come to realize more and more that the greatest disease and the greatest suffering is to be unwanted, unloved, uncared for, to be shunned by everybody, to be just nobody to no one."

Mother Teresa of Calcutta

I remember the day I left Germany for a distant place called America. It's as clear today as it was back then, when life's trial was an evolving adventure. I recall standing motionless and staring at the train tracks with the wide-eyed wonderment of a five-year old. Even now, past scenes jog my memories back to life.

With a sorrowful look, I turned to Tante. "Do I have to go?"

"Yes, it's time. You're going on a great journey that will take you to a far away place called America."

"I don't want to leave; I want to stay with you," I pleaded.

She stooped to my level, and with her eyes tearing she forced a reassuring smile. "I need to stay here and take care of all your friends; and you have to be brave." She captured a runaway tear from my cheek before continuing. "Can you do that for me?"

"I think so." In a fearful tone I asked, "what if I get lost?"

"You won't. Do what you're told and be sure to give them your full name, Peder Rolf Stromnes just as it says in the passport and everything will be fine."

She handed the boy a little red book. "This is very important so keep it where you can find it. People will want to look at it."

"I don't want to go." I pressed against Tante and hugged her with all my might. "I want to be here with you."

"I know," she whispered, "I'll never forget you, but now you're going to be with your very own Mom and Dad. They love you very much and can't wait to have you with them." She gently pried loose my firm grip and extended me to arm length. "We'll meet again someday, I promise." She gave me a kiss, rose, placed me beside Hans (her ground's keeper) and quickly turned to walk away.

I know she was sad, I could see it in her stooped shoulders. I think she didn't want me to see her crying. With a rush in her voice, she said, "Be brave my kleine Pater."

I watched her walk away until she was out of sight. Then, I turned to Hans. "Are you coming with me?" I asked, looking up.

Hans was very, very tall. If I stretched to my fullest and stood on my tiptoes, I could almost touch the belt that held up his baggy trousers.

"No. I've got work to do around the school." He handed me my belongings, which were bundled together and tied securely onto the end of a pole.

The distant whistle of a locomotive turned my head, even before it rumbled into view. My eyes were riveted toward the huge engine as it rolled to a noisy stop - spitting and hissing every inch of the way.

I asked nobody in particular, "Do you know where New York is?"

Ignoring my question, Hans took my hand and walked me to the conductor. They exchanged a few words, punctuated with approving nods. Hans handed over a bundle of papers.

The shorter, older fellow looked down at me over his perfectly round belly. "What's your name, Son?" the conductor asked.

"Peder Rolf Stromnes - Tante said I had to say all three to make sure everyone would know who I was."

"Well, that's a pretty smart idea; you wouldn't want to get lost."

"Lost! Am I going to get lost?" I blurted out.

"Now, now, don't worry; we'll take good care of you." He handed me a bar of chocolate.

I waited until I was seated and the train began moving backward, before I pulled out the chocolate bar and inspected it. I wasn't sure what it would taste like. I liked the smell and decided to take a bite. The creamy texture and sweet taste was new, but I enjoyed it.

I spent most of the ride looking out the window. On occasion, the conductor stopped by to say hello. I didn't leave my seat too often, because I was afraid he wouldn't be able to find me. My aching muscles accentuated my discomfort - the trip was very long.

I have no memory of how I got from the train station to the airport. I do recall buildings flashing by my window and people all around me talking about a place called Munich and later Frankfort. I'd never seen such crowds, buildings and cars in my entire life. I felt queasy with all the newness tumbling into my life and being shuffled between different people, of whom none were very talkative or pleasant.

By the time we arrived at the airport, my stomach was growling; every muscle groaned its disapproval of the trip and I had to go to the bathroom. After explaining my predicament to a uniformed guard, he took my hand and we wove our way across a corridor crowded with people. "That's the bathroom; I'll wait for you here." I entered a smelly cubical room. The stench almost stopped my urge. I did my business and then hurried out for some fresh air.

The airport was intimidating. I found it difficult to keep up with the long-legged guard, because the wrappings around my feet were coming loose. He seemed in such a hurry. We eventually stopped at a counter where he handed over a pile of papers to another gruff looking official. He focused his attention on a small, red document, examining it very carefully. On occasion, they would break off their conversation, look at me and then continue talking.

"Ready to get onto the plane?" the fellow with the ticket asked.

"What's a plane?" I responded.

"You'll see in a minute." When they finished their conversation, he nudged me along with a guiding push.

A long passageway directed a crowd of us toward a set of steps leading out doors. After a short walk from the terminal to the plane, I climbed a long set of stairs that took me into the belly of a new experience - a plane. Suddenly, out of the darkness, the most beautiful woman I'd ever seen took my hand. She knelt down to my level and gave me a big smile. Her eyes were sky, blue and she had the shiniest, longest sandy - blonde hair.

"I'm Kara and I'm going to take care of you. Okay?"

"Okay," I said with a smile extending the full width of my face. I was already beginning to feel better.

Once within the seating area of the airplane, all I could see were rows of heads perched beside each other. I felt relieved when a few rose and they were attached to a body. Kara lifted me onto a seat wide enough for me to curl up and sleep in - if I'd wanted to.

She glanced at the piece of paper I'd extended toward her. "Now listen carefully, Peder." Her serious look was directed straight at me. I could tell she was about to say something very important. "You have to stay in your seat until I say you can leave. I need to help some other passengers get settled in, but I'll be back as soon as I can. Do you understand?"

"Yes," I promised. "What if I want something?"

"Contact any person who is wearing the same kind of outfit I've got on. We're all here to help make your trip to America fun." Her warm smile and quick wink assured me not to worry. I watched her walk away, admiring her blue and white uniform. I especially liked her bright, red shoes.

Whenever possible, Kara would stop by to say hello, and bring me snacks to eat and assorted drinks. Later, when the lights lowered and the area became quieter, she rewrapped the cloth around my feet, tucked me in a blanket and read me a story. I wish I could remember it.

"It's a long trip," she said, "So try and get some sleep. Before you know it we'll be in New York City, where you're going to meet your new mom and dad. Isn't that great?"

"I don't know. I guess so." I fussed around like a little puppy trying to get comfortable. It wasn't long before I'd curled myself into a tight ball. I looked up at Kara and said, "I wish you could be my mom."

She flashed me her warm smile and with a quick wink answered; "Think of me as a great friend who likes you a lot." She stooped over and gave me a peck on my forehead.

"Thanks." I closed my eyes and felt safe. It had been a long, tiring day and I was very tired. After a bit, I fell asleep amidst the little noises all around me, and the steady droning of the engine.

Kara nudged me awake. "We're here, Peder; time to get off the plane."

The plane ride was fun. What's not to enjoy when you receive attention from an attentive stewardess? But things were about to change.

I arrived in New York City on May 18 wearing a tattered pair of trousers cut from an old G.I. blanket and makeshift cloths covered my feet. A used t-shirt covered my chest and shoulders. Once off the plane, I wasn't prepared for the throng of people rushing all around me. I was petrified when Kara handed me over to a grumpy old man who waddled so fast, I was running to keep up with him. I felt bounced around like a rubber ball on a playground. I wanted to cry, but knew that wouldn't be brave, so I didn't. I remember Tante telling me, "Be brave Peder, it's the best way to make it through difficult times."

Nothing seemed familiar, which made the movement of time flow as slowly as molasses. I was startled when I suddenly recognized two remotely familiar faces. The couple before me crouched down to my level - welcoming me with open arms. When I got closer, the man was speaking a funny - sounding German, but I understood him. I hadn't uttered a single word to anyone since I spoke to Kara. I wasn't even sure if any sound would spill out of my mouth.

A young, slender lady with wavy brown hair brushing against the nape of her neck spoke next. She appeared short, slender, with dark, round eyes and delicate features. It was even harder to understand her German, but I knew what she was trying to say - she was happy to see me. Her words were brief but clear. "Do you want to be our son?" she asked, with a soft smile, in broken German.

I nodded, not knowing how else to answer. She beckoned and I awkwardly walked into her outstretched arms. Everything around me was loud and confusing, but I understood her firm hug and felt safe.

The man offered me a ride on his shoulders and I accepted. From my higher perch, I could finally see where I was going and what was happening all around me. I felt better gliding above the rushing flow of people. Now at least, I wouldn't be trampled to death. It was a long trek to their parked car, but once inside the quietness felt calming.

I wasn't wearing any shoes, just wraps that had finally unraveled. The lady reached for my feet, but I quickly withdrew them. She spoke to me but I couldn't understand anything she said. I looked at the man who gave me the ride on his shoulders. He smiled and said, "I'll tell you what they're saying."

"Would you like a pair of new shoes?" she asked.

"Shoes?"

"Yes, for your feet."

With a sense of bewilderment, I asked, "For me?"

"What's your favorite color?" the man added.

"Red. During my plane ride," I continued, "the lady who watched out for me, she wore red shoes."

"Then red it will be," he trumpeted.

A police car's siren blared as it sped by us. I pressed against the woman and buried my face in her blouse.

"Art, he's shaking," she implored.

"Just hold him, he'll be okay. God only knows what sirens remind him of."

"I think it relates to the war experiences he had as an infant," the woman, Trudy, suggested. "As a psychology major in college, I remember reading case studies that explained how infants, hearing loud sounds or sudden explosions, recalled the fear years later."

"When the children grow older do they remember why they're frightened?" Art continued with piqued interest.

"Over time and with lots of counseling some of the children became aware of the source of their anxiety."

"Poor little fellow." The man reached over and began rubbing my back; I flinched but kept silent about my discomfort whenever somebody touched my shoulders. I didn't want them to know of the beatings all of us received at the orphanage. I felt that if I wasn't brave they might not want to keep me. The woman pressed me closer to her side; I began to relax.

The screaming sirens repeatedly interrupted the stillness of our ride. Finally, we located a shoe store in midtown Manhattan. Once inside, I began to settle down and loosen my grip of the lady's hand. I directed my full attention toward a monstrous rack of shoes. The rows extended from the floor to the ceiling and wrapped around three walls.

I looked around before uttering my first words since the frightening blare of the sirens, "Do they have any red ones?"

The first task was trying to find a size that fit my small feet. It wasn't long, however, before I was shoehorned into a shiny pair of red shoes. I liked them so much; I wouldn't take them off - even to put on a pair of socks. They were on my feet and I wasn't about to lose the first real shoes I'd ever worn.

Exiting the city was an adventure. I sat on the woman's lap and never took my eyes away from the window. The buildings were higher than I could see and when we entered a long tunnel, I shut my eyes until the woman assured me it was safe to open them. Once away from the city, we stopped for a bite to eat. I ate an entire hamburger, spooned in all the ice cream set before me and slurped down a soda that made me burp.

When we got back into the car, the man held up a box. "We have one more gift for you. Are you ready?" We all smiled together.

"Ready? Open the package."

I did. Inside, buried deep within a mound of shredded paper, I uncovered a stuffed monkey. He had a round head with two red marble eyes and a big, pencil - thin grin, a soft, reddish terrycloth body and a long tail.

"His name is Curious George. Tante told us you were a curious boy, so we thought you might like a friend to cuddle up to when you go to bed," the lady said in a whisper.

At first I didn't know what to say. This was the first true gift I'd ever received that I could call my very own. I looked at the man and then the woman sitting beside him. I carefully peered into their eyes and softly said, "Thank you . . . Mom; thank you . . . Dad." I hugged them both and then snuggled between the two of them with Curious George tucked securely under my left arm.

Once on the road, the hum of the car lulled me to sleep. I didn't wake up until the next morning.

It was May 19, 1949, my first full day in America.

We lived in a trailer park on the outskirts of McGuire Air Force Base, Fort Dix, New Jersey. It served as government housing for lower-ranking officers. My dad was a lieutenant. I loved the trailer because I was never too far away from my parents. We always ate together during breakfast and dinner and I slept on a couch only six paces from their sleeping area. We stayed there for a little over three months and I seldom felt alone. On occasion, however, loneliness crept inside me.

At first, when the lights went out and the crickets chattered throughout the night and the brightness of the moon slipped around the edges of the drawn curtain, I drifted back to Germany. Of all the memories a particular one emerged on a regular basis.

One day, a man and woman went on a fieldtrip with all the children and Tante. We hiked to the first meadow of a tall mountain to enjoy its beauty and get away from the heat of the lowlands. When we returned home, I saw Tante engaged in a smile-filled conversation with the couple, who had spent the entire day with us. Before they left, the man came up to me and shook my hand. The lady tried to kiss me, but I withdrew. I wasn't sure what she was going to do - in a blink they were gone.

It took me longer to forget them. They were different from the other visitors who would slip in, look around and then rush out. When someone wanted to look me over, Tante wouldn't let anyone poke or jab at the various parts of my body or examine my teeth - which I disliked the most. If a finger made its way into my mouth, I expressed my displeasure with a firm bite. The couple that stayed with us on the meadow were always friendly, however, eventually they too left. I don't remember ever seeing them again but there smiling faces were always in my mind.

As always, sadness touched each of us when a friend stopped showing up for breakfast or disappeared after lunch. On occasion, I'd wonder if any person would ever pick me out of the group. I began to believe no one would ever want me. The passage of time was bearable only because I loved my Tante and the things she taught us in school.

*   *   *

Now, I was glad to be in America and living with this man and woman, but I missed my Tante. On the hardest nights, I would bury my face into the pillow and press against Curious George for added reassurance. I didn't want my new parents to hear me crying. I didn't want them to send me away.

Late in August, we received a notice upgrading our accommodations. We were being moved out of the trailer park and into family housing, located on the outskirts of a little community called Wrightstown, New Jersey. It didn't take us long to transport our meager belongings into the modest two-story apartment. Dad explained to me why we had been awarded a better place to live; "I've been selected as the new Base Chaplain."

At the time, I had no idea what he was talking about.

The tiny apartment felt like a castle to me. I even had my own room, which I didn't have to share with a bunch of other kids. The room also had a door that opened and closed, but I seldom closed it - and never at night. The trailer was great, but now I had my own private space.

Our new dwelling was ready in time for the start of school. Since I could barely speak or understand the language, I was placed in kindergarten with Miss Manyon.

The first few months, Mom sat in the class and served as my interpreter. We would walk to school together and then stop at a store for some treats on the way home from school. She always let me have a cone filled with a scoop of walnut ice cream. By Christmas, I was proficient enough in English to attend class without my mom being present. After the holidays, I was told some disturbing news. Dad was transferred to an overseas assignment. Mom told me it was in a place called Korea. I felt the nagging notion that I was responsible for my dad leaving us.

Next to my mom and Tante, Miss Manyon was the kindest and most wonderful woman I'd ever known - even more than the stewardess. She instructed all her students, "Never consider any question dumb."

That was important to me because I was filled with questions and she patiently answered every single one, with a knowing, encouraging smile. After awhile, classmates began communicating with me and including me in their group projects. What I appreciated most was my teacher's willingness to work with me on an individual basis. I could always go to her for help.

I didn't make many friends during my kindergarten year, but still managed to enjoy the class activities. By year's end, I understood the language very well, but was weak in my speaking ability. I particularly hated my pronounced German accent. Some of the older boys didn't like it either.

At the end of my kindergarten experience, Miss Manyon recommended I skip over first and be allowed to enter second grade. I did so with some reluctance. My second year began without the watchful and attentive care of Miss Manyon, my mom or any new friends. Mostly, I missed my dad.

It took some explaining from Mom to convince me everything would be all right. She kept reassuring me that Dad needed to be in Korea to help the men and women who were fighting a war called The Korean Conflict. "That is why he needs to be away," she reiterated.

"Why?" I asked again.

"It's part of his job," she responded.

"I don't like him being gone."

"I know it's hard on all of us."

"Will he get hurt?" I persisted.

"I hope not. We'll pray every night that he will be safe. Okay?" She hugged me so hard, I knew she was worried.

Dad was good about writing and mailed us letters on a weekly basis. Whenever his letters arrived, we'd immediately snuggle up together on the living room couch; Mom would read and I'd listen to the stories retold from the pages laid out before us. I paid particularly attention to the stories about the little Korean children he'd picked up off the streets, late at night. Their parents had been killed and begging for food was the only way the boys and girls could get something to eat. He referred to them as orphans. At the end of each story, Mom would explain to me that I too had been an orphan. I always felt sad for the children and wondered if they would ever find their mom or dad. Each night before I went to bed, we would both pray for my dad's safety, all our friends and the orphans. It made me feel both happy and sad at the same time.

In a sense, I was fighting my own war at school. During recess, I was invited to play only when there were war games. In every battle, I was killed as the evil Nazi soldier. I hated the game, but it was the only time I wasn't left alone on the playground. Two of the third-grade boys were bullies; they always taunted me, made fun of my accent and called me hurtful names - like kraut or Nazi.

It was during this time that Mom taught me the phrase, "Sticks and stones may break your bones, but names can never hurt you."

The hardest time of the school day for me was getting to class. To walk from the housing area to the school, I had to cross an empty lot. Most mornings, the two bullies waited until I was halfway across the field before they came after me. Even though I was quick, on occasion they'd catch me. They'd knock me to the ground and then start kicking and hitting me. I had to give them some credit, they were always careful not to bruise my face or any part of my exposed body. I was quick to pick up on that maneuver. I made a point of wearing shorts and short-sleeved shirts - even when it was cold.

I never told Mom or Miss Manyon about the bullies; I was too ashamed. When my bruises were discovered, I explained it away as a playground accident or being clumsy. I don't think Mom believed me.

I figured it was my problem to resolve. I came up with a few good ideas. First, making friends with the crosswalk guard was a must; second, switching around my departure time for going to school; third, finding alternative routes to take. On occasion, I hid in the weeds and made a dash to a spot where the crossing guard would be looking for me. If the bullies were close on my heels, he'd blow a whistle and stop them in their tracks. This would give me enough time to zip by him, run across the street and into school before they could catch me. It was a cat and mouse game, which I eventually won. One week, I was dodging around to avoid them, the next their harassment stopped. I think the crossing guard threatened to tell their parents what was going on.

The incidents with the bullies and being ignored on the playground made me more determined than ever to lose my German accent and hide the fact I wasn't an American. I hated being picked as the German soldier. It drove me to work diligently for good grades (which found me a small group of friends), and to seek out classmates who lived in my neighborhood. But above all, I vowed never to utter another German syllable - even at home.

By third grade, I appeared as fully American as a kid could get. I dressed like all my classmates, my accent was completely gone and some of the boys and girls started asking me to be on their team or work on their school projects.

Halfway through my third year of schooling in Wrightstown, my dad's being gone bothered me more and more. My discontent and questions became persistent. Mom tried to address my mounting concerns with patience and reassurance.

"There's a war going on and he needs to be away a while longer."

"Why can't he be home with us?" I pleaded.

"It's his job and people over there need him."

"I don't like him being gone. Is it my fault?"

"I know it's hard for all of us. And no, it's not your fault." She cupped my face in her hands. "We have to have patience. Soon we'll all be back together again as a family."

Like water coming to a boil, my emotions ran over. "I don't believe you," I screamed. I ran into my room, slammed the door and cried for hours. I felt abandoned when Dad left for Korea and responsible for his leaving us.

During the winter of my third year in Wrightstown, Mom ran into my room waving a letter in the air. "Your dad was promoted to Major!"

"Is that good?" I asked.

"It means that he's doing a great job. I think it's related to the special project he has been involved in."

"Project? I don't know what you mean, Mom."

"It's all in the letters he's been mailing us. It's the children, Peter."

Dad was good about corresponding with us. We would receive one or two letters every week. As the months turned into his first full year, he began sharing information about a special project he had undertaken. His writings were filled with news about orphans he'd found on the streets of Onyang. With each new letter, Mom would retell and update this unusual story unfolding amidst the conflict in Korea. After awhile, I knew the tale as well as she. In the oral tradition, we strung the letter's messages together in chronological fashion. It was an adventure so fascinating I had it memorized.

At dusk, Dad and his Korean driver would take a jeep into the neighboring town. Once there, children by the dozen would run up to them begging for food, clothes and even money. Dad's driver would tell the children to scat and go home. A handful would remain, buzzing around the jeep like mosquitoes, even after the older kids had been shooed away. My dad asked them, "Why are you still hanging around?"

Each of them explained they had no place to go or parents to be with. They were struggling to figure out how to stay alive.

Hearing the heart - wrenching stories of how each of them had lost their parents moved him to act. He piled the smallest of the children into the back of his jeep and, under the blanket of darkness, slipped onto the airbase. Once safely in, he drove them to a large tent, which he'd set up the night before on the outskirts of the military grounds, filled it with borrowed cots and proceeded to hide the children from the military command.

As the soldiers became aware of my dad's efforts, they secretly smuggled in food, clothes, blankets and an assortment of games for the children. Everyone knew it was illegal with the potential of severe consequences if the operation were discovered under the very nose of the base commander.

Every week, Dad would venture back into town looking for orphaned children between the ages of three and six. More quickly, than expected, the numbers jumped into the forty-plus zone and kept on growing. Dad knew his days of concealing the project were limited - there were too many orphans to clothe, feed and keep concealed. Only one viable option made sense: bring the base commander into the picture.

My dad's primary hope rested on the knowledge that the General was a regular Sunday morning worshiper; he attended the midweek Bible study and was a man of abiding faith. Over the first year of the war, their relationship grew into a deep, mutual respect for the other's responsibilities. Finally the day arrived. Everybody was nervous, mostly for Chaplain Brenner and the children.

Over and over my dad wrote, "What I'm doing is right. All I can do now is leave it in God's hands and pray the General embraces my vision - building an orphanage."

When the Base Commander arrived, he stood before the tent filled with orphans. He stood straight and tall, barely a muscle twitching as he took in the stories. When finished, the C.O. turned to my dad and spoke with an air of authority, which cemented people in their tracks.

"This is what chaplains are supposed to do. Whatever you need, I'll support you. Call my aide and set up an appointment to see me as soon as possible, in my office." As quickly as he had arrived, he walked away.

Whenever Mom told the story she started to cry.

"Why are you crying?" I asked. "Isn't Dad doing something good?"

Mom used my Dad's humanitarian effort as a springboard to begin talk about orphans and my early beginnings. I was nearing my 8th birthday and just starting to get an inkling how my life had actually started before the train ride carried me out of Prien, the town in Germany where I had lived with Tante. She explained that my birth parents were Norwegian; I was born in Germany and orphaned because of the war. At the time, I couldn't comprehend how she was connecting the importance of what Dad was doing in Korea with what she had just told me. She impressed upon me how giving lost children new hope was what they had done for me. In the same breath, she wanted me to know how fortunate they were to have found me in Germany, and how we were now a family.

I was happy to have her as my mom and I told her so. I wasn't sure what to say about being an orphan. I knew I didn't like feeling like a German. It was disgusting. It did, however, get me to thinking about my past. Why weren't there a flood of memories to recall? I could feel anger, disgust and confusion weaving together into a tight knot in my stomach and I didn't know if I should even try to untie it. I thought it best to ignore what I couldn't understand. I decided to bury this knowledge hoping to drop it in some dark hole deep enough to be forgotten.

It wasn't to be.

During late spring of 1952, we received an amazing letter. Dad had just been given the option of reducing his active duty time in Korea by extending his tour of duty overseas. If we wanted, we could be reunited again as a family by joining him in Japan. Mom talked about the move during lunch and we agreed it would be a wonderful opportunity to learn more about another culture. During the week, she managed to telephone Dad and discuss the options available to us.

I came home from school one day and saw Mom so fidgety, I guessed she had important and urgent news pressing to burst forth from behind her beaming smile.

"We're headed for Japan," she told me enthusiastically.

It seemed like my whole life was a series of new adventures. Dad was excited, Mom was elated and I was more than ready to leave Wrightstown, New Jersey.

Dad had his orders extended for another eighteen months and our departure date was set for three months down the road - just in time for summer. I remember looking at the map and thinking that Japan was on the other side of our world globe.

YAKOTA, JAPAN

"My tour of duty in Yokota, Japan will encompass all of your fourth - grade year and a portion of the fifth." My dad stumbled over his words in an effort to put a positive spin on a new situation. It was okay with me. I was more concerned with how to make new friends in a foreign country.

Eighteen months was barely enough time to scrape the surface of the culture, traditions and beauty of this unique country known as "The Land of the Rising Sun." I was fascinated by the people: their almond-shaped eyes, slight builds, shiny black hair, the way they greeted people with a bow, managed to eat with chopsticks, could sleep on the floor in homes with paper - thin sliding doors and removed their footwear before entering their homes. Everywhere I turned, my senses were filled with pagoda-shaped buildings, the fragrance of cherry blossoms, exquisite flowers of every imaginable color, sand art, men pulling rickshaws to transport people through the crowded streets and narrow alleyways, strange but beautiful music and the captivating eloquence of the snow-capped Mount Fuji. While in Japan, I also learned how to swim, and play third base for a little league baseball team. If there was anything negative to speak of, it was a discovery Mom made. She noticed that whenever I did a lot of reading or we went on long car rides during the night; my right eye would begin to ache. On occasion, I'd even get severe headaches. She decided to ask an ophthalmologist about her concerns.

After an extensive eye exam, we discovered I had a weak left eye. The doctor was very considerate to take the time to explain what might have happened to bring about this condition.

"It is commonly referred to as a lazy eye (Amblyopic) because the muscles in the stronger eye compensated for the weaker eye by doing most of the work."

The doctor went on to explain, in greater detail, the possible causes that could have resulted in my having this eye condition. First, he reassured us that the eye was not diseased. The next few minutes were unnerving to hear. He explained that the brain for some reason, does not fully acknowledge the images seen by the amblyopic eye. It appeared to him that my condition was a neurological active process. The loss of vision takes place in the brain. If one eye sees clearly and the other sees a blur, the brain can inhibit (block, ignore, suppress) the eye with the blur (hence lazy eye). Anything that interferes with clear vision in either eye during the critical period of birth to 6 years of age can cause an Amblyopic condition. The most common causes of lazy eye are constant strabismus (continuous turning of one eye) and blockage of an eye due to cataract or trauma.

I could see that the word trauma caught my mom's attention. I wondered if she would tell me what was on her mind and explain what the doctor was saying.

"That would explain his headaches, Mrs. Brenner," the doctor continued, "Your son didn't receive proper medical attention in time to catch his Amblyopic condition. I also suspect, his lack of a balanced diet exacerbated the weakening of the muscles in his left eye."

"Is it too late to be corrected?"

"Not completely, we may be able to regain some muscle strength. Right now his left eye is at 20/200 and the right eye an exceptional 20/15."

With an added tinge of hopefulness in her voice, Mom asked, "How?"

"We can put a patch over his stronger eye and see if the weaker muscles in the left eye will strengthen some." The doctor leaned back in his chair before continuing. "Because the treatment is being administered so late, I doubt that the improvement will be too dramatic."

"Why?"

"The patch or frosted eye glass should have been implemented before Peter reached the age of five; eye muscles are fairly developed by then."

"Will he require an operation?" Mom inquired.

That got my attention in a hurry. The doctor could see the apprehension appear, as my ashen face accompanied a set of already clammy, cold hands.

He smiled. "No, an operation won't be necessary."

"What will happen to my eye?" I interjected.

"When we take the patch off the strong eye, it will start doing the work of seeing again. The left eye will revert to being lazy," he explained.

"Should my son try the patch or frosted glasses?"

"I'd recommend it for several months. It might improve the muscle strength enough to give Peter better depth perception than he now has. It's worth a try."

For the next nine months, I wore some combination of a patch or frosted glasses that covered my right eye. I still swam, was able to play baseball, and learned to accept my condition. I could see, and that was what was most important to me.

More importantly, the discovery and living in a foreign country tweaked my curiosity about my years as an orphan. For the first time, I began wondering about those empty years and the effects it might have had on me. Mom could sense my interest and for the first time just touched upon a period of my life I'd heard little or nothing important enough to remember.

The doctor's visit was a strange ending to an exciting tour of Japan.

SPOKANE, WASHINGTON

During the winter of 1954 our family was transferred back to mainland America. George Wright Air Force Base was on the western outskirts of Spokane, Washington in the northeast corner of the state. Again, I didn't know anyone or the details of the area we were settling into. More disconcerting, I was about to walk smack into the formidable wall of another school year as a stranger.

Departing and arriving in the middle of my 5th grade year was stressful. When you leave, early roots are snipped before any relationships can take hold; Arriving late into an established setting makes it twice as difficult to make new friends: cliques have been established; popular classes are filled; and program quotas have no breathing room for expansion. In Yokota, Japan the elementary school was located on the airbase. In Spokane, all military dependents were bused into town and distributed among the town's various public schools.

It was January; the ground was already covered with snow the height of a small car and it was freezing. The challenge lying before me seemed impossible to overcome. My first winter month felt like enforced isolation: The snow was deep, the wind cutting and Mom bundling me up like a mummy; but mostly the feeling came from within the halls of a school filled with strange faces. The sense of loneliness was becoming all too familiar.

Adjusting and adapting were more than just words; they were becoming a way of life. The isolation and loneliness is heightened if you're an only child. My dad would say, "Peter, you can stay home and feel sorry for yourself or get out in the world and make positive things happen." It was here that I learned a very important lesson. I needed to find a quick way to be accepted into a new group. Sports became my vehicle for acceptance. I worked hard to become an excellent baseball player and also earn good grades. One or the other invariably served as a means for developing a viable pool of friends.

I also learned how the military way of life is an overt expression of a caste system: the higher the rank or command position, the better your benefits. We were rewarded with housing in an elite area of the base reserved for commanding officers and department heads. As the new base chaplain, Dad was granted the privilege of a home among upper-tier officers. Our brick house looked and felt like a mansion. It was larger than the combined spaces of our trailer, the Wrightstown apartment and our house in Japan. We were the youngest family in the neighborhood. Dependents my age were scarce.

I decided to create my own private world. It was filled with piano lessons, playing with our new family addition - an Alsatian Husky that looked more like a wolf than a typical German Shepherd - climbing apple trees in our backyard and inventing solo games to occupy my mind and time. I spent hours shooting marbles, riding my bike around the streets and reading.

Eventually, I got tired of being by myself, so I set my mind on finding a friend. The unlikely connection was a nickname. Everybody in school called my math partner T.J. One day, during class, he referred to me as P.K. (Preacher's Kid). From that moment on, we became the best of friends. On weekends, he'd come to the base and we'd explore the woods around our house, pick and fill containers with raspberries, climb apple trees, and bike to the pool for an afternoon swim. Every day after school, we'd walk to the diner owned by T.J.'s parents. His dad always greeted me with a hamburger and large vanilla shake. In turn, he knew his son enjoyed visiting me at the base.

The move to Washington State was a turning point in my life. In the early spring of 1955, I enrolled in a class to prepare for the honor of becoming a naturalized citizen. My German accent had long since disappeared. My friendship with T.J. inadvertently revealed a means for concealing my past from even the closest of friends. T.J. wanted to know more about me, and I had to figure out how to answer his questions without being dishonest. His questions were innocent enough, but my answers were evasive.

"P.K., do you like being a military brat?"

"It's alright. I really don't know anything else. Do you want to live here all your life, in one place?" I asked.

"Sure, but I like the way you get to see so many different places."

"It sure keeps me hopping around."

"Peter, with all the moving around you did, do you know where you were born?"

I hesitated, trying to formulate an answer. T.J. was my best friend and it wouldn't be fair if I weren't honest; I also didn't want him to think I was a German. It was then that a classmate of mine in Japan popped into my head. He was born in Rome, Italy but was an American citizen from Texas. T.J.'s questions, coupled with the knowledge of what I'd learned from an earlier friend, provided me with a safe explanation.

"I was born in Germany," I stated matter-of-factly.

"Wow. In Germany," T.J. blurted with wide - eyed astonishment. "Are you a German?"

"T.J., you have to realize lots of kids in the military are born overseas, but are still Americans."

"How can that be?"

"Easy. They are part of the military, which makes them American citizens even if they're born overseas."

"That's unbelievable. Imagine, born in another country but still an American."

"It gets complicated, but that's basically what happens to many of us."

We slurped down the last of our milkshakes and switched to more immediate matters - like taking a walk to the river that flowed through the center of town. It was fun watching all the fishermen reel in their catches. For some of them, I guessed it was going to be supper for the family. I felt content leaning over the bridge's railing observing the rippling water and all the activity along the embankment. Mostly, I was pleased with myself for finding a way to hide my embarrassment and not losing a friend.

In the fall of 1954, Mom and Dad had spoken to me about becoming a naturalized United States citizen. It would require my attending classes, studying for a test and then being sworn in by a circuit judge. By April of 1955, I would have lived in the United States for five years and be eligible to enroll in the program.

One evening, Dad pulled out a metal container from the back of a closet and began shuffling through its contents. With a sense of satisfaction, he pulled out a small, red passport.

"Know what this is son?" He held it up for me to see.

I looked at the red cover and shook my head, "I'm not sure. Maybe?"

Dad handed the official document over to me. I inspected it with great interest. The size and redness of the booklet appeared familiar to me - like I'd seen it somewhere before. Finally it came to me: The passport in my hand was one of many official documents Hans first exchanged with the train conductor and later with a guard, who presented to an airport official before I boarded the airplane in Frankfurt, Germany, headed for America.

I opened the gold - lettered document and stared. On the inside cover was a picture of a 5-year old boy. I asked, "Is it me?"

"Yes." Dad came closer and pointed to the embossed area. "This is proof that your natural parents were Norwegian."

I carefully weighed my next question. "I'm Norwegian, not German?" I looked at my parents, alarmed at the sudden burst of energy accompanying the words from my mouth. "Why didn't you tell me?"

"We did, but now you're older and can better grasp the importance of what you're holding in your hand and what we tried to tell you," Dad explained.

Mom pointed to the picture. "That's how you looked when you got off the plane in New York. You had longish blond hair shaped like a bowl with thick bangs," she said with a chuckle.

"I'm glad you gave me a haircut," I said with a hint of a smile.

"You're going to become a naturalized citizen of American, son. We felt this was the right time for you to know that the blood flowing through your veins is 100 percent Norwegian."

I felt a lump in my throat as I rubbed my fingers slowly over the embossed lettering. After a few moments I said, "I'm glad," then looked up at my parents and added, "Thanks."

Later that evening, as I was getting ready for bed, I looked at myself in the mirror. I had just splashed a handful of ice - cold water on my face. The evening ritual invariably accentuated what appeared to be a scar creasing the left side of my cheek. I ran my forefinger down the length of the cut. For whatever reason, it appeared more prominent this night - and that bothered me.

I began exploring the thought of not being permitted to become an American citizen. Surely the scar wouldn't be enough evidence to reveal that I was an orphan born in Germany. What if they disliked me because I was born in Germany during World War II? Would they believe I was a Norwegian? I wondered if I had any German accent that would betray me; what if they saw the scar. Could the blemish link me to something ugly? What if it disqualified me from becoming an American?

I finished my routine and headed off to bed with my head filled with disturbing "what if" thoughts. Once under the covers, I closed my eyes - only to wrestle with my restless spirit. Tossing and turning, I drifted off into a fitful state - somewhere between a deep rest and semi - wakefulness.

I found myself staring at a room filled with children standing at the foot of their cots. The head of the beds were pressed against the wall, arranged side-by-side, and lining both sides of a long, barracks like room. They were waiting quietly, patiently for the large woman, dressed in white from head to foot, to pass before them. She carried a shortened horsewhip tightly in her right hand, pressed against her leg, all the while wearing a dour look on her face. On occasion, she'd slap the switch against her thigh - cracking the stillness of the room. A few paces behind her walked a bullish man with gnarled fingers and a pimply face. A mousy woman dutifully trailed him. The bulky fellow was inspecting individual orphans who caught his attention. He was gruff and the woman was silent. As they marched down the line, they eventually stopped before a slender boy, who must have been about four. The woman in white barked out instructions as the man poked and jabbed at the boy's arm, shoulders and side. The child turned away, slapped at the man's hand and tried to step back, only to bump into his bed. It was obvious the orphan didn't like what they were doing. The man called the little boy a "bastard," grabbed his face and forced open his mouth. He resisted, incurring the wrath of the bulky woman, who repeatedly struck the kid's back and shoulders with her whip. The bully continued to pry open the mouth. He began to probe the boy's teeth and tongue with his dirty fingers. Suddenly, the man screamed, pulling out his bleeding finger. He backhanded the orphan to the floor. With her switch, the witch continued striking the back of the fallen child. In defiance, he turned to look at her. She lashed at his face, opening a deep wound across the left cheek. The brute turned and grasping his bloody finger stomped out of the room with the mousy woman stumbling to remain close on his heels. The housemother raised her arm and the whip came down a second time, drawing blood. The room erupted in defiance with screams, crying, yelling and banging on the floor. The child lay on the floor, holding the side of his face and glaring at the woman in white.

I opened my eyes and felt my heart pounding with the force of a hammer. I screamed and held a hand over the left side of my face, rocking uncontrollably until I felt someone holding me. It was my mom.

Becoming An American

I was one of only two children in the Naturalization class, but that didn't bother me. What was unnerving was when I first entered the room each person seemed to be speaking a different language. It sounded like the chatter of little birds. When the instructor came into the room, I shut out all the noise and concentrated on listening to what he was about to say. I wanted to learn as much as possible about the history of the United States and its form of government, so I could become a citizen.

We learned an array of fascinating facts about the political make up of the country: what constituted the three branches of government; how the checks-and-balances system worked; the importance of leaders like George Washington, Thomas Jefferson, Ben Franklin and Abraham Lincoln. I liked President Lincoln the most and was very impressed with the U.S. Senate. Since there were only two U.S. senators per state, I felt they must be really important. We had to know who the state governor was, as well as the mayor of Spokane. Everybody memorized the Pledge of Allegiance and the words to God Bless America. I was infatuated with the history of the pilgrims coming over on the Mayflower and settling in Plymouth . . . The fight for Independence . . . the Civil War . . . and President Franklin D. Roosevelt's New Deal.

I memorized every story set before me. I was confident with what I knew. However, it was a sleepless night which proceeded my historic day.

I was one month and three days shy of being 11 years old. At 4'4" and 70 pounds, I anchored myself firmly in the front row, facing an imposing podium. It loomed before me like a mountain. Without warning, and as loud as the crack of thunder, a uniformed man bellowed, "Everybody rise for the Honorable Judge Sam M. Driver." In one motion, every person in the courtroom was standing.

The judge wore a long black robe. He quickly scanned the 128 members of the new class standing before him before settling an extra moment on Rachael, who was ten years old, and me. We both were born in Germany. A faint smile creased his face as he asked everyone to be seated. In unison, we sat. I can't remember everything he said, but was absolutely certain he looked right at me. I adjusted my tie, but wished I could have been invisible. Before Court Clerk Stanley D. Taylor swore us in, Judge Driver reminded us of our duties as citizens of the United States:

"You must exercise your voting privilege, serve on juries when called upon and take an interest in your government. Your vote must be intelligent and informed; you are responsible for knowing the candidates and the issues. The people who represent you in Congress look to you for guidance. It is up to you to form a well thought out opinion on public matters."

He went on talking about a social order and how members of a community are dependent, to a certain extent, on others. I have to admit his droning made my eyelids heavy. His final statement, however, gave me chills.

"By the authority duly invested upon me by the United States District Court, Spokane, Washington, I hereby declare each of you on this 15th day of April, 1955, citizens of the United States of America."

With a final declaration, he pounded his gavel with authority on the top of the podium; I was handed an important - looking document. I stared at it before turning my head in search of my parents. They were right where I'd left them. I beamed at them and they lovingly gave me a wave. Suddenly, every person in the room was congratulating the person next to them. When I made it back to my parent's side, we too started shaking hands, hugging anyone within arms reach, and extending our congratulations.

When the commotion settled down, I looked at Dad and asked, "Would you please read this paper for me?" Dad took the document I'd handed him and slowly read the following:

Be it known that a term of the United States District Court of the Eastern District of Washington, held pursuant to law at Spokane on April 15, 1955, the Court having found that Peter Rolf Kalk Brenner, then residing at Quarters 8 - b, George Wright Air Force Base, Spokane, Washington, intends to reside permanently in the United States when so required by the Naturalization Laws of the United States, had in all other respects complied with the applicable provision of such naturalization laws, and was entitled to be admitted to citizenship thereupon ordered that such person be and (s)he was admitted as a citizen of the United States of America.

In testimony wherefore the seal of the court is hereunder affixed this 15th day of April in the year of our Lord nineteen hundred and fifty - five and of our Independence the one hundred and seventy - ninth.

CERTIFICATE OF NATURALIZATION
PETITION NO. 10556
Peter Rolf Kalk Brenner

I looked at the document that was signed by Stanley D. Taylor, the clerk of the United States District Court. "Is this mine?" I asked.

"Yes, son; you are now an American citizen of this country, like us. How does it make you feel?"

With great pride and honor, I straightened myself up to my full height and said, "I now have a home."

I couldn't understand why Mom was crying. For the first time in my life, I felt as though I belong somewhere; it was the happiest day of my life.

CHAPTER II

On the Move

"I was born to a woman I never knew and raised by another who took in orphans. I do not know my background, my lineage, my biological or cultural heritage. But when I meet someone new, I treat them with respect . . . For after all, they could be my people."

James Michener, Author

Cross County Trip

I felt more grown up as an American citizen. The fact that I wasn't growing taller, however, bothered me.

Mom regularly tried to reassure me not to worry. "Peter, one day you'll start sprouting up like a weed," she said. "In time, you'll be tall enough."

"I don't like being called a squirt or half - pint," I lamented.

"Don't fret over it, everything will be just fine," she promised me.

Dad was more practical. He taught me a response. "Try deflecting the negative with a positive."

"What's that mean?" I exclaimed in utter frustration.

"Easy. Toss out a phrase that simultaneously injects humor and acceptance."

"What does simultaneously mean?"

"It means together. Like so: Why, I'll be knee - high to a grasshopper," he said with a deadpan face.

"I still don't understand."

"The expression alludes to being short, but paints a funny picture," Dad explained.

My initial giggle evolved into a body - shaking, eye - watering laugh.

"What do you say about that, you squirt?" Dad said as he started tickling me.

Roaring uncontrollably, I sputtered, "Why, I'll be knee - high to a grasshopper."

We both fell off the couch onto the floor laughing until our sides hurt. Mom just looked at us, shook her head and went into the kitchen to pour us something cold to drink. I think she really wanted to pour a pitcher of water onto our heads.

By the end of the day, Dad gave me a second phrase to counter negative attacks from disrespectful people; "Well, I'll be a horn - toed swallow." I finally felt well armed for my next encounter with any name - calling classmate. By the next day, I'd come to an important decision. I decided to always try to be positive in the presence of negative.

School was out, I had a final milkshake with T.J., we sold our dog and I watched our belongings being packed and loaded once again into a monstrous, curb - hugging moving van. It was time to get on the road. Early the next morning, we rolled out of Spokane, Washington headed for Montgomery, Alabama. As with all our other moves, we had a family gathering to discuss our pending trip. I had the atlas opened to the United States; Mom was thumbing through the pages of her travel guide when Dad called the meeting to order.

I spoke up first. "This looks like an awfully long trip, Dad."

"No problem, I've taken a ninety - day leave of absence. This will be the longest vacation we've ever had together as a family." He leaned back with the most satisfied and relaxed expression I'd seen on his face for some time.

"Three months: two on the road seeing the sights, visiting with friends; and four weeks to settle into our new dwelling," Mom added.

"Will I have a full year at the new school?"

Dad replied: "Yes, but only for your sixth grade. I too will be attending school. I was selected to attend the Air Force's Commanding Staff School in Montgomery, Alabama. It's only a one - year program, after which I'll be assigned to another base."

"Where's Montgomery?" I asked.

He pointed to the spot on the opened page of my atlas. "It's the capital of Alabama."

"Where are we going before we get there?"

Dad puffed up his chest and proclaimed, "Everywhere."

Mom piped in, "or whatever we can cover in eight weeks." She spread out a sheet outlining our two - month itinerary. "We plan to visit some of our military friends in Oregon, California and Texas, spending some time in America's greatest National Parks-like Yosemite, Grand Canyon, Petrified Forest and Carlsbad Cavern, with added stops in the cities of Portland, San Francisco, Anaheim, L.A., Vegas, Santa Fe, Phoenix, Dallas and New Orleans."

"I hope we don't get lost," I said, half kidding.

"We won't. Your dad's got a great sense of direction and I've got the travel - guide."

"And I have the map," I said with a broad smile.

The summer of 1955 was a memorable journey. The natural wonders, historic sites and incredible cities were parsed out among the three visits with family friends. We stayed the better part of a week at the Reed Cattle Ranch outside Portland Oregon; parts of two days and one night with a couple whom my parents had met during my dad's tour of duty in Kitzingen, Germany following World War II; and one night in Texas with a fellow chaplain with whom Dad served during the Korean Conflict. Each stopover served as an oasis amidst the neon lights beckoning weary travelers, the humid hot days that drained our energy, and the deluge of sights and sounds drowning our senses. But the mix painted a mental montage of a spectacular summer never to be completely forgotten.

In Oregon, at the Reed Ranch, I was encouraged to participate in a cattle roundup. It was a two - day, one - night roundup with the objective to corral cows roaming the open range. I was hoisted atop a horse twice my age that answered to the name of Snowball. His job was to stay steady on the main trail and make sure I didn't tumble off his back. I felt like a genuine cowboy riding my steed across the range handling odd jobs and being with real wranglers. Mom and Dad stayed back at the ranch. My respect and appreciation for the cowboy rose to new heights as I admired the chilling, star filled night and endured the heat of a blazing sun the next day. They were a vanishing culture, which had helped shape the landscape of America. To be part of that toughness, even for just a slice in time, touched me. It deepened my appreciation to be an American.

Our next stopover was for only one night in Riverside, California. Dad had met the young couple in Germany during the allied occupation following the end of World War II. Even as a young child, I could sense that the visit appeared to be especially important to him. While Mom supervised my pool time, Dad spoke extensively with our hosts. They often tossed quick glances in my direction during the course of our stay. I had the distinct feeling that I was often the center of their conversation.

I asked Mom about it. She answered, "They feel very close to your dad. He officiated at their wedding. It was just after the end of the war and the wedding made it possible for her to join her new husband in the States. She was referred to as a War Bride."

"Do you know them?"

"Not as well as your dad."

"Why?" I continued.

"I wasn't at their wedding."

Later in the day the dark - haired woman came over to talk to me.

"Hi. Your dad tells me you are a naturalized U.S. citizen."

I gave a Cheshire cat grin and with great pride responded, "Yes. I even have a certificate to prove it."

"I hear you're Norwegian."

"Did my dad tell you?"

"We have something in common," she said with a twinkle in her eye.

"We do? What?" I asked in an inquisitive tone.

"I'm also Norwegian and still have a little accent to prove it."

"Wow, I've never met someone from Norway."

"Indeed, we have something very special in common."

I quickly moved on to an important question that had just popped into my head. "Are you also an American citizen?"

"Just like you, I too had to go through classes to become a naturalized citizen. That gives us even another connection." A timer suddenly buzzed calling her back to the kitchen and interrupting her warm smile. She lingered awhile, looking me over from head to foot, before heading back to the kitchen. She said,

"Have to go. I'm glad we had this little chat."

"Me too," I called back.

My mom gave a faint nod as she looked in my direction.

"I have something in common with her," I announced. "She's an American citizen just like me."

"I know. Isn't that exciting?"

I felt warm inside, like I'd just taken a full sip of hot chocolate. The feeling stayed with me for the whole visit.

I spent the rest of the day swimming in their backyard pool. After the sunset, I divided my time between comics and finishing a Hardy Boy's mystery book. The next morning, we were off, but not before the woman came up and cheerfully stated, "I enjoyed having you over and hope you might visit us again, soon."

We got into our car and slowly backed out of the drive way. My last image of her was a simple wave as we sped on our way.

The stretch from the Grand Canyon via Carlsbad Caverns to Dallas, Texas was a long, hot drive. To pass the time, I read Hardy Boy mysteries and drew pictures. When all I could hear was the hum of the tires, I'd think about the family we'd visited in Riverside, California. The woman seemed so interested in me. The fact that we both were Naturalized Citizens, Norwegian and had lived in Germany fascinated me. I began wondering if she knew something about my past.

Our third stop was Dallas, Texas. It was a sprawling city plopped in the middle of Texas. It was here that we visited Chaplain Robert Taylor and his beautiful wife, Millie. He was over six feet tall. His face was strong in a handsome way and the slight Texas drawl put one instantly at ease. His wife could have been a model. She was tall, with elegant facial features, kind eyes and flowing chestnut - colored hair that settled softly on the top of her shoulders. They knew my parents since before the Korean Conflict. Chaplain Taylor (I was told) survived the Death March to Bataan as a prisoner of war. He was still recovering from lingering injuries inflicted upon him during his forced march and imprisonment. They lived off the base in a spacious home befitting a war hero, who had risen to the lofty position of Chief of Chaplains and the rank of a two - star General. There was an aura about him radiating strength, reassurance and respect. My dad and Chaplain Taylor never spoke about their time in Korea around us. Like Riverside, California the Taylor's discussions with my parents were indistinguishable murmurings. Again, I sensed I was often the topic of their conversation.

As we crossed the border and drove into Alabama, I reflected on our cross - country trip. We played all sorts of car games to keep us occupied during the long days on the road. I liked Twenty Questions: identifying and making a list of where the cars we saw came from, seeing who could count the most cattle out of their side of the window before passing a cemetery - which would then result in the loss of all we'd seen - memorizing State Capitals and recalling fascinating facts about the places we'd visited. On occasion, while driving through Texas, my dad would select a long, straight stretch of road. This was my time to hop out of the car and retrieve all the bottles I could find alongside the road. When we drove into the next town, I'd cash in the bottles at a nickel each and use the money to buy souvenirs, enjoy an ice - cream cone or treat myself to a 12oz. bottle of pop.

It was a great vacation. I realized how comfortable I felt traveling across nine states and over 3000 miles. Whenever anyone asked, "Do you like living and traveling all over the place?" I'd answer, "Yes. It's all I know."

MONTGOMERY, ALABAMA

People and places have a way of shaping our environment. Base housing at Fairchild Air Force Base in Montgomery, Alabama was significantly different from our home in Spokane, Washington. The moment I stepped into our new accommodations, I gasped. My new bedroom appeared to be a converted closet designed to house Lilliputians. It was hardly large enough to accommodate a single bed with a tall, narrow dresser standing guard just far enough from the foot of the bed to allow its drawers to open. The room was no wider than my body fully outstretched to the tips of my wiggling fingers. I'm certain the tight living quarters encouraged the inhabitants to stay away from the apartment from early morning until late into the evening.

It wasn't a problem for me. Mom had me dressed, fed and at the bus - stop by 7am. All the children living on the base were transported forty - five minutes to a cross - town elementary school. The pecking order for seating was simple; get there first. As soon as the bus rolled into the school parking lot and opened its door, we tumbled out and scattered to our classes.

Being transient dependents, we knew how to quickly identify our particular interests. I applied and was accepted into the precision marching honor guard unit. They had already been selected to march in the Macy's Thanksgiving Day Parade. Since late summer, the unit had been preparing precision routines for its trip to New York City. I wanted to revisit the city I'd seen when I was only 5 years old.

During the course of the year, I formed friendships within the marching unit. Tony, a born and bred Southerner became my closest buddy. A week or two before we were heading north for New York he asked me "Are there many 'Damn Yankees' in New York?"

"I guess," I answered. "It's a huge, crowded city, from what I can remember."

"Are you a "Damn Yankee?' he inquired?

"Probably; I lived up in that part of the United States for three years."

From that moment on, he called me "Damn Yankee."

When we came back from the New York trip, I told my parents all about the marching, food, sights we'd visited, and that I'd discovered I was a "Damn Yankee."

"What!" my mom sputtered. "What does your friend call you?"

"A 'Damn Yankee'," I repeated.

My dad, who had kept silent throughout the conversation, eventually piped in "I'm going in to see the principal. He needs to know what's going on here. That's no way to address anybody - especially our son."

"Oh, it's not just me. All of the kids from the north are called that name." My parents shook their head in disbelief.

The next day, Dad went in to see the principal. Later that evening, the three of us got together to hear what resulted from the office visit. My Dad couldn't suppress in his laughter any longer. He finally blurted, "Your friends don't even realize the significance of what they're saying. They think the word damn is the prefix to Yankee and a perfectly proper word. Their parents refer to northerners as 'damn Yankees' in such a matter of fact manner; their children think it's just a name we're called."

Nothing came of the incident. Tony and I remained close friends for the entire school year.

The afternoon bus ride home from school always had fewer students than in the morning. I had no clue from one day to the next whom I'd be sitting next to. The mix was diverse. I sat beside every skin hue and geographic division one could imagine. That's why I tuned in to every word Dad said about a woman called Rosa Parks. It was December of 1955.

I couldn't understand why a tired, hard - working black woman couldn't choose to sit in any seat on the bus. I asked my parents, "Why does a colored woman have to stand at the back of the bus, when there are plenty of available seats at the front of the bus?"

"It's a terrible law designed to discriminate against the colored people," Mom answered.

"There's no sense to it, Son," Dad elaborated, "except that people want to keep others in their place. It's wrong to deny anyone their freedom to move about freely."

"It's not that way on our bus. Rollin is as dark as chocolate and we always sit together in the front row of the bus on the way home from school. Why can we do it?"

"Your bus is not considered public transportation; it's a base bus used to transport military dependents," Dad explained.

"I'm going to tell Rollin it's wrong what they're doing to this woman."

The following day, I organized my first protest. I arranged for every person of color to partner with a white friend and sit together during the bus ride. Some of the girls took it a step further by holding hands with their seatmates when they stepped off the bus and onto the school grounds. It wasn't much, but it made all of us feel better. We even started hanging around on the playground and eating together in the cafeteria.

The only people who had trouble with our actions were some of the administrators of the school-principal, a few teachers and some parents who were hanging around the area. The parents were the noisiest. When we stepped off from the bus they would yell and call us names. I remember them calling us "nigger - lover". I think the administration thought we'd stirred - up a hornet's nest that would result in angry parents complaining. There were, however, some changes made. Every morning, when we arrived at the school, an adult boarded the bus and had us file out one - by - one; a second person quickly escorted us toward a side entrance of the school, and immediately instructed to go directly to our classroom. I believe the administrators didn't want parents to see us walking together or holding hands. We were told that the changes were for our own safety and protection. It took a few weeks before everything settled down. Now I knew why they called us "Damn - Yankees". They didn't like our friends.

KANSAS CITY, KANSAS

As Dad forewarned, we were headed for another assignment the week school let out. Mom insisted we use the summer months to become familiar with our new surroundings and begin forging friendships with our neighbors. Dad was promised a three - year assignment as the new base chaplain at Richard - Gebauer AFB, Kansas.

Mom was so excited about the prospect of staying in one location for more than eighteen months, she convinced Dad to buy our first home. It felt like a mansion compared to the cracker - box apartment we'd just left behind in Alabama.

We bought a pretty, two - bedroom house tucked away in the heart of Prairie Village, about a dozen miles from the airbase. Shawnee Mission Junior High School, a huge, state - of - the - art facility, was only a couple of miles down the road.

During our new civilian - type life, the entire family immediately became active with a local American Baptist Church. It was only a 15 - minute walk from our house. Roger was my best friend and the minister's son. I liked the fact that we were both kids of a preacher.

I immediately became active in the church's Boy Scout Troop. Roger and I rose rapidly up the scouting program and earned the rank of Life. We even earned an additional five merit badges toward scouting highest honor - Eagle Scout. Our friendship became close because of scouting; we went on camping trips together; we learned how to administer first aid; mastering water lifesaving skills was the most challenging; and the cooking merit badge the hardest.

When the baseball season rolled around, I tried out for one of the local little league teams. My team was awful. I only remember winning one game all season. But I didn't care; I made the team and we were playing baseball. By season's end, Mom gave me the sad news. It was one of the few times I'd ever seen her cry, when she started telling me about our next move.

BENNINGTON, VERMONT

The military informed Dad that he would be assigned to Toule, Greenland beginning the summer of 1957. It would be a non - accompanied tour lasting only nine months. My mom was heartbroken. She decided, rather than staying in Kansas alone, she and I would spend the year with her parents in Bennington, Vermont. Just talking about the decision brought a new smile to her face.

We sold our home and I began my 8th grade in the Green Mountain State known for its maple syrup and famous freedom fighter Ethan Allen and the Green Mountain Boys. I later learned that Grandma Moses, who painted local landscapes of Vermont until after she was 100 years old, had a museum on the outskirts of town. The town's location on a map served as a stickpin point holding down the southwest corner of the state.

We knew our stay would only be for one year. My greatest surprise was being around so many relatives. For the first time in my life, I was talking and playing with first cousins. It seemed as if a third of the town's 13,000 residents were related to a Fenn, Burgess or Shea.

Grandma Pauline and her husband Guy introduced me to a grab bag of new experiences. Guy took me snowshoeing and taught me how to bait my fishing hook with squiggly worms, how to track a wounded deer he shot, and how to recognize which berries were poisonous or a tasteful treat. Cousin Peter took me hunting for frogs (we ate the legs) and taught me how to ice skate and play hockey. We would go tubing down the river, cheer Howard, Peter's big brother, on during a high school football game and ski at Hogback Mountain. Grandma Pauline was the landlord for a seven - unit complex. She helped me to master the skills of house painting, making minor home repairs, washing the dirty sheets, helping around the kitchen, and her most favorite secret where to spot a herd of deer at dusk. She also instilled the attributes of hard work, pursuing dreams and respecting others.

I was too small to play football and too short for basketball, so Mom insisted I learn how to play the trombone. I redirected my energies toward music. I practiced and played well enough to make the school's marching band. I'm certain my experience with the Montgomery marching unit was a real plus for me. I made the baseball team, but, being an outsider, didn't get much playing time. The final fanfare of our nine - month odyssey was my being the first Boy Scout in the district to earn the rank of Eagle by the age of thirteen.

Interfacing with extended, loving family members loosened a logjam of gathering thoughts. I was acutely aware of having been an orphan. Without my saying a word, Grandma Pauline knew what was bothering me. She took me aside one evening and said, "Remember, Peter, you come from good stock. Your bloodline is Norwegian, even though you're being brought up an American. The past is always a part of you, so be proud of who you are."

I nodded with a weak smile. She knew I'd heard classmates mumbling the word orphan behind my back. Nobody talked about it to my face, but the whispers were loud enough to hear.

"This is a small community and whenever a stranger comes in, he becomes the topic of the whole town. The people are not trying to be mean, they're just wondering. Remember, you'll always be my favorite." She handed me a chocolate - chip cookie hot off the cookie sheet. The chocolate was still gooey.

"Thanks." Her love calmed the turmoil swirling within my head. However, once the questions became better formulated in my mind, the circumstances surrounding my coming to America began tumbling to the fore. During an unscheduled moment, I asked Grandma, "Am I really an American?"

She always answered with the same statement, "You sure are and much more; that's why I love you just the way you are." The pronouncement was always accompanied by a noisy, wet kiss on the cheek.

LINCOLN, NEBRASKA

Leaving Bennington, Vermont made me as sad as I was the day we left Spokane, Washington. To divert my attention, I returned to an ongoing concern. It was similar to hitting ones toe to divert attention from a headache. During the drive to Lincoln, Nebraska, I asked Mom, "Why am I so short?"

Her response was more than I'd bargained for. "Nobody knows for sure, but some doctors claim your height is affected by the care you received during your formative years. Your first three years in orphanages were particularly difficult times for you."

"What do you mean?" I turned to face Mom but could still see Dad stealing a glance my way as he drove down the highway.

In a straightforward but sensitive way dad ventured into uncharted territory for the first time. He elaborated. "During the war, food was scarce. Children in orphanages didn't get the first run of fruit, milk, vegetables, cheese fish or much meat for that matter. Those items were allocated to the fighting soldiers; and after the war, the bulk of the food supply was redirected toward families trying to rebuild broken lives."

"When you're a baby," Mom added, "the right kind of food is very important. I imagine your surroundings might have been dirty, and proper medicine in short supply. Illnesses were high among wartime babies. We learned that during your first year, you contracted scarlet fever."

I sat silently looking out the window. I didn't know what to say. Actually, I was depressed to hear what they were saying. The more I heard about my pass the more anxious I became. All I wanted was to be a little taller so I could be a better baseball player. I could hear Mom's muffled voice trying to penetrate my troubled thought.

"In time, you'll grow and be just fine."

"I hope so." In silence, I turned my attention back to the rolling hills of Pennsylvania.

Our arrival in Lincoln, Nebraska marked the start of my high - school experience. For the fifth consecutive year, I was going to be bused to a new school. Once again, I would have to figure out how to make new friends.

The base bus ride took us to an inner - city school. It featured several gangs consisting of girls, blacks, Italians and Asians. Fights during lunch period were the rule, not the exception. Adults were seldom seen on the playground area. I think they made it a point to linger in the teachers' lounge and pour an extra cup of coffee, or shuffle papers around the top of their classroom desks to avoid leaving the sanctity of their classroom. During the first week of school, I didn't say more than a dozen words. The second week, I told Mom about the conditions and said, "I'm not going back to that school. I'll get eaten alive." Then I told her about the fights. Little did we know, Nebraskan, Charles Raymond Starkweather, accompanied and assisted by his fourteen - year old girlfriend, Caril Ann Fugate, would, later in the year, murder ten people over a period of eight days. Caril was a member of a girls' gang at the high school. Starkweather and Fugate were about to make history. They would become America's first single - episode mass murderers.

By the third week of school, Dad had arranged for me to piggyback a ride from the base to St. Mary High, a private Catholic School located on the opposite end of town. Enrollment there was already at full occupancy, but Dad heard of an area high school, which still had available space for incoming students. I rode the bus to St. Mary and then walked the extra mile to Southeast High. Since the Catholic school released its students before I could walk back in time to catch the bus home, I elected to try out for the track team. The team practiced right after school, which made my pick - up time better for my parents'. Fortunately, I was fast enough to make the team and run the 100 - yard dash and 440 relays.

It was in Lincoln where I first saw a tornado. We were sitting on the porch when a funnel appeared moving in our direction. We watched it bearing down on us. Within a minute, dad scurried us toward the basement. Suddenly the noisy tornado made a 90 - degree turn heading east over the Mississippi River. The next morning we read that the funnel had destroyed a high school by the name of Ruskin Heights. All the letters were blown off except the ones that spelled RUIN.

Lincoln was a SAC (Strategic Air Command) Air Force Base. Dad spent most of his time driving or being flown to out - of - the - way locations. Once there, he'd conduct services and provide counseling for the young airmen who manned silos housing underground nuclear missiles strategically positioned on the borders of North Dakota and Montana as part of America's Cold War defense program. The assignment was considered an isolated tour of duty. We didn't see too much of him during the year, since a third of the time he was on call and another third of his time he was activated and isolated with the flight crews. I didn't like him being away so much of the time.

The greatest gift I received during my freshman year was a brief growth spurt. I grew five inches. At 5 feet, 5 inches, I felt like a giant. More importantly, I ran track and made the school baseball team as a centerfielder. Baseball became my passion. I was still too small for football, an okay size as a point guard in basketball, fast enough for track, but perfect for baseball.

I practiced every opportunity available to me to improve my arm strength, speed, stamina and fielding skills. My hitting, however, needed the most improvement. I couldn't pick up the pitches quickly enough to initiate a power swing. The majority of my hits were singles and doubles. It was the coach who noticed I was having trouble hitting the ball with consistent authority. He wanted me on the team because of my fielding skills and speed on the base paths. It wasn't until our move to Massachusetts that I discovered why I wasn't seeing the ball well.

CONCORD, MASSACHUSETTS

Similar to the other assignments - overseas in Japan, the year in Spokane, Washington, the time at Maxwell - Gunther AFB in Montgomery, Alabama, Fairchild AFB in Kansas City, Kansas, and Bennington, Vermont - the Brenner trio packed up their belongings again, and this time returned to New England for our new lodging. My upcoming sophomore year would mark my seventh school in seven years (4th thru 10th grade).

My spirit still remained high for the move to Hanscom Field, Massachusetts. All military personnel except Generals lived on Low, Middle or High Street. The Generals lived in imposing homes on Circle Road. Since Dad was the Base Chaplain, we lived on High Street. Our apartment was scrunched in the middle of a three - unit complex.

The high school was only a 15 - minute bus ride to historic Concord; the town where the Minute men of the American Revolution first stood their ground to battle against the red - coated British soldiers. "The shot heard around the world" was fired across a little stream marked by a bridge, still standing, no more than a mile from the school. The town was home to some of the most famous writers of their time: Louisa Mae Alcott, Ralph Waldo Emerson, and Henry David Thoreau. Thoreau's Walden Pond was nestled in the woods on the southern border of town.

We were promised three years at Hanscom Field. I was excited at the prospect of finishing out my final three years of high school in the same location. Everything clicked during my sophomore and junior years. I was playing centerfield for the baseball team, joined a bowling team and became a trophy - winning bowler. I took my first real girlfriend, Sue, to the junior prom, my grades were excellent and the family vacations included the three of us.

I also became an ardent Red Sox fan and was selected to attend the Ted Williams summer baseball camp for "promising ball players." It was at the camp that a coach detected a minor flaw in my hitting. It was due to the weakness of my left eye. The muscles in the stronger right eye were compensating for the weaker left eye by doing most of the work. It was the reason I had trouble picking up fastballs. The hitting instructor suggested a few minor adjustments to my batting stance that included an open stance improving my ability to pick - up the pitched ball more quickly as it came out of the pitcher's hand. He also suggested I learn how to become a switch hitter-it would enhance my chances for making a team. It did.

Life was excellent, bordering on outstanding. I was confident my senior year would be the crowning chapter of my high - school experience.

During the summer of 1960, my world crumbled.

Dad was offered, not assigned, a plum assignment as the Command Chaplain stationed at Toule Rosier, France. The new responsibilities would virtually guarantee him an early promotion to the rank of full Colonel. He accepted.

I was furious. "No, I'm not going!"

"Peter, this is a promotion move for your father. He has to take it," Mom pleaded.

"Great for him, I'm happy he's doing so well. I'm not budging," I stormed.

"France will be a wonderful place to live. We'll travel all over Europe during the summer . . . you'll love it . . . honest . . . it'll be an unbelievable experience for you."

"I can stay here for my senior year. I know there are friends who would let me live with them. I could join you right after graduation," I argued.

From behind, I heard a firm, steady voice. "We're not leaving you behind."

I turned and addressed my dad, "Baseball, a girlfriend, my senior year, close friends; how can you take all this away from me? I've never complained about our hopscotching around, attending different schools and having no close friends. You can't do this to me. It isn't fair. Why are you asking me to leave everything I love behind?" My face was red and tears were welling up in my eyes.

"We're going. Period." I could hear dad's voice rising and the decibels ratcheting up.

I stepped to within inches of his face. "I didn't become a part of this family to be a piece of luggage carted around the world," I fumed.

Mom stepped between us and made the defining argument. "We're family and being together is our highest priority. We've been separated too much as it is. We're not leaving you behind."

My hands balled up into fists. My simmering anger was about to boil over. I was so furious, I was afraid of what I might do. "I hate you both!" I yelled, then pivoted like a soldier and marched off to my room, slamming the door behind me.

I didn't apologize or initiate a conversation with my parents for over a week. I fabricated a reason to be out of the house every chance I got. I bared my soul to Sue and every friend who would listen to me. The military dependents understood; the civilian friends couldn't believe I was leaving them during my senior year. It was the most miserable move of my life.

VERDUN, FRANCE

Later that summer, we moved to Toule Rosier, France. The base was only a couple of hours from the western border of Germany in the Alsace - Lorraine region. The city of Strasbourg was less than a three - hour drive southeast of the base, and Frankfurt lay the same distance northeast of our location. The most impressive tourist attraction was the resort town of Baden Baden; a little town nestled in the northern edge of the Black Forest - made famous by the Hansel and Gretel fairytale.

I didn't care.

All military dependents, embassy children and children of CEO businessmen were housed at the regional school in Verdun, France - just a short ride from Luxembourg. My mom insisted we rent a French villa halfway between the base and the military boarding school. The house was in the little town of Spada, near Saint Michel on the Meuse.

It didn't make any difference to me.

The farther from my parents I could get the better. It was my intent to have my own isolated tour of duty. If Dad could go off to Korea, Greenland, pursue a post - graduate degree and visit godforsaken SAC outposts; I could embrace the freedom of attending school at some desolate location away from them.

However, a strange transformation came over me on my way to becoming a pain in the derriere (the first French word I learned). The boarding school was an excellent place for me to live. Every student in the school knew what all of us had gone through before arriving at Verdun. Oh, our experiences varied some-but where also the same-where we lived, how often the moves came about, renewing struggles to make friends, disrupted education and occasional RESENTMENT. We were a military family and my disappointments were similar to other friends going through similar struggles. Life was unfair and all of us reserved the right to be angry. It made no difference if we were children of enlisted or officer parents; if our background was Army, Navy or Air Force; or what responsibilities defined our parent's livelihood. We understood each other and that was our bond.

Time has a way of smoothing over raw feelings. Eventually, I enjoyed my occasional excursions to Spada and trips to the Air Force Base. My Dad was doing well with his new high - powered responsibilities and Mom enjoyed speaking French with the villagers. I, in turn, learned to appreciate the rich diversity of our mini - campus atmosphere.

I missed my friends in Concord, but realized adjusting and adapting would have to remain a defining aspect of who I was. I could embrace it or remain entrapped in a self - imposed web of anger. The first option suited my personality and I decided not to fight my situation for the time being. There would be more important battles later.

It's amazing how critical events in a person's life can be experienced in a short time frame. It's even more remarkable how those events, be they traumatic or tremendous, bring clarity and meaning to one's life.

On a blustery, cold winter morning, I decided to catch a ride with Dad to the airbase. I needed to sharpen my ball handling skills and improve upon my jump shots if I wanted to entertain any chance of making the high school basketball team.

It was a slippery, narrow, curving rural road with snow concealing a sheet of ice beneath its pristine beauty. Suddenly, Dad lost control of the car and in an instant we smashed headfirst into a tree. The impact threw my dad's head into and partially through the windshield. When he jerked back his face was severely cut. His face looked like raw meat recently sliced. "Are you alright, Peter?"

"I can't move my legs! There's no feeling." I looked at the dashboard that had snapped down on top of my legs. "I think I'm paralyzed." Suddenly, I felt a sharp pain in my chest.

As my Dad opened the car door, he called back in a reassuring tone. "I'll get help . . . Stay calm . . . I'll get help in no time."

Somehow, he stumbled out of the wreck with his face covered in a sheet of blood. Fortunately another car was coming down the road. He flagged down an oncoming automobile and somehow managed to open the driver's car door and slumped onto the backseat. The next instant they were headed for the airbase that was only a few miles away. I later learned that when they reached the gate, in broken French, Dad ordered the driver to continue through the stop sign. As he gave directions on how to get to the infirmary two Military Police started chasing after them. At the parking lot of the hospital, Dad opened the car door and fell unconscious onto the pavement. The Military Police quickly assessed the severity of the situation and rushed my Dad into the hospital. Within moments, he was wheeled into an operating room, while the desk personnel were pulling up his medical file. To their chagrin, they noticed that Chaplain A.E.K. Brenner had an extremely rare blood type. With thousands of soldiers stationed on base only 4% of the population had his blood type. One of the military police heard what they needed and interrupted the frantic efforts at the front desk.

"My buddy and I have the same blood type as the Chaplain. If you need us, we're here."

The two were immediately taken to the O.R. room, placed on either side of the patient and began being prepped for an immediate, double transfusion. Their presence, at that moment in time, saved my father's life.

My dad must have told somebody that I was still at the accident scene. All I could envision, as I sat paralyzed from the waist down, was my Dad's bloody face.

I felt relieved when the sound of an ambulance's siren caught my attention. It wasn't long before I was being treated for my injuries just down the corridor from where my Dad lay. My legs had gained feeling and some motion. Of greater concern were the 3 broken ribs pressing up against my lungs.

To my surprise, Mom was at the hospital when I arrived. She said she'd felt that something was wrong, got in her car and drove to the base. It was a "Twilight" moment to say the least.

Lying on a gurney next to my dad with two strangers giving him blood and Mom talking to me got me to thinking. Could anything be worse or better in such a short period of time? I decided to give a little prayer of thanks before the pain pills put me into another world. My final image was the sight of a doctor entering the room with a huge smile on his face. At that moment, it made all the difference-even the ribs didn't hurt as much.

It was in July, following my high - school graduation and entering college, that Mom and I made a trip to Oslo, Norway to visit my Norwegian relatives. Dad had kept in touch with them; but elected to wait until I was older before trying to help me understand the significance of their presence in my life.

It also amazes me how the proximity of good and bad events in one's life sometime converges within unexplainable closeness. They become reminders of how lucky one is when each experience serves as a meaningful moment to review and later savor. Such were the cases in the winter and summer of 1961.

The summer following the car accident, mom and I headed off for Norway.

We stayed with the Brodwall family. Julie was introduced as my aunt and her two sons, Jorn and Erik, were my first cousins. Erik was just little, but Jorn and I got along just fine. I was amazed how well everyone spoke English. The visit provided a peek into my past. I remember looking intently at my cousins and Aunt to see if there was even a remote hint of some physical resemblance; I wasn't certain until I met the two beautiful Toxborg girls-also first cousins-that I recognized a family resemblance. I could clearly see our similarities: Their blonde hair matched the color of mine, puffy cheeks with a prominent dimple on the left side of their face mirrored the one I had, their sturdy stature and small facial features - ears pressed against the side of the head, a tiny nose and broad foreheads - all resembled my features.

Karin Toxborg was one of five sisters, including Bjorg, who were scattered throughout Norway during World War II. Bjorg (B.J.), the woman I'd met in California following my naturalization, had suddenly become an item of interest for me. Without a shred of doubt, the summer visits on the banks of the Oslo Fjord dispelled any lingering doubts I might have had about being Norwegian. I knew the blood flowing through my veins was Norwegian.

I felt awkwardly proud and relieved at the same time. I was filled with new questions, but I hesitated to venture on with an in depth look. I was still wary of the unknown; it shrouded a slippery bank leading to a mysterious darkness. I wondered if casting new light into the past would be too revealing.

We visited the Brodwall family three consecutive summers. I always felt accepted and with each visit my courage grew bolder. Naturally, I became curious about my own particular history. I felt assured that my past was somehow grounded more amidst the Scandinavian mystique than the German soil of disdain.

CHAPTER III

My College Years

"Autobiography begins with a sense of being alone. It is an orphan form."

John Berger

It was an unusual journey that brought me to the borders of Norway. Soon, I would be attending college in Germany, a two - year program sponsored by the University of Maryland, Munich Branch. Eventually, my travels and education would take me back to America. However, there was restlessness within me through out my stay in Europe.

The new wealth of information left me conflicted. My American parents had adopted me from some unknown place in Germany. Questions about the mystery loomed before me: Who was the absent sister, Bjorg? How did I get to Germany? Where was I born? Was my father Norwegian? If my mother really was still alive, why was I adopted? Unanswered questions kept scratching my mind.

With the start of college, my nights became anxious and my life disconnected. There was an angry, confused rebel inside me and he wanted out.

I spent my first two years of college in Germany, on the grounds of McGraw Kaserne. The Army base provided a mini campus with two dorms and class space for students enrolled in The University of Maryland, Munich Branch graduate program. The two - year program attracted, much like Verdun's regional high school, dependents of embassy and military personnel.

I used the program and its facilities as a base of operations. I wasn't about to let studies in French, German, math and psychology interrupt my travel plans. The long weekends were filled with backpacking adventures in the German Alps, relaxing on the French Riviera, train rides crisscrossing the landscape from Rome to Amsterdam, Brussels to Moscow, Madrid to Paris and Dubrovnik to Berlin, and flights to Norway.

I downed many a beer - filled mug in the evenings during Munich's October Fest, and the Swabbing Street Festival. Between festivals, several of us managed to observe the local life while peering through the beer of a half - filled mug. With little effort, I grew proficient in German and improved upon my conversational French. Dressed appropriately, I'd pass for a German. The pathetic reality was, I didn't feel guilty about my lifestyle - an irresponsible student pissing away his parents' money.

My grades fell faster than a meteor. By the end of my first year, only high Bs in German and drama kept me in school with my academic standing teetering on the brink of probation. I may have been almost failing academically, but I was socially popular. Surprisingly, I was selected for the position and responsibilities of Dorm Proctor for the start of my sophomore year. I really think it was because nobody wanted to ride herd on their friends. My fluency in German and French continued to dramatically improve throughout the year, opening up a prestigious opportunity for me, barely managing to keep my grades respectable, to represent the University of Maryland at an international conference. Students from throughout Europe gathered in Munich to discuss incentives designed to enhance international cooperation and better communication among world leaders. Aimlessness combined with my undetected anger, lurking like a circling shark beneath the surface, I smiled my way around the weekend conference.

On November 22, 1963 my carefree attitude ended with the suddenness of a torpedo attack. Like a stricken ship pieces of my emotions lay strewn before me. When the conference concluded, our Kaserne contingent caught a speeding trolley making its way back to our campus located on the outskirts of Munich. It was approaching midnight and we'd been sequestered from the outside world for more than two full days and nights of lectures, presentations and films. Besides being drained of every ounce of coherent thought, we were a bit tipsy, a byproduct of mixing hard liquor with champagne, as laughter and raucous behavior reinforced our "ugly American" image.

Amazingly, I was the most aware and sober of the inebriated group. For no particular reason, I noticed that every single person on the trolley was staring at us. I detected sadness in their eyes and a darkness shrouding the atmosphere. I would have attributed it to my own condition had they not, without exception, turned their attention back to the tabloids they were reading, lifting the newsprint high enough to conceal the pain etched on their face. The bus driver noticed my curiosity and beckoned me forward. I moved slowly past the seats and accepted the tabloid he extended to me. A deathly silence filled the trolley. I translated the bold print heading plastered across the top third of the tabloid to read, "President Kennedy has been killed." I slowly read and reread the first paragraph. *How could we not have known? It had to be a hoax.*

Filled with disbelief, I stumbled back up the aisle to rejoin the group - tears welling up in my glazed eyes. "President Kennedy has been killed," I murmured in shock.

"Killed?"

"Where?"

"When?"

"How?"

The rapid - fire questions left me gasping for more air. I waited a moment before answering; "He was assassinated by some crazy guy called Lee Harvey Oswald. Our president was shot while campaigning in Dallas, Texas." Like a rock thrown through a pane of glass, my words cut and left us emotionally bleeding. Like everyone else around us, we were in shock.

"Look!" A member of the group pointed to pedestrians walking like zombies up and down the streets. Every single person was reading from a tabloid similar to the issue I'd read to my friends. Individuals were visible but barely definable; even the lights seemed dim, managing to emanate just enough of a glow to create an effect of an entire community in mourning. Like an ominous fog, a spirit of gloom blanketed the city.

We looked at each other and simultaneously wept. Within moments, all of the riders were crying with us. I believe it was a night when all our lives were changed - mine was.

Classes were discontinued for a week.

Area chaplains arrived on campus to conduct a memorial service and be available for students who needed counseling. Some students escaped home to be with family. Since my parents were stationed in Tripoli, Africa, I decided to spend the week by myself, sequestered in the darkness of my room, and reserve the desert rendezvous for Christmas break. I still needed to sort out some conflicted feelings.

President Kennedy's tragic, horrific death shocked everyone, but rattled me to the depth of my senses. Having lived in Concord, just outside of Boston, for two years forged, for me, an affinity with this young, articulate, intelligent president; who gave all of us a sense of hope that might be yet realized. I was suppose to be an example of what young people could do for their country and here I was frittering away my life with forgettable parties, blank faces and empty nights. In an instant a madman's bullets took away MY leader. I knew I had to climb out of my pity - pool. I promised myself to somehow find a way to turn my life around. The question was, was it too late to salvage my pathetic existence? As a starter, would I even be able to resurrect my plummeting collegiate prospects?

I faced my last semester needing a C average to avoid expulsion from the University of Maryland's program. It came down to my final psychology exam. After three hours, with cramped muscles, stiff fingers and an aching back, I handed the professor my blue workbook and stated, "I need to pass this exam to stay eligible for admission into any college."

Professor Weber looked at me and asked, "How do you feel about your essays?"

"I think it's my best, to date."

"Did you study?" He thumbed through my booklet while observing my reaction.

"Yes, but I don't know how I feel about the answers."

"How much better is better?" he asked.

"I have to have a B+ to maintain an overall C minus average for the semester." My voice was almost a whisper.

"How hard did you prepare?"

"Harder than for any other exam this entire year," I voiced with a surge of confidence. I straightened up and locked my eyes with his.

"Let's hope it was enough." He gave me an encouraging smile as he dropped my exam on top of a mounting pile of blue booklets filled with other hopeful dreams.

That night, I prayed for the first time in over two years. It was a simple request repeated throughout the night. "Dear Lord, I have been lost, but want to be found. If it be your wish, give me another chance and forgive me for my actions." Even though I prayed, I suffered with my thoughts the entire night and into the early morning hours.

That afternoon, I was the first to enter the psychology classroom. My exam book lay off to the side of the pile with a note: "Peter, I'm glad you studied and worked so hard; sometimes the effort is worth more than the grade."

My heart sank. I opened to the front page and skimmed through the booklet. Not a single red marking had been made anywhere on the entire exam. I wondered if Professor William Weber had even read it. Tentatively, I turned to the last page and saw the bold red letter. It was a B+. The sudden rush of air escaping from my lungs startled me. It felt as though I'd been punched in the gut. After catching my breath, I realized the professor had given me the rare opportunity to redeem myself. He trusted the integrity of my word. I tossed my booklet into the wastebasket, but kept the note and headed back to the dorm.

It was time to start packing. It was incumbent upon me to figure out if any college would risk accepting a student on probation. I was going back to America confident things would work out - somehow.

WICHITA FALLS, TEXAS

I arrived in Wichita Falls, Texas, my father's final assignment as an Air Force Chaplain. He was retiring from the military, while I was leaving behind disturbing memories and a rebellious nature at bus stops, train stations and airports throughout Europe. It was time to move on. Yet I could feel a mounting storm building within me. It pulled at me, like a dog tugging at my pant leg. I kicked it away too fearful of what I might discover.

The isolated Air Force training base occupied an arid wasteland interrupted by rolling tumbleweeds, prairie dog towns covering acres, and an ever - present array of crooked - neck vultures picking clean the daily road kill. I remember sucking in the dry heat and thinking, I deserve this hellhole.

My cumulative grade - point average made my college transcript about as impressive as newsprint adorning the bottom of a birdcage. Oh, I could nevertheless amble across the grounds of the University of Maryland College Park campus or sweat it out at Baylor University in Wichita Falls, but neither inspired me.

As options, they felt like rumbling thunderstorms reminding me of past failures and unanswered questions. I had vacationed three consecutive summers with my Norwegian cousins from Oslo; yet my birth mother was still as elusive as a wisp of smoke. With each trip to Norway more questions surfaced around me. Why wouldn't they talk about her? How did I get to Germany? Who was my father? What did they really think of me? Each unanswered question fueled the discontent storming within me. Angrily, I had roamed Europe and minimized my studies while focused on my questions. The voice in my head needed answers to the questions.

No matter, whatever my feelings, the immediate choices began looking inevitable as the rejection letters accumulated on the kitchen table - like junk mail. My despair mounted as another school year neared with deadlines looming just around the corner.

During the sweat of a 100 - degree day, my dad interrupted the doldrums of my self - imposed pity. "Peter, you look piqued. What's the problem?"

"College, Dad," I said with a hint of sarcasm. "I don't mean to appear ungrateful, but Baylor and the University of Maryland don't exactly whet my appetite for learning."

"And Munich did?" he countered.

I shrugged my shoulders in an attempt to dismiss my embarrassment and the truth of my dad's question.

"I've got something in the works," he ventured over a sweaty glass of iced - coffee.

"What do you mean in the works?"

From behind me, my mother entered the kitchen and answered, "Another contact."

Dad took a huge gulp of his drink before setting the glass atop the table. "I've contacted a family friend, who I believe can help us out."

A glimmer of hope appeared in my voice. "Do you mean a college?"

Dad stood, walked to the sink and peered out the kitchen window. He lingered for a while, surveying the vast emptiness before him and sighed as though he knew the landscape was a painting nobody wanted to buy.

"I know you hate it here and I don't blame you for an instant." His voice lowered to a whisper as he continued. "I've asked a lot of you in support of my career." He turned to face me and waited until Mom took his arm and gave a knowing smile. "We want to thank you."

I blinked and stepped back. I didn't know how to respond. This gratitude had materialized like a rabbit out of a magician's hat. "I don't understand. What do you mean?"

"It's time for me to put you first, Peter. I'm retiring after this tour of duty, and forcing you to stay here with us, in Texas, is just unfair. In fact, it would be selfish on my part."

I sensed how awkward he felt talking to me in such a manner. "Dad, I'm fine. Correct me if I'm wrong, but you two haven't had too much to brag about during my past three years? Have you?"

He ignored my question and instead flashed a grin he'd been hoping to give for years. "Dean Pierce, of Emerson College, Boston is a family friend. He might be able to pull some strings and help us get you enrolled."

"Boston!" I exploded. The next question fired out of my mouth like a rocket. "Emerson?"

"Yes. It's a communicative arts college . . ."

"I know, Dad. It's also private, very expensive and not next door to Wichita Falls."

"Yes, we know." He replied with a chuckle.

"But I've already applied and haven't heard a word from them."

"He's considering my request as we speak. I imagine some of your tangled knots need a little more work to unravel, if you know what I mean?"

I plopped down onto the kitchen chair. A heavy silence filled the room before I had the courage to speak.

"Dad, if I am accepted into Emerson College, I'll make both of you proud. I promise."

He came over to me and pressed my face against his chest; "Peter, we've always been proud of you; now it's time for you to respect yourself."

EMERSON COLLEGE, BOSTON

My three years at Emerson served as an emotional life jacket. The changed setting and second chance to study at an institution I'd wanted to attend, turned my life around.

As I boarded the Four Star Trailways bus, my dad reassured me, "Your college years will be the best years of your life; and I'm including the past as well as the future." Dad decided I needed private time to contemplate my future - and he figured a long bus ride would be the best remedy for what ailed me. Mom did what she always would do during a departure. I could feel her one hand discreetly slip an envelope into my back pocket while with her other hand, she simultaneously gave me a lunch bag accompanied with a kiss. I'm certain Dad knew that traveling money and my favorite goodies were going to accompany, once again, during yet another journey.

At that moment, I wasn't 100% sure everything was going to be okay. As the bus started pulling out of the station, I began wondering what I would find in Boston. I had three days and three nights to contemplate my future and for the first time in my life was glad my legs were short and able to fit behind the seat in front of me. I decided to start giving thanks no matter how small. Ultimately, my hope was that the importance of Emerson College would be its ability to heal my spirit, build up my confidence and be a resource for making life - long friends.

In October of 1964, I was invited to pledge Phi Alpha Tau. Being accepted into the brotherhood was my life jacket in a sea of uncertainty. The Tau brothers became extended family; admission into Who's Who and earning Honor Society grades dramatically improved my confidence; I made the baseball team as its starting third baseman; became actively involved with the Student Government Association and its president during my senior year; and I honed my skills in the art of public speaking, debate, public relations and Radio/TV broadcasting. I even dated some. More importantly, I made close and trusted friends. I couldn't have asked for anything more.

But a strange thing happened on the way to earning my degree: I became aware of extraneous disruptions poking holes into the smooth surface of my college life. For no explainable reason, crowded rooms, sirens blaring in the middle of the night, surprise noises and sudden mood changes disrupted my ordered world. I felt off balance, and keeping my teetering emotions on an even keel became a worrisome issue. I kept the feelings to myself, too embarrassed to talk to anybody about something I couldn't understand. I just smiled and moved on. However, I needed someone I could confide in and not feel like a jerk. My parents were too far away. I decided to turn to my two trusted fraternity brothers - Jerry and Steve - but how?

One wintry night I conjured up an idea that warmed-up my insides like a good cup of hot coffee. Following my graduation, I would invite my two buddies to join me on a summer odyssey - a six week, cross-country trip.

They accepted and so the planning for the summer of 1967 began.

CROSS COUNTRY ADVENTURE

During the spring of '67, I received my acceptance letter from the Hartford Seminary Foundation. My grand design was to merge two fields of communication - radio and television broadcasting with a religious emphasis-into one discipline. I also convinced myself that a summer experience with no ties or obligations was necessary for my spirit and overall health. What could possibly give me better direction or more rejuvenating energy for future challenges than a carefree, loosely charted summer adventure with two of my closest college friends? On the surface it made no sense, but deep down, I knew it was perfect.

I was 23 years old and more than ready to kick - up my heels for a six-week adventure crisscrossing the United States with two fraternity brothers. Jerry and Steve still had their senior year at Emerson College to look forward to, but neither had ever taken a cross - country trip like I was proposing. The idea fascinated them. Considering our meager finances, our itinerary was ambitious. I'd convinced my fellow travelers that heading straight to Omaha, Nebraska as fast as possible-skipping all the tourist sights east of the Mississippi River-would give us more time to explore national parks, hike trails, spend time on the beach, gawk at natural wonders and visit historic sites. They agreed. The goal was not to exceed $10 a day, per person for essentials: gas, lodging and tolls. Personal expenses, mementoes and food were left to the individual's discretion.

In Iowa, we began assessing our driving strengths, weaknesses and preferences behind the wheel of Steve's rented Rambler Rebel: for example, how many hours before a driver relinquished his turn in the driver's seat; whether there should be two people awake at all times; who would take the night shift, the city run, etc.

I was elected to drive the first late - night stretch. All of us, however, were actively engaged in the game, "Twenty Questions." There were few cars on the road and getting scarcer by the minute. I rumbled by an occasional car as we roared our way along the highway toward Nebraska. We were so involved in the game, none of us noticed the flashing lights or heard the blaring siren. I was the first to notice the patrol car, but not until it had filled my rear - view mirror with bright, flashing red and green lights. I quickly pumped the brakes and eased the car onto the shoulder of the road. In my side - view mirror, I saw the dark silhouette of an approaching patrolman. My muscles petrified.

"May I see your driver's license and the car's registration papers?"

"Yes sir," I said sheepishly. I was so nervous it took me a few moments to tug the wallet out of my hip pocket. Steve, rummaging through the glove compartment, found the packet housing the required car registration. He passed it over for me to take. I handed the items to the patrolman with a half smile. The other half was stuck in my throat. I guessed him to be about 8 feet tall and over 300 lbs. He carefully reviewed the information.

Without looking up, he asked, "Tell me, young fellow, do you know how fast you were going?" He snapped his face up as he directed the beam of his flashlight onto each face one at a time pausing, long enough to get a good look.

"No sir," I choked.

The question, "Why not?" was accompanied by a stern look. All three of us started blurting out our version of the game, "Twenty Questions." He must have thought we were crazy. He raised his hand for us to stop.

"Where are you from and what's your destination?"

Again, we started rattling on about how we were college students from Emerson College in Boston, and why we were heading for California . . .

"Stop," he barked.

We shut up tighter than a cork in a wine bottle.

"Now listen to me. Do any of you have even a remote idea why I am concerned about you guys?"

I thought it a strange question: but, being the driver, felt obliged to answer, since my pals had mysteriously developed a sudden and severe case of laryngitis. "I was driving too fast?" I ventured.

"You guessed right on the first question. Congratulations," he said sarcastically. "As a rule, people drive too fast on this stretch of the road and especially late at night. However, that is . . . not . . . why I am shaking my head in disbelief. Why do you think I am so shocked by your behavior?"

"We were going really fast?" I offered weakly.

"No," he screamed. His face turned as red as a tomato.

I shook my head from side - to - side watching the blood vessels of his neck double in size. At that moment I figured we were going to jail forever. A broad grin ran across his face so wide, I could see his shiny gold tooth despite the darkness of the night.

"Do you realize I was the only car on the road?"

I opened my mouth, but before I could utter a sound, he continued. "You are the first driver who has ever passed my well - marked police car going 85 mph with no other vehicle in sight."

The three of us let out an audible gasp. I felt my freedom slipping away behind iron bars, or at least the need for a hole to crawl into.

"Now here's what I'm going to do. I believe your stories because nobody could have thought up such a cock - and - bull yarn in so short a time. You're getting a warning accompanied by a rider."

"A rider?" we chimed in unison.

"Yes a rider. When I get back into my patrol car, I am radioing ahead to alert the five states you are headed for. They will have your descriptions, the make and color of your Rambler, plus the explicit order to keep you under continual surveillance. In short, if you so much as fart or burp in the wrong direction, the three of you will be looking out from behind bars until you are up for retirement. Is that clear?"

I can just imagine the look he saw on our faces. We nodded in approval at his generous terms and agreed to be extra careful in everything we did.

"Here's the warning." He slapped it into my hand along with my I.D. and the car registration. I in turn, passed it on to Steve with Jerry looking on.

"I suggest you switch drivers and find a place to sleep."

As the patrol officer drove off, Jerry spoke up. "Guys, I enjoy driving at night."

Our first - late night excursion together taught us lots about our driving capabilities. We learned Steve found night driving tedious, due to an eye condition; my left eye became tired from the brightness of oncoming headlights, due to weak muscles, my problem since childhood, and Jerry loved driving during evening hours.

We shared a lot about ourselves during the course of our six - week adventure. My buddies were the first people, other than family, to hear selected segments of my sketchy past: I told them I had lived in an orphanage until I was five, lived on military bases around the world as an Air Force dependent and enjoyed being an only child. They shared family stories, career goals and embarrassing incidents. On that desolate drive across Iowa, we made a covenant to keep each other's stories confidential. Their promises became of vital importance to me when we reached the Pacific shores of California.

Due to our limited budget, we made a point to arrange overnight visits with personal friends, college buddies from Emerson and relatives as often as possible to minimize our expenses and say hello. At Lake Tahoe, we stayed with my college friend Mike Kletter. We gambled a little, swam a lot and later in the evening had a great meal with the family. Later, we had a two - night respite with Steve's cousins in Los Angeles.

They knew we were coming and welcomed us the moment we arrived on their doorsteps. Before we were even unpacked, they started talking baseball. The Dodgers were in town for a three - game home stand and, if we were interested, they would treat us to a ballgame for our second night in town. I begged off, asking Steve and Jerry if I could borrow the car to visit a longtime friend of the family. They knew how much I loved baseball, so they figured the visit had to be important. They agreed to my request.

I left after breakfast, promising to return by the time the baseball excursion was over. I looked at my two buddies and said, "The people I'm visiting will provide me plenty of new information to talk about on our way to Las Vegas."

The hum of the car's tires speeding on the highway transported my thoughts toward the impending rendezvous with B.J. (Bjorg). It was hard to comprehend the idea that this was only the second time I'd be seeing the woman dad believed to be my biological mother. The first time didn't count. I was only ten, recently naturalized an American citizen and on the start of a six-week family excursion from Spokane, Washington to Montgomery, Alabama. It was 1954 when I first met her - I was more interested in the backyard pool and dodging two toddlers crawling about the living room floor. It felt like eons ago.

As each mile sped me closer to the town of Riverside, the thought of B.J. being my long - lost Norwegian mother churned inside me. Dad was insistent I carve out at least a day for a brief visit. Due to heavy traffic, the drive took more than two hours. I was glad; it gave me time to think things through.

I spent the time consolidating the many conversations I'd had with my parents regarding B.J.'s relationship to me. I began reviewing the reasons why this visit was important.

August 6, 1946, a young Second Lieutenant, known by the name of Johnny, received his discharge orders stating that in two weeks he'd be headed back to the United States. He had one major complication: he had fallen in love with an attractive Norwegian woman who worked at the canteen area of the American Red Cross. Their two - week romance and his pending orders resulted in a hastily arranged marriage before the justice of the peace. It was the only way they could arrange for the woman, Monica, to join her husband - to - be, stateside. He was departing for America in a few days and she would follow later. Alone. However, before the departure, the teenage girl insisted they culminate their relationship with a Renewal of Vows church wedding. The two contacted the base chaplain, who was stationed outside the quaint town of Kitzingen, Germany. On August 8, 1946, Chaplain Brenner honored their request and conducted their second wedding service. Johnny went stateside and the new bride followed on a War - Bride troopship. Her vessel took more than three weeks to make the journey across the Atlantic Ocean. It wasn't until much later that my dad discovered Monica was B.J. and Hunter was called Johnny.

Before I realized it, a road sign signaled that I was nearing the town of Riverside. Five miles later, my exit popped into view.

Earlier in the week, I'd called B.J. and Hunter, hoping the family would be home and receptive to my stopping in for a quick visit. They were.

Finding the place was easy. Hunter's directions were perfect. Recognizing the house also proved easy. I pulled up alongside the curb in front of their home and spotted the pink flamingo, which had been on the lawn when I was ten years old.

B.J. and Hunter were standing at the front door.

Hunter came across the yard to greet me. B.J. stayed on the porch. "Hi Peter, glad you could make it," she called out cheerfully.

"Thanks," I responded from within the car. "I was really looking forward to this day. Is it okay to leave the car parked on the street?" I got out, closed the car door behind me, and accepted Hunter's extended hand.

"The car's perfect right where it sits. How was the traffic, bad?"

"A little slow in some places, but not too troublesome considering what I'd been anticipating."

Off to the side, I could see B.J. motioning for us to join her. Her decision to wait for me at the door made me feel awkward. I quickly dismissed it, as I attributed my feelings to the same nervousness that was probably churning inside her. Once we were within arm's reach, she gave me a quick hug before directing me into the house. The dwelling area seemed smaller than I had remembered. I credited it to the fact that I was only a fifth grader when we first met, and their family had more than doubled in number since my last visit. The clan staring at me now had grown from two toddlers to five siblings - two girls and three boys.

The afternoon went well. I sensed that Sandra, the teenage daughter, took an immediate liking to me. The feeling was mutual. After our barbecue dinner, she pestered her parents to let me take her out for some ice cream. Meanwhile, her two brothers hopped on their bikes to explore the neighborhood before it got too dark, while the little ones were being made ready for bed.

Over a large bowl of ice cream, Sandra and I talked. The informal setting afforded us quality time to learn more about each other. I also wished I'd had some private moments to talk with her mom. It didn't materialize and the reason was obvious: too much commotion going on with five kids and an out - of - town visitor. The extra time with Sandra, however, initiated a relationship that strengthened even as we shared our feelings over my dish of maple - walnut ice cream and her ice cream sundae.

By the time we returned to the house, the two little ones were already tucked in their beds and the two older brothers were back from cruising the neighborhood. B.J. and Hunter were settled in front of the television, relaxing with a nightcap and watching the final hole of a golf tournament. They turned to greet us.

We engaged in idle talk for the next hour or so. Eventually, with a modicum of protest, the three older siblings got ready for bed. After one hug and a couple of high - fives the trio vanished as if a sorcerer had waved a magical wand. It was getting late; reluctantly, I had to be on my way. We chatted some more before I made my way to the door. When it was time to leave, I gave Hunter a firm handshake and pressed my cheek against B.J.'s. What she whispered in my ear shocked me.

"Peter, when I saw you walking up the driveway, I knew you were my son."

It took my breath away. She gave me a firm hug accompanied by a knowing smile.

"My parents have spoken of you often," I said. "I'm glad this trip worked out so well for all of us." I paused an extra moment before continuing. "Another time, I hope the two of us might have an opportunity to talk."

"You are always welcome here," B.J. answered. She glanced over and spotted her second oldest son, who had discovered an excuse to come out to the kitchen. He filled his glass with some juice, chugged it down and then looked at me. Satisfied, he started back toward his bedroom.

"Did you take a close look at him, Peter?" B.J asked. "Can you see the similarity?" As if on cue Brian stopped and turned to look at us before disappearing down the hall. I think he heard his mom.

I nodded. "Yes, we certainly borrowed from the same gene pool."

A few minutes later, I was in the car turning the ignition. The sudden roar of the Rambler was my signal to be on my way. I waved goodbye before steering the car down the street and around the corner. Once out of their sight, a deep silence invaded my space as I drove back toward Los Angeles. The only chatter I could hear was in my head.

I had to agree, Brian definitely came from the same gene pool. We both had dark blond hair, small noses and ears that pressed against the sides of our heads. The set of our eyes, broad foreheads and dimples all suggested we were siblings. It was obvious the Norwegian side of the family was strongest in the two of us. I flipped down the visor and stared at myself in the mirror. For the first time in my life, the idea of having a brother was real.

It didn't seem long before the lights of L.A. filled the night. I arrived back at the house within thirty minutes of the returning baseball fans. The rest of the evening was spent replaying every inning of a game the Dodgers won. I wasn't surprised that everybody's words sounded like radio static on a stormy night. My thoughts were centered elsewhere. Later, after the household became still, the three of us slipped silently downstairs to grab more snacks and leftover conversation. We sat talking around the kitchen table well into the early morning hours. Even as weariness pressed against all of us, my fraternity brothers insisted I tell them about my mysterious visit. Bathed in the soft glow of a Mickey Mouse lamp, I shared some secrets, which only my mom, dad and I knew. My voice lowered, guarding against any possible eavesdroppers, forcing Steve and Jerry to lean closer toward me.

I shared the obvious.

"Thanks for the use of the car; it provided me a fantastic opportunity to visit family."

"Family!" blurted Jerry and Steve.

I emphasized silence by placing a forefinger across my lips. "What I'm about to tell you is for your ears only. Agreed?"

"My lips are glued," Jerry whispered.

"Same here," Steve signaled with a zipper motion across his mouth.

"I think I met my natural mother and had supper with her family."

"What are you telling us?" Steve continued.

"As I was about to leave, she said, 'Peter, when I saw you walking up the driveway, I knew you were my son.'"

"Why did you doubt?" Jerry asked.

"She looked different than I'd expected. I thought she'd be a blonde and she wasn't."

"You've been watching too many movies," Jerry laughed.

"Have you seen her before?" Steve continued.

"Not as an adult. When I was 10 the family took an extended vacation from Spokane, Washington to Montgomery, Alabama . . . we stopped in for a day."

"Was your dad there?"

"I really don't know anything about him. Dead for all I know."

"What was it like?" they both chimed.

"Strange. In one afternoon, I was in the presence of a mother I know very little about and 5 siblings."

"Did any of them look like you?" Jerry asked.

"Yes, the middle brother. We have the same facial features and blond hair. He even has a dimple on his left cheek like me."

"Nothing like instant family," Steve chuckled. "How did that make you feel?"

"It's strange growing up as an only child only to discover, on a sunny afternoon, you have three half - brothers and two half - sisters."

The ensuing monologue focused on describing the house, identifying the various family members and relating my time with Sandra. I kidded some to hide my new - felt awkwardness. I ended with, "If my mother has another son, I can say I have two complete brothers and one whole sister."

They had to ponder a moment to digest what I had just said. On that note, I clicked off the Mickey Mouse lamp and we tiptoed off to our respective sleeping quarters.

My eyes closed, but sleep eluded me for several hours.

I knew so much more, yet so little. If B.J. is my mother, why don't I look more like her? Why did she leave Norway? Where was I born? It was the first time I really started wondering specifically about B.J. and how to relate to her and the rest of her family. Question flooded my thoughts tugging me in varied directions. How and when did I get separated from B.J.? Where was I brought up during the war? Why has she never visited me? Does she really believe I'm hers?

Before sleep overtook me, I made one determination. I decided I would find a way to mentally distinguish between the two of them. Not surprisingly, it surfaced out of a conversation with Steve and Jerry. Their questions always referenced B.J. as Mom: "What did you think about your mom? Did your mom look the way you thought she would? Do you look like your mom? - I felt a tinge inside whenever they referred to B.J. as my mom. To me she was my natural or biological mother and I would refer to her as Mother or B.J. For me, Mom was the person who held me when I was hurt, read to me before going to bed, celebrated my birthday with a party, and knew that maple walnut was my favorite ice cream and baseball was my number - one sport. Mom was the woman who adopted me when I had no home. It made sense to me that the person who raised me deserved the intimate and endearing title of Mom. I knew nothing of my father. This afforded me the liberty to call Dad, "Father" if I was inclined to do so. It felt strange, thinking about how to delineate this suddenly new relationship in my life. When would I call B.J., Mother? - As opposed to using her first name, Bjorg? As sleep began to take its hold over me, I had the strangest premonition that this decision wouldn't be laid to rest for some time.

Ten days later our journey was over and lasting friendships were solidified.

CHAPTER IV

New Awakenings

"What difference does it make to the dead, the orphans and the homeless? Whether the mad destruction is wrought under the name of totalitarianism or the holy name of liberty or democracy?"

Mahatma Gandhi

Electing to pursue religious studies at a seminary was not a popular decision during the Vietnam War. The seminarian's primary conflict rested on motivation.

Local draft boards had the authority to grant seminarians 4F status, if the accredited, religious institution could provide enrollees a certified letter of acceptance into a degree - granting program. Many college graduates utilized this unique exemption as a means for dodging the draft and thus avoiding military service. These "draft dodgers" blended in among applicants who genuinely wanted a career in ministry. The difficulty was distinguishing between the two. A significant number warranted the derogatory label, but most were responding to a "call" to service. The lines became even more distorted when many seminarians, and their professors, began actively protesting against the Vietnam War. The public's knee-jerk reaction was to lump everybody together like a ball of clay and view all seminarians as draft dodgers.

My particular situation added another dimension to the dilemma - my dad. I admired his work especially during the Korean War and never lost sight of his devotion and effort to help the orphans lining the streets of a war torn

Korea. My father was a wonderful illustration of the important role chaplains performed while surrounded by the chaos of war.

I remember asking him, "Dad, how did you make it through the war?"

"I knew what I was called to do. My task was to establish a ministry of presence."

"I don't understand? You were ordered to Korea."

"I'm referring to my presence as a person of faith. The weapon I carried was my faith. A gun, M - 16 or grenades were not a part of the arsenal I utilized in support of the troops. I moved in and amongst the soldiers. My survival kit included a miniature bible for every soldier who wanted one, prayers for all occasions and always a listening ear. They knew I'd be there to hear their fears, hold their broken bodies and strengthen their spirit. My job was to help them not to be afraid of death but to do their job, whatever it might entail."

"I don't know if I have that kind of strength, Dad."

"That's why you go to seminary. It's where you clarify your relationship with God and learn which of your strengths will best serve His purpose to bring a sense of peace in a person's mind."

Whenever I doubted my commitment to the ministry, I'd think back to that afternoon conversation. I'd been accepted to the Hartford Seminary, and often recited the nursery rhyme my mom taught, "Sticks and bones may break my bones, but names will never hurt me." In a silly way, it gave me strength to know my commitment to ministry was genuine.

In September 1967, I began my first year at Hartford Seminary confident it was the right move. It wasn't long before my decision of how to serve God was challenged.

There was a movement being heard in the corridors and classrooms of seminaries across America. I felt the energy and couldn't resist its pull.

William Sloan Coffin, a chaplain at Yale Divinity School, was advocating civil disobedience against the Vietnam War. An articulate international figure for justice, and a vehement opponent against the involuntary draft, Dr. Coffin organized a coalition of seminarians, religious leaders, ordained clergy and professors to unite under the banner of "Clergy against the Vietnam War." He had the magnetic draw of a Pied Piper. Across the nation an army of followers was rallying to his call for action - a silent, non - violent protest march on Washington, D.C.

Hundreds along the eastern seaboard rode buses, hopped on trains and drove cars to meet at an armory on the outskirts of the nation's capital for a massive rally. The following morning, I joined thousands from around the country. We gathered in front of Lincoln Memorial for a pep talk by prominent religious leaders - Martin Luther King, Andrew Young and Jesse Jackson, Harvey Cox - advocating nonviolence as a means for securing peace.

The method was profound in its simplicity.

We would march in silence from the Lincoln Memorial to Arlington National Cemetery. We were instructed not to say a single word to each other, ignore taunting, grant no interviews and keep our eyes forward. We were also instructed to walk in step with the person in front of us. Our uniforms consisted of robes, vestments, religious symbols and a vow of silence.

The call was made and we began our walk. I remember mikes stabbing at us with the sharpness of a Centurion sword, people throwing profanity like rocks hurled at harlots, and verbal threats tossed over us like a blanket of hate.

Throughout the thirty-minute march, I felt no fear, only pride in the manner of our protest. In silence the sound of our steps resounded across the airwaves of the media world, our steps were televised across America as the message of **peace** resounded as beautifully and powerfully as a choir singing in one voice.

Throughout the duration of the march, I recalled the stories of the orphans my father saved during the Korean War. He risked his career to do what he knew was right in the eyes of God. During the march, my own World War II beginnings began surfacing as a litany of questions awoke in my consciousness.

- How many children will be orphaned in this war?
- How long will the lost child remain forgotten?
- How many of the neglected lose hope amidst their broken lives?
- Is war the way to peace?
- What damage awaits the orphan who survives the ravages of war?
- Can a broken past ever be fully repaired?

I knew the truth was becoming engrained in my mind like stain seeping into wood. The march changed me; but, more importantly, it made me aware of having been born an orphan. As my thoughts formalized, I felt the full force of fear and resolve within the same breath. My definition of war crystallized like a philosophical thought that was calling for a parchment to be scratched upon. I jotted down a few words shaped by the feelings formulated during our silent march for justice.

Just Wars?

"There are no just wars, only wars justified by governments maneuvering for power, corporations filled with greed and individuals seeking unwarranted wealth. Sometimes, war forces participation but the losses experienced by the living are never completely forgotten, only silently waiting to rise up and be heard again under the canopy of another dark day."

Rev. Peter Brenner

A casualty of my stance was the loss of a close, college friend - Medwyn. He was a classmate of mine at McGraw Kaserne, Germany. We kept in touch through occasional correspondence and frequently recalled memories of good times during our first two years of college. With the escalation of the Viet Nam war, our letters became more frequent and vitriolic. He joined the Army and was shipped to Vietnam as an artillery officer. I was adamant and unrelenting in opposition to the war. I felt I had softened my pen by sprinkling in supportive statements regarding the troops struggling to carry out their orders on behalf of our country. But it wasn't enough. Our letters became caustic and angry. Eventually they stopped. Our friendship had become a casualty of the war.

I had ignored my dad's wisdom. "Your presence as a person of faith is your weapon in war." I realized that I didn't have to mitigate my feelings toward the war, but rather, I needed to be more sensitive when dealing with others of divergent views.

I lost a valued friend because of my self - righteous need to be heard. I should have guarded against tuning out his feelings and raising the volume of mine. It made me wonder if my "Call" was merely an echo losing its force every time it banged against a wall of conflicting opinions.

Hartford Seminary was the perfect place for me to address the many questions and doubts that continually invaded my thoughts on a regular basis. The most difficult time came when the activities of the day concluded, my studies were put to rest and I lay down, exhausted and hopeful for a quiet night of rest. Often I was afraid to even close my eyes because of a repetitive nightmare that haunted me at various stops along my odyssey of self - discovery.

THE DREAM

The car weaved precariously down the narrow mountain road. At every bend, only two wheels managed to hug the curve before smacking down on all fours for the brief straightaway. The young driver pressed down on the accelerator, forcing the bulky, green Hudson to lurch forward into the night.

"Slow down," the young lady, implored. "You're driving too fast."

"I know," was the curt reply.

"Then slow down before you drive this heap into a tree."

"No!" The tone was unwavering in its resolve. The driver snapped his head to the right.

The woman was still there. Her fine features were taut with fear; white knuckles indicated her fingers were pressed firmly into the dashboard; the color drained from her cheeks, left a pasty white hue surrounding her hazel eyes, round as marbles; dark waves framed the sides of her face accentuating her wide - eyed look. Her laser stare seared into him. It was as though she were willing him to stay on course.

The car surged toward the oncoming bend in the road.

A sense of urgency highlighted her plea. "Peter, stop this madness. You are going to kill us if you continue driving this way." Then she vanished.

"Peder, keep your eye on the road! Slow down," the new girl, a teenager, pleaded. "You're frightening me."

The driver blinked and then rubbed his eyes. He gasped in disbelief, unable to force his eyes off the face of the Norwegian girl. Her smooth, silky hair spilled generously over her shoulders, complementing the high cheekbones and ruddy complexion. Her blue eyes mesmerized him.

His heart skipped an extra beat every time the changing image of the women switched back and forth, like the sides of a spinning coin - first the dark - haired New Englander, then the blonde Scandinavian girl. Glued to the transformations, he was oblivious to his surroundings and ignored their plea, as the county road disappeared out from beneath them.

Screams reverberated within the car, but it was too late.

Crashing through the guardrail, the automobile sliced between two trees before the nose of the green Hudson tilted downward. At first, it seemed like the car was floating in slow motion, but soon the descent accelerated.

In shock, the driver could only stare. Below them waited jagged rocks and crashing waves as the trio plummeted toward certain death? The young man turned to face His two passengers. Their images continued alternating back and forth. Then they stopped. Together, the two women smiled.

A scream filled the room. I panicked until I recognized my own voice banging against the walls. I was sitting upright in the bed as though an iron rod had replaced my spinal cord. The darkness shrouding my vision heightened my other senses. I could both hear and feel my heart pounding against my aching chest. I was soaking wet. My breathing labored in an erratic manner. I inhaled whatever air I could force into my lungs. It seemed forever before my pulse slowed and I felt a sense of calm return. I was alive and not smashed against the boulders at the bottom of some nameless cliff.

It was the same dream. It started at the end of my summer trip and began intensifying a couple of weeks prior to my arrival at Hartford Seminary Foundation (HSF). Now it was coming more frequently and I didn't know what to make of it.

I dropped back onto the bed struggling to gather my strength and trying to assess what had just transpired. One singular overwhelming thought became unnervingly clear: the river crashing against the rocks below was getting closer following each episode.

I felt the dream was a precursor, an omen of things to come. It frightened me. I needed to address this horrific nightmare before it was too late. The outcome appeared obvious: death on the rocky coast of nowhere.

Confronting my fear of dying was not going to be easy. My mind already felt like a crammed elevator filled with uninvited guests. Another pending crisis would only jostle around, press to the back and shove to the side issues already struggling to get out. I was praying for the door to slide open and provide an escape from the unavoidable options looming all around me.

I snuggled back under the protective warmth of the blanket. I lowered my eyelids and an assorted list of questions scrolled before me.

Who were the women in my dream?

Was I ready to be a minister?

What should or could I do?

I analyzed each item closely. Continuing with my studies was my most pressing concern. The other questions would have to wait; or so I thought.

I slowly pulled the covers over my head, curled into a fetal position and lay perfectly still. I imagined being a caterpillar enveloped within its cocoon. I wondered if I would ever be free of my disturbing thoughts or remain forever entombed by ignorance. I stretched my body to its full length before tossing off the blankets. Motionless I sat on the edge of the bed. The sunrise of a new day beamed its rays into the bedroom, forcing me to squint in self - defense. I slid off the sheets and made preliminary motions to get ready for my first year of graduate studies. I prayed the dream would stop or understanding would reveal itself.

Gary was a new friend of mine during our first year at HSF. I believe he sensed my struggle. One day, a month before our spring break, he joined me for lunch and made me an enticing offer. It had the same attractive air as the summer trip I proposed to Jerry and Steve.

"Peter, I've got a great idea."

"Okay, fire away."

"A trip to Mexico," he ventured.

"Mexico?"

"During spring break, we can go to Acapulco," he said with a Cheshire - cat grin.

"Gary, I couldn't go even if I wanted to." I turned away with a hopeless shrug and continued poking at my lunch.

"If it's money, it won't be a problem."

The statement sounded simple enough. I returned Gary's look and answered, "Maybe for you."

"Listen up." Gary moved closer to me and whispered, "I've already figured it out. We'll take a plane to my parents' place in San Antonio, Texas." He held up his hand to stop me from interrupting. "My parents always encourage me to bring a friend home - their treat. We stay with them a couple of days, get driven to the border to pick up a red-eye bus run (overnighter) and stay at an inexpensive motel on the outskirts of Acapulco. It's doable. Besides, I'm betting you've never even been to Mexico."

"I like the idea. I'll check with my parents and see if they will advance me some spending money. I've got a feeling that an offer to take a trip to Mexico would be something they'd encourage . . . I could use a break . . . who knows, I might not even be coming back to this place as it is."

"I guessed as much. That's why I want you to come with me. I can't imagine two more years here without your puns to keep me in stitches. Who knows, this trip might give you a good reason for sticking it out for another two years."

"Don't plan on it."

"I'll get the ball rolling on my end and you figure out how to make it happen at yours." Gary nodded in agreement. "This coming summer will be a memorable trip; trust me."

After classes were out, we flew to San Antonio, Texas. After a couple of days of sightseeing, Gary and I packed for our trip to Mexico. We arrived early at the bus station; affording us the opportunity to select the two front row seats overlooking the stairwell. The setting felt like a B movie, and we were at casting central scrutinizing each individual boarding for the shoot. The passengers were living caricatures of everyday - life: a mother herding her five children like little chicks to the back of the bus, a lanky giant bending at the waist to avoid banging his noggin on the ceiling, an elderly couple struggling to climb the steps before slowly inching their way to the first available pair of seats, and two gorgeous teenagers chattering so incessantly, I wondered if they could take in enough air to continue their conversation. An hour later, the entire entourage was squeezed into place. Another forty minutes passed before the luggage was shoved, kicked and scrunched into spaces half the needed size. Finally, the bus driver revved up the engine while a young, attractive attendant gave the thumbs up, indicating the seats were filled and the show was ready to roll.

Gary and I reviewed our itinerary embedding it in our thoughts for the duration of the trip. I read a couple of chapters of my mystery book until the bumping and swerving of the bus gave me a splitting headache. Fortunately, our seat location provided us with a panoramic view. When night swallowed the light of day, we opened our boxed meals and devoured their contents.

Throughout the ride, our smiling, dark - haired attendant assisted passengers with pillows, blankets and periodic information and historical facts germane to the area we were passing through.

Weariness set in, Gary and I asked permission to hang our legs over the metal railing, separating us from the stairwell. She granted our request recognizing we barely had enough room to shift our feet sideways and parallel to the seat. Once settled, I drifted off into a restless sleep ignoring the incessant rustling and indistinguishable conversations tickling my ears.

A blast of cold air on my face interrupted my sleep, as piercing screams began penetrating the silence. My eyes snapped open. Barely beyond my reach lay a twisted, splintered tree limb. It took a moment for me to register the gravity of what had just transpired. The front of the bus had been sheared away in the shape of a V - its point being where the attendant had once sat. Before me stretched nothing but open space. Gary and I looked at each other. We were covered with broken glass. Staring at the empty spot immediately to our left, we knew the slender attendant had disappeared beneath the twisted steel and rubble. The driver was screaming, trapped behind the steering wheel and clawing at a stump where his leg had been moments before. The inside leg of my trouser was cut - like someone had taken scissors to them. The metal banister was slammed flush to our seat, allowing my legs to freely dangle in the air. Gary was already assisting an older person across the aisle. I slid forward onto the remnants of the steps, tore off my jacket and retrieved the tie I'd shoved into one of its pockets. I edged to the driver and used my tie as a tourniquet to stop his bleeding. Placing my jacket against the back of his head, I tried to reassure him help was on the way. The next instant, bedlam exploded among the passengers as each began to recognize what had happened to them.

Out of the darkness, a deep voice barked instructing every person to exit through the emergency door at the rear of the bus. I felt a slender hand with a firm grip take hold of the tourniquet. I looked up. A middle - aged woman, with a calm smile, looked down at me and in broken English, thanked me for what I was doing. Then, she insisted I follow the rest of the passengers off the bus and to safety. I'm certain she must have been a doctor or nurse.

Once off the bus, I located Gary. He informed me another bus was already on its way to transport everybody to the nearest town where a major medical facility was waiting our arrival. When the bus rolled in, we all filed out of the bus and into a receiving room where physicians and nurses assessed the extent of each person's wounds. The sun began to peek over the horizon casting an eerie light across the sky. Medical assistance was being administered to those most seriously injured.

Gary and I looked at each other.

"Peter, are you okay?"

"I think so, how about you?" I touched my face to wipe away what felt like warm water. It was blood. My finger touched up against a sharp object. It was a piece of glass. I gingerly pulled it out. Gary too was splattered with blood. "We're covered with broken glass."

"Wow, you're right." Gary carefully moved his fingertips across his face and began picking out the larger pieces.

"I've got an idea. I'll extract the pieces of shrapnel I can see and you pluck out the glass embedded in my face."

"I've got a tweezers in my backpack; that'll help with the tiny pieces."

We spent the duration of the ride carefully extracting various sizes of glass; first from our face and then our scalp. By the time we reached the recovery station, we were a bloody mess. We received immediate medical attention by a woman draped in a white robe and a stethoscope hanging from her neck. She also assisted us in the task of filling out all the proper forms and clearance papers before quickly setting us on our way. They even provided transportation to our hotel. The whole process seemed surreal. It was as though they wanted to quickly brush us away, like dirt under a rug, so our presence wouldn't be noticed. I couldn't help thinking they didn't want an international incident reported.

Once at our hotel, we sat on our beds analyzing why everything was rushed through so quickly. Ointment, bandages, bloody clothing and a large bottle of aspirin were the only real evidence of what had happened a few hours earlier. The authorities had whisked us away and then washed their hands of us.

We later learned that the bus attendant was killed in the crash; the driver had lost the lower portion of his right leg, but would live; and several passengers had broken bones and severe lacerations. The newspaper reported the bus driver had fallen asleep at the wheel and crashed against the rocky hillside about two hours north of Acapulco. If the bus had veered to the left, we'd have tumbled over the embankment, probably to our deaths. It was a sobering moment to grasp how fortunate we had been. In the article there was no mention of any American passengers riding on the bus.

With our remaining couple of days, we managed to enjoy some of the local excitement. Just outside the town of Acapulco, adjacent to a restaurant pressed against the hillside, sits the LaPerla. The view alone is worth a visit. Below sits a cliff with four brave men lining up to dive into churning ocean water. These "Clavadistas" (cliff divers) put on five shows a day, diving into a narrow rocky channel. They must time the ebb and flow of the waves to allow for enough water to refill the narrow gorge so as not to hit the rocky bottom. They make it look easy but it's a scary, dangerous maneuver to master. The "LaQuebrada" (high divers) are professionals risking their lives on a daily basis, to entertain wide - eyed tourist.

During the last night of our trip, Gary and I lifted our glasses of red wine, looked at the divers one last time and toasted our good fortune. Both of us couldn't imagine why anyone would risk his or her life on a daily basis. We'd just survived a harrowing experience and being safely grounded felt reassuring.

I looked at Gary and said; "I've decided to continue my second year at Hartford Seminary."

Gary grinned and answered, "I'd guessed as much."

"You certainly seem confident with your assessment," I remarked, a bit surprised by his tone of absolute assurance.

"God spared us and I can't fathom why; except that He did. One doesn't walk away from a message as clear as what we've just survived. We both would have lost our legs at the knees if that young girl hadn't allowed us to break the rules."

"And neither of us would be talking now if the bus had gone over the cliff instead of into the side of the mountain," I emphasized.

We both turned to watch another diver drop some 45 meters and slice gracefully into the crystal - blue water just beyond rocks jutting out from the mountainside. As the young man surfaced from the depth, I laughed.

Gary's forehead furrowed, bringing his brows together, "What's the chuckle all about?"

"You did say, 'this will be a memorable trip, trust me.' It's similar to a phrase I was told by a woman when I was five years old." We lifted our glasses and toasted each other one more time and said, "Thank God."

*   *   *

Living on the monastic grounds of Hartford Seminary was not conducive to meeting women. This was obvious by their reaction whenever I uttered the dreaded words: "I'm a seminarian." It was evident to me that most women were not attracted to men pursuing a career in ministry. It was as if we'd had an infectious disease - tolerable, but only at a distance. I concluded, that to a woman, treading onto Seminary grounds was to her akin to visiting a leper colony. By the end of my first year, I'd convinced myself establishing a relationship with a woman would be close to insurmountable.

Classes had just gotten underway. I was in the first week of my second year of a three - year Master of Divinity program. One bright and glorious September morning, the temperature was warm enough for shorts and a T - shirt rather than blue jeans and a sweater. I ambled across the quad, past the stone chapel and toward the main administration building some fifty yards away. I headed toward the archway separating the main building from the faculty offices. Emerging from the opening were two joggers heading straight for me. They appeared to be college - aged women, and that warranted a closer look. I drifted to the left, positioning myself along their projected route. As the duo neared, their attractiveness became even more evident. The taller girl's sweeping blonde hair immediately caught my attention. The shorter, dark - haired girl smiled as she ran by me.

I nodded.

My heart skipped an extra beat to keep pace with my accelerating pulse.

I counted to three before glancing back to observe their departure. The brunette must have had the same thought running through her mind; she turned her head to glance back. Blood rushed to my cheeks the instant our eyes met.

She hesitated a brief moment before redirecting her attention to catch up with her running partner. I continued to stare as their figures became smaller and smaller and my hope grew larger. I was confident their animated gestures and chatter were about me. When they disappeared from my line of vision, I turned around and headed back toward the archway lamenting my missed opportunity. What a fool I was for not reacting in a more assertive manner - like tackling either one of the girls and whispering, "I love you more than life itself." Now they were gone and the likelihood of reconnecting with them seemed remote at best. I could hear church bells tolling in the distance, and wondered if God was trying to tell me something. Either way, I was confident that persistence and patience would prevail if I stayed resolute to my hope of encountering them another time. I could only hope they were from the area and regularly jogged across the campus.

It was another perfect Saturday in autumn. Multicolored leaves blanketed the ground. For the admiring viewer the fall colored trees turned clear - glass into stained - glass windows, and predictably the temperature was just crisp enough to be refreshing.

I needed a break from reading Dietrich Bonhoeffer's prison letters. Hitler had jailed the theologian for his role in plotting to overthrow him. The book was intense and inspiring at the same time. I could only immerse myself with his struggles for short periods of time. His plight struck a nerve, which made me feel uncomfortable.

I turned away from the open pages yawning before me. Casting my attention around the room, I marveled at the magnificent chamber surrounding me. The Seminary's library/reading room was sequestered on the second floor of the administration building. It extended the full length of the building from east to west. Its decorative ceiling rose to a second level, where oil paintings of past scholars stared down upon students with an oracular wisdom. Bookshelves lined the entire north and south sides of the two - story room. The grand entranceway interrupted the south wall. Three alcoves embracing bowed windows were symmetrically located on the opposite side of the room. Each window afforded a panoramic view of swirling leaves extending across the green lawn toward the chapel and resident quarters.

I wondered if Bonhoeffer had ever experienced such an idyllic setting while studying in Germany. Did he have any inkling of what lay before him? Was his courage always within him to do what he felt was right and just? What would press him to join forces with others to have Adolph Hitler killed, all the while risking prison and possible execution? As I considered these matters, I felt the questions were directed more toward me than saying anything about him. I dismissed these fleeting excursions into foolishness.

Turning my attention back to the magnificent setting and pondering my commitment to do God's work, I felt so safe and secure. I wondered if that was the attraction that drew me toward ministry. Or was the seminary a place to hide? Maybe I was running away from my hidden past. I even wondered if I was afraid to be categorized as a thrown away, German orphan, a misfit of society. My thoughts were conflicted between the action of Bonhoeffer and my need for security.

Students interested in being by themselves sat on wooden benches beneath the arched windows. Facing east, they could check the hands of an imposing clock ticking away to inform us how much time was left before our next class. On occasion, light chatter would interrupt heavy silence. During exam week, I felt the mere scratching of my pencil traveling over paper, or my rummaging through research work was too disruptive for the level of intensity emanating throughout the chamber.

Even though I felt imprisoned by the need to get my assignments read, the warm rays streaming through the window were diminishing my enthusiasm to continue working. I turned to look up at the clock. Time had slipped away from me. I was late for my appointed rendezvous. Quickly gathering together my books, I tucked them under my arm and rushed toward the exit leading to a lower level via the grand staircase. On the first floor, the maroon - colored square tiles and high bowed ceiling led me to a single oak door. Beyond it stood the archway.

It was just minutes before noon and time for my hopeful encounter with the two elusive joggers. It had been four weeks and my optimism was beginning to wane. I pushed the heavy oak door. It flung open, almost hitting a young woman on my left, who was bent over tying the laces of her running shoes. The sweep of her long hair caught my attention. I stood motionless. Startled by the door, she straightened upright and turned my way. It was the blonde girl. I gasped, praying the sound had gone unnoticed. I felt like an adolescent on his first date, not a twenty-four year old trying to remain calm while collecting his bearings.

I inched forward and broke the awkward silence with a meek "Hi."

She looked at me and smiled.

"Run here often?" I mumbled, as though I had just filled my mouth with a handful of marbles.

"Excuse me, what did you say? Tossing her silky mane away from her face, she revealed a radiant smile and sparkling blue eyes.

I estimated her height to be about 5'9". This made her almost tall enough to make me feel uncomfortable. Under the current circumstances, however, it didn't really matter. I wanted to know more about her friend, who was shorter. When a guy is 5'5" height becomes a minor concern. I was tall enough not to feel short, but short enough to wish I were taller.

In a more articulate manner, I asked, "Weren't you and another girl jogging through here a few weeks ago?" I could hear ringing. It took me a second to realize the chimes were church bells and not just in my head.

"Yes. You waved at us," she said with a chuckle.

"Guilty," I pleaded with raised arms.

"Well, I've really got to get going."

"Wait." Feeling empowered, I persisted, "What's your name?"

"April."

I pressed forward. "Do you live or work around here? Are you going to school?"

"I'm a senior at Hartford College for Women. We're just across the street." She pointed.

I felt better with her willingness to tell me where she was from. "Please, wait one moment." I fumbled through my briefcase until I uncovered my notepad and a long, yellow pencil. Triumphantly, I held up my treasure as evidence of my intent. She gave a hearty laugh. I had to admit she was getting prettier by the moment. "I've got an idea," I volunteered. "Here's my name, phone number and my friend's name. What do you say we make it a foursome? I tore off a piece of paper with my phone number, extending it and my pencil toward her. "What do you say?"

"And what are you asking?" she teased in an impish tone.

"Simple, a friend of mine and I would like to take the two of you out for dinner and casual conversation." I waited; nothing but stillness pressed against my ear. The silence was too awkward for me to remain mute. "Talk to your friend. If the two of you are remotely interested, give me a call; if not, maybe you and I could continue this conversation another time."

April gave a quick smile before taking the piece of paper. "I'll call," and just like a rush of wind, she was gone. I bundled together my fallen books and strewn papers. Nothing came of the radiant smile or implied promise.

It was the same old story: girls don't like seminarians. I had convinced myself that was the problem. However, the April incident got me thinking, maybe it was my fault; maybe I'd never find a soul mate for the simple reason that being an orphan, a castaway of society, I wasn't good enough to deserve a close and meaningful relationship. I began etching this interpretation of me in stone.

My middle year at HSF was a notch below okay. I didn't date; my grades slipped a bit; a melancholy air occasionally invaded my thoughts when I was feeling sorry for myself; and my disturbing dream returned with greater frequency. I started questioning my commitment to stay in seminary. The idea of ordination seemed like a cork bobbing about in a sea of confusion. It made sense for me to start honing in on other opportunities.

At the start of our studies, every student is assigned an advisor. After my incident with April, I decided to have a long talk with my designated guru - Ken Cannady.

In our first session, I expressed doubts, concerns and the possibility of my withdrawing from the Master of Divinity Program. With his encouragement, I enrolled in the seminary's Clinical Pastoral Education (CPE) Program, being taught at Hartford Hospital.

"If you hurry," he said, "you'll just make it before the deadline. I know for a fact that there are still openings for the class. It would serve as your second - year internship experience."

The more I thought about it, the more enticing the idea of CPE became. The field - education program was specifically designed for students considering a career path toward becoming a hospital chaplain. More importantly, it was a full year of counseling and self - examination. That's what captured my immediate attention.

I elected to continue with my second year of studies. I wanted to give the CPE program a try. I liked the idea of receiving supervised psychotherapy from a clinical psychologist, plus an opportunity to develop counseling skills. It felt right.

Within the first three months of the program, I had visited all but one of the wards at Hartford Hospital. One day, Ken Cannaday, my professor called me on it in class.

"Peter, don't you feel it's time to visit the Children's Ward?"

I silently ignored the question, shuffling through papers and hiding behind an air of business hoping he'd forget I was there. It didn't work out that way.

In a sharper tone, he reiterated his concern. "Well? What do you say?"

Aware of the cutting edge of his voice, I lifted my head and tightened my lips. Throughout the classroom, slumping students straightened and stopped what they were doing. An unsettling hush, like a rolling blanket of fog, settled over the room. The awkward silence was interrupted as my classmates began rearranging meaningless sheets of paper to occupy their nervousness.

Ken's voice softened as he turned away from me and addressed the entire class. "It's imperative that each of you visit every ward in the hospital. Next week, I want your most recent verbatim with a patient on my desk. Class is dismissed."

He turned toward me again. "Peter, before you leave, I need to speak with you for a moment."

Once the room emptied, I preempted Ken's attempt to say something. "Sir, I tried visiting the children's ward three weeks ago, but when I heard the babies crying, I froze. I couldn't make it through the entrance way."

"That's unusual. Why?"

"I don't know."

"Have you tried to go back?"

"Once, a couple of days ago. I made it to the desk but began feeling sick to my stomach and dizzy. I was going to tell you but just hadn't gotten around to it. I don't know what to do."

Outside, a howling wind quieted. Ken stared at me. Suddenly, I was awash with guilt. How could I not reach out and help crying babies, silent children or suffering teenagers? What was wrong with me? The thoughts had invaded my thinking before, but not enough to move me to make the extra effort to open the door and enter the wing of wailing cries. I lowered my head in disgust.

Ken rubbed his chin several times as he paced slowly before me. "I've something which might help you. Visit later in the evening, after most of the children and babies have already been put down for the night. I'm certain all but a few of the children will be asleep. Pick one and have a conversation with only that child. Write everything down and then have your verbatim ready for our next class."

"But what if I can't?"

When you go for your visit, let me know and I'll make a point of being close by. If you need me, I'll be in the chapel. Okay?"

I nodded. "I'll try again this weekend."

"I recommend Sunday; it shouldn't be too crowded. Don't worry; we'll work thru this together."

"Thanks." For the moment, I felt reassured.

Ken was right; the whole hospital seemed quieter as I approached the main entrance. I entered the pediatric wing without incident. It wasn't until the elevator door opened onto the floor of the children's ward that my chest tightened. I stepped through the door to be met by a smattering of dissonant cries. Inching forward, I dragged my feet toward the entranceway. I felt as though I was plodding through a muddy quagmire. The cries became louder, but I trudged down the corridor to the door and entered the wing. My thoughts transported me back to my earliest of years.

All I could see were beds lining both sides of the room. They were pressed so close together that to get out, each child had to climb over the end of their steel cot. The crying became wailing as the deafening noise enveloped me. I covered my ears and fell back against a door. All the children were looking at me with pleading, empty eyes; they were gaunt, with pale faces devoid of smiles. There were so many of them; they seemed to stretch as far as I could see. Each was reaching out in an effort to grab me, calling out for help, asking for food and wanting to be touched. I closed my eyes, struggling to lock out the images and the chaos swirling around me. I forced myself to focus. Suddenly, I saw one boy sitting quietly on the bed. He held out his arms and, without a sound, called out for help.

I was looking at myself when I was a child. It startled me. Like a stream of running water, fear flowed over me. I started to wail like a baby. I felt forlorn and disoriented. A hand settled on my shoulder. I opened my eyes and, in an instant the room emptied.

"It's alright, Peter, I'm right here." Ken squeezed my shoulder and guided me out the door into the hallway. The evening attendant gave me a quizzical look.

"What's happening to me?" I screamed. "Am I crazy?" I pressed my back to the wall and slid slowly to the floor. Exhausted, I whispered over and over again, "What's happening to me? Am I crazy?"

Ken joined me as we sat together on the cold, hard tile of an isolated hallway. Each time I repeated the question, he answered, "You'll be fine, trust me."

It was two weeks before I felt comfortable enough to come back to class. Ken used the time for private consultation, until I was strong enough to attempt another visit to the children's ward. He likened my incident to ghosts rising out of a dark hole. The ghosts were the unanswered questions of an unknown past. Crying baby's evoked experiences I had gone through as an orphan.

"So, I'm not as crazy as I think?" I asked.

"No, you're not crazy at all."

"How did you know I was an orphan? I never told you."

"I called your adoptive parents. Even they don't know much about your years as an orphan; they told me you were born in Germany during the war. "I suspected that when you told me what you saw."

"There were so many crying children," I explained.

"Actually, Peter, the wing was almost empty. There were only a few children who were awake. They were quietly asking for water or help to go to the bathroom. You imagined something that was very real to you," Ken reassured me with a warm smile. "Your dad said they found you at a place called Prien. Do you remember that?"

"I remember Tante Marella and that the building was close to a lake."

"How many children lived there with you?" Ken asked.

"I don't remember. Not many. Maybe eight or nine?"

"That suggests that you lived in another orphanage prior to Prien. Do you recall anything before Tante?"

"No. Well, I did have a dream which frightened me."

"What kind of dream?"

"It involved a little boy being hit and treated like disposal trash." I started to choke on my words.

"Your dreams remember, Peter. You just don't realize it. When you visited the critical unit of the children's ward, it jarred loose lost memories. Knowing that alone is going to help you face, I imagine, an extraordinary past."

"Ken, should I visit the children's wing?" I shifted in my seat and rubbed my hands together. I could feel droplets forming on my brow.

"When the time is right, you'll know what to do. As for now, it's obvious crying babies make you uncomfortable."

"Why?" I pleaded.

"The why will still needs to be uncovered. For now, when you're ready to go back to the children's ward, I want you to single out only one child.

Blank everything else out of your mind and walk straight for the one who first catches your attention. Approach him as a friend."

"What's wrong with me?" I chocked.

"There's nothing wrong with you, Peter. I believe, that when you entered the room, you stepped back in time. The incident placed you at the mercy of one of your earlier orphanages. It's not the crying that frightens you, Peter; it's the reason for the crying that triggers the mystery you need to uncover."

"And I will, someday," I responded with a faint degree of renewed confidence. "I think."

I trusted Ken enough to broach him with an additional fear - my dream with the two women in a car heading for the cliff. It was recurring enough times to begin frightening me. He listened intently as I reiterated the horror that was disrupting my sleep on a regular basis.

Our sessions covered a span of 8 weeks. His analysis was so simple; I was annoyed I hadn't figured it out for myself.

In summary, he explained, "You're struggling with your relationship between two mothers. In a sense, it's killing you inside. I believe you need to explore your past with your biological mother. Your dream is going to haunt you until you uncover more about your hidden past. Your natural mother is the only one who has the key to unlock the past . . . at least part of it."

I nodded, gave a big sigh and answered, "I guess I'm the one who can take the initiative, but it scares the hell out of me."

"And it will continue to do so until you face it head on."

"Damn, I hate it when I agree with you." We both laughed. I knew Ken was right, and that was unnerving to me.

I went back to the ward and managed to single out a smiling, happy and never complaining 5 - year old boy. He and I became good buddies. I soon learned that he only had two months to live. I believe I helped him appreciate his final four weeks. What he never realized was that he helped me even more. He made me laugh; taught me the importance of living each day as a gift; how to tap into my inner strength; and that I still had time to discover the lost five - year old boy within me, who needed to be set free.

I knew I wanted to be in ministry and realized it would be at a cost. The war in Vietnam and critics' claims that seminarians were draft dodgers left me in a puddle of anxiety. Every battle scene filling the television screen made me anxious; loud sounds, wailing sirens and crying babies filled my mind and distracted my efforts to study. It was beginning to reflect in my grades. I wasn't sure that my call to ministry was authentic or that I'd ever find a woman who would be attracted to me. Nothing seemed to make sense. I was in my mid - twenties and already felt old, emotionally worn and tattered like an old jacket ready to be tossed aside. I needed an away place and extended time to reorder my disheveled thoughts. I found an answer posted on a 3 by 5 postcard.

In our student union there was a bulletin board filled with scrapes of papers noting opportunities for summer employment. Most of the ads were promoting small church openings in some, desolate, out of the way location. I ignored all of them. However, one inconspicuous piece of brown paper caught my attention. It was entitled, "A Christian Ministry in the National Parks." The return address came from the National Council of Churches out of Riverside, New York. It piqued my interest. That evening, I mailed my letter to Warren Ost and the National Parks Ministry.

Within a week, I received a promotional packet. I tore open the envelope and was instantly moved by the beautiful photos, encouraged by the job descriptions and challenged with the multiple forms requiring detailed information about why I wanted to enroll in their kind of work. The program was offering a "worker/priest" format for ministry. If accepted, I would be assigned a secular job for pay and serve as the hospital chaplain at the park's clinical center. There are only three national parks that had enough tourists to warrant a hospital ministry program: Yellowstone, Yosemite and the Grand Canyon. Each required a seminarian to serve as its chaplain. I felt encouraged. I was already enrolled in a CPE program - and that would be a big plus in my favor. Serving as a hospital chaplain in the National Parks Ministry program would be outstanding preparatory work. Before the evening's final mail pick up, I filled out the application form and had my request for assignment on its way. Yellowstone was my first choice.

It seemed like an interminable amount of time before I received a letter from the Parks Ministry's office. When the letter arrived, I hesitated before opening it. What if I'd been rejected? I already had a parks and recreation job waiting for me in Philadelphia, but it wasn't in a National Park setting. I gingerly opened the letter. The first two sentences lifted the anvil pressing down on my chest.

"Dear Mister Peter Brenner, you have been accepted as a participant in our Christian ministry in the National Parks program. We were unable to assign you to your first choice, but are confident you will find Yosemite a suitable location for meaningful ministry and a memorable experience . . . ."

Finally, I'd been accepted.

My goals for the summer were simple: no serious relationships, lots of fun, plenty of backpacking and hiking, journaling and time to corral my thoughts.

I could barely contain my enthusiasm to get on the road for California. In 1969, classes at HSF concluded by early May. The mass exodus included students, seminarians, administrators and professors loading up their cars to evacuate the premises. I was in the front of the line and behind the steering wheel of my VW "Love Bug" driving toward the setting sun. I looked back at the campus in my rearview mirror and felt such relief.

I needed some distance from a Vietnam War that was still warring on me; I wanted time away to make sense out of an emotionally draining year in CPE, and space from an academic pursuit that seemingly provided little help in reassuring me that I'd made the right decision to enter a career in ministry. The only call ringing in my head was the option of not returning for my third and final year at HSF.

My early arrival at Yosemite National Park proved to be a distinct advantage. My reward was a spacious, double - occupancy tent with a hardwood floor. Of the two plain wooden dresser drawers, I selected the one farthest from the entranceway. In the space of thirty minutes, I had my clothes neatly folded and positioned in the appropriate drawers and in an orderly fashion. Once satisfied and reasonably settled, I ventured out to explore my new setting.

It was a brief walk from my lodging area to Yosemite Village - the center and heart of civilized life in the valley. It didn't take long to identify the best eating places, the information center which provided maps that highlighted detailed evaluations of the best trails for hiking, plus a booklet delineating the appropriate tools and basic supplies necessary for backpacking in the high country. There even was a pamphlet loaded with important facts and services being provided by the Park's clinical services. I ambled over and took a quick tour of the small but efficient medical facility that would be my primary ministry for the summer. I also located the gas station, where my secular job would get underway in a couple of days. The entire compact community was nestled among the granite mountains and alongside them flowing Merced River.

Within a week, I was exploring the trails and marveling at this gem of God's creation. The hiking trails provided time away from crowds and a brief period for reflection before responsibilities and exuberant tourists started to shape my days.

I sensed it was a necessary place to be at this juncture in my life.

By early June, all but a few of the park and ministry workers were registered as the program got underway. On Friday the 13th, Chaplain Davis, our program supervisor, scheduled a campfire gathering alongside the banks of the Merced River and under the ever - present majesty of Half Dome. Daylight had not yet given way to the beauty of sparkling stars and the marble - white glow of the moon. It was an impressive setting to welcome the team together.

We began with icebreaker games - a non - threatening way of learning more about each other. Thirty minutes into the activity, we heard a noisy car bumping its way over the rugged terrain. It rattled to a stop with glaring headlights blinding every one in the area. A fellow worker jumped out of the driver's side, scurried to the passenger's door, opened it and helped a tired looking young girl out of the car. I could sense she was overwhelmed by the sudden appearance of a crowd waving in her direction.

"Hi guys, I'm Tom. Sorry we're late but the plane was delayed." He nudged his dark - haired companion forward, away from the car lights and into the circle surrounding the fire. "This is Anna, but she goes by Bonnie."

With a valiant effort, Bonnie greeted us with a weary smile and soft, "Hello."

Tom took Bonnie by the elbow and seated her on top of a stump near the blazing flame.

It was only then I could really see her face. Her hair was short, with bangs a bit disheveled but standing watch just above dark eyes. She was shorter than Tom - and he wasn't terribly tall. I tossed a casual glance in her direction. All of us were checking her out, and I'm certain this wasn't what she'd envisioned for her initial introduction to a pack of strangers.

Suddenly, Tom pierced the stillness with his annoying tenor voice. "Bonnie finished taking her finals this morning and then rushed to Dayton, Ohio to catch a plane to California. She's majoring in music and will be a senior at Wittenberg University."

"Thank you, Tom," Chaplain Davis interrupted. He approached Bonnie and grinned. "You must be pretty worn out. Just sit here and catch your breath while we continue."

I think I heard her give a sigh of relief just before she said, "Thank you."

In the course of the evening, every member of the Park & Ministry team became better acquainted with each other. We knew things were coming to a close when Chaplain Davis handed out our assignments, schedules and rules. He was giving closing remarks when a commotion flared up at the edge of the fire.

Bonnie was on her hands and knees, sifting through the leaves and the area around her log. With a pleading look and panic in her voice, she said, "I've lost one of my contacts . . . I've got to find my lens . . . I can't see without it."

In one motion, the entire crew surrounded her and carefully began to examine every wood chip, pebble, acorn and leaf in our square foot of responsibility.

A voice piped up. "Bonnie, where were you when you realized you'd lost the lens and what were you doing at that very moment?"

"I was standing right here; I brushed some hair away from my face and the next instant it was gone. It's got to be right here - she swung her arms in a circular arc hoping to identify the area needing to be scoured.

I shook my head at the daunting task before us before edging into her designated area, lowering to the ground and methodically scrutinized every inch of earth before me. I was stunned when I saw a glitter and spied, sitting atop a leaf, something shiny. I carefully retrieved a plastic disc, held it up and asked, "Is this it?"

It was.

Even amidst a chorus of cheers, Bonnie strung out a list of thanks to anyone who could hear her above the din. Finally, she looked at all of us and said, "I'm sorry, but I'm about to drop and still have to check in. Again, thanks for everything."

Tom stepped forward and announced, "I know the routine; I'll take her to the registration desk." He turned to Bonnie and smiled.

And just like that, the two stepped out from the fire's glow and into the darkness of the woods. I felt sorry for the girl and couldn't help wondering if this was an omen of her summer. If so, I wanted no part of it.

The Yosemite summer proved to be a soothing ointment for my troubled soul. I felt healing take place each night I spent in the upper regions of Tuolumne Meadows, hiking the trails, climbing to the top of Three Sisters and surveying Yosemite Valley from atop Inspiration Point. The panoramic view of the entire region, from atop the granite giant, Half Dome, inspired me. Recorded within my mind were evening hikes lit by the brightness of sparkling stars casting a silver glow upon the rustic trails. The wary animals of the region greeted me with hesitant but curious stares. Mist from Yosemite Fall washed off the dirt and sweaty film that showers were unable to clean away. My journal pen continued to address empty pages and then fill them with the miracle of God's presence as one experience after another touched my spirit and renewed my soul.

One historic event that summer will always be emblazed atop my list of moments to remember. One afternoon, late in July of 1969, for one brief hour, every person in the valley and in the high country, I believe, had his or her ear pressed against a radio. Neil Armstrong was making history around the world as he took "One small step for man and one giant step for mankind." Amidst the beauty and grandeur of God's creative wonder, people stopped doing their routine activities and paused to listen to the words of an astronaut explaining the miracle of walking on the moon. In Yosemite Valley nothing was moving and not a sound could be heard. I'm certain that even the animals in the high country became as silent as those of us remaining motionless on the valley floor - filled with awe. It wasn't until the first step had been taken that voices and sounds could be heard. Everything in the valley came to a standstill allowing people to talk, chatter, laugh and pontificate on the accomplishment we'd just heard. It was a whisper that built to a crescendo; it was a moment indelible carved upon the mind - never to be forgotten.

Bonnie and I began a congenial acquaintance, but as the summer unfolded, like pages in a storybook, our relationship became increasingly more important. Our paths often crossed during campground visits promoting our outdoor Sunday - morning services. We looked forward to our occasional chats, which evolved into pleasant conversations. Chance meetings gave way to extended walks and lunch alongside icy old streams freezing our dangling feet.

I fought the urge to forge a meaningful friendship with this Wittenberg girl, but to no avail. I was smitten by her looks, drawn to her smile and connected when sharing our life experiences. By August, I was calculating ways to bring us closer together. I selected her 20th birthday for a trip to San Francisco.

It was the tipping point in our relationship.

I extended - and she accepted - an invitation to attend a major - league baseball game. I also encouraged her to spend an overnight in the city. She was an ardent Pittsburgh Pirates fan capable of spouting facts, stats and figures at a machine - gun pace. We laughed, ate hotdogs, cheered until we were hoarse. Any girl who could enjoy a baseball game as much as I did and knew so much about baseball was all right by me. After the game, we toured the city before going to a friend's place for the evening. She trusted me with her safety and I honored that trust.

Soon Bonnie would be heading back to college for her senior year. Two important decisions had been made in my mind. I had decided to complete my third and final year at Hartford Seminary Foundation. I also knew the depth of my loved for her and had already decided I wanted to marry her. I was confident her feelings would be the same.

My first decisive step began with a romantic dinner at the luxurious Ahwahnee lodge. After the meal we stepped outside and walked across a manicured lawn to a quiet corner nestled off to the side of the Lodge and surrounded by glorious flowers. It was the moment when the sun disappears below the mountaintop, but still casts its yellow glow across the sky. I sprung the question. "Bonnie will you marry me?"

She looked at me, hesitated, and softly said, "Don't you think things are moving too fast?"

"Maybe. But I know I love you; that's something I'm certain of."

She shook her head and looked toward the granite giants guarding the valley. "Peter, I'm sorry. I need more time to sort out this important decision. Please understand." She touched my hand and I reluctantly understood her hesitation.

The rest of the evening tasted like a bottle of spoiled milk. I managed to keep my composure and be a perfect gentleman. Inside, I felt like a train wreck. An evening kiss righted my rocky emotions. I realized the time probably wasn't right. I also knew that I couldn't let Bonnie escape and disappear out of my life.

I pressed her hand into mine and said lovingly, "I'll wait."

She tried to suppress a chuckle but I saw her shoulders move. This encouraged me. We walked to Yosemite Village where I gave her a goodnight peck. As she walked away, I knew, without a sliver of doubt, she loved me. She just didn't know it - yet.

I spent the entire fall communicating with Bonnie and setting up a mid-Ohio recruiting program by Hartford Seminary. Of course, I volunteered to head - up the project. The Seminary accepted my proposal and arranged to send me on a trip to the Ohio region - of which Wittenberg was included. I arrived during the week of Bonnie's Organ Recital. Amidst both of our responsibilities, she agreed to visit my parents and me during our Christmas break. She came to Philadelphia, and for the second time, I asked her if she would marry me. She accepted the ring and my offer.

On Saturday, June 27, 1970, one year and two weeks after our Friday the 13th campfire gathering, we were married in Charleroi, Pennsylvania. Her father, a bilingual, Slovok, Lutheran minister, officiated and my father assisted in the ceremony. Bonnie's brother, Cyril (himself a recent seminary graduate) was a groomsman and stood beside Dave Pople (a classmate of mine at HSF), along with my two great Emerson friends - Steve Baltin and best man, Jerry Greenstein. Bonnie's attendants were close friends from Charleroi, Pennsylvania and Wittenberg college.

* * *

Following June graduation ceremonies for both of us and after Bonnie and I were married at her father's church in Charleroi, Pennsylvania; we secured summer jobs in Hartford, Connecticut. As a temporary bridge to the future, I became the summer landlord of a small apartment complex on Farmington Avenue, just inside the West Hartford border. We each landed a part time summer job in the mailroom of Hartford Seminary. With free lodging set and enough subsistence money to pay our bills, we aggressively pursued all opportunities available for establishing creditable careers in education and mass communication. By mid - summer, Bonnie secured an elementary music position in Middletown, Connecticut. My Emerson College communication training still pulsed through my veins compelling me to explore the possibilities of making it in some field in religious communication. It wasn't quite what I had envisioned, but as the summer came to a close, I embarked on a two-and a half-year excursion into the world of film promotion and production, plus multi - media presentations. We rented an apartment on West Street in Rocky Hill, Connecticut. It was close to Middletown and an easy jumping off place for my media work.

In August of 1970, I jumped at the opportunity to work for Dick Ross and Associates. As one of two New England Regional Representatives, I was responsible for contacting religious organizations and pre - sale of group tickets for the film *The Cross and the Switchblade,* starring Pat Boone and Eric Estrada. Prior to the film's release, I set up advertising, radio and TV interviews for the celebrities and secured all the detailed arrangements for the gala grand opening of the movie. It was an adrenalin rush zipping from town to town throughout my designated region and juggling the various responsibilities. It was a heady experience, rubbing elbows with movie stars, reading my reviews in the entertainment section of the newspapers and gawking at a television interview featuring my own spin of a feature movie coming into town.

But nothing would measure up to match the turn of events that embroiled Bonnie and me on Thanksgiving Day, 1971. I had just completed a successful Grand Opening with Eric Estrada and Pat Boone in Springfield, Massachusetts. Mr. Boone immediately left the scene to be with family or another engagement. Eric Estrada was sort of milling around without any apparent agenda in mind. I decided to ask him if he had any plans for Thanksgiving' If not, would he be open to join Bonnie and me for dinner. To my surprise, he was available and accepted the offer.

I called Bonnie. "Hi hon, would you mind if I brought a guest to dinner tonight?"

"No. I guess not. We don't have much but I'm sure I could scrape up another plate of food. Who are you bringing?"

"Eric Estrada."

I heard a gasp before the phone hit the floor. "Who? Who did you say?" Bonnie choked.

"Eric. He's by himself and has nowhere to go until tomorrow. I thought it would be fun for us to get to know him better."

"Peter, we don't have any furniture in our apartment - not even a table or enough chairs. Even the food is going to be on plastic plates. I'll never be ready in time. You did say tonight, right?"

"Bonnie, he won't mind. He's a struggling actor who's got no place to go. It'll be a great evening. I'll see you in a couple of hours. Bye." I decided to hang up before Bonnie could change her mind.

The evening was a smashing success. The three of us had a great meal and wonderful conversations. We spent the whole night talking about how each of us was in exactly the same place in our lives - embarking on our dreams. We were three young adults enjoying the stories and history that brought us together. Every time I think of the evening it warms my heart. And Bonnie was a smashing success.

The dynamics, however, changed dramatically when winter arrived with its icy storms and deep snows. The risk of cancellations forced Dick Ross and Associates to relocate its promotional efforts and New England regional representatives to the warmer climate of Florida. Instead of being home for most of the evenings, I would fly out of Hartford on a Sunday night and not return to Connecticut until late Friday. On occasion, I was required to stay an extra week, only to be compensated with one extra day tacked onto my return home. It wasn't long before the excitement turned stale, and the bright lights lost their luster to the loneliness I felt in an empty hotel room.

I decided to look for new employment.

During one of my flights back to Hartford via New York City, I heard commotion coming from the front of the plane. I asked a stewardess what the fuss was about and learned Otto Preminger was a passenger in the first class section. I don't know what came over me, but I decided this was a golden opportunity to meet an icon in the film industry. I felt driven to arrange a meeting with him. But how and what would I say? Suddenly an idea popped into my head.

Taking a deep breath, I strode boldly forward, parted the curtain and spotted the shiny head of an imposing familiar - looking figure. I hesitated, and then moved to his side. In perfect German and barely moving a muscle, I introduced myself and asked if he would allow me to share a World War II story.

He looked up and glared. In German, he growled, "Wass machts du da?"

My heart stopped as my mouth opened to say, "I want to tell a story you might find insightful." It felt like a week before he responded.

"It better be good, I'm a busy man." He waved his hand for me to sit down. "I'm ordering a drink. If you want, I'll make it two."

Surprised, I sat down. I could hardly believe my situation. My plan to meet him had worked. I was actually sitting next to the man who directed one of my favorite movies: the blockbuster, *Anatomy of a Murder*. Trying to untie my tongue was my next immediate concern.

The drinks arrived. He looked at me with eyes that seemed softer than the minute before. This giant filmmaker and infamous tyrant actually appeared human.

My heart started to beat again.

"It's good to speak in one's mother tongue. Don't you agree?" He began.

I gulped and nodded before continuing, "I'm rusty with my German." His statement put me on guard. I didn't like the phrase mother tongue and being mistaken for a German bothered me.

"Shame on you, you're doing very well. However, I sense you would like to switch back to American?"

"Yes, if you wouldn't mind. In fact, at the age of five, I was determined never to speak German in public and only when required."

Otto's bushy eyebrows rose. "Was it the war or your playmates?"

I was taken aback by his insight. I gathered myself together before responding, "It was both. How did you know?"

"Simple deduction; you don't look German yet your accent is distinctly Bavarian and you speak perfect American. You said you wanted to tell me a story about WWII and yet you're not old enough to have fought in the war, but could have been a baby during the mid - forties. My guess is you're an orphan and your playmates made fun of you. Am I right?"

I was speechless.

His friendly demeanor put me at ease and the interest exuding from his face encouraged me. It emboldened me to begin my story.

For the next half - hour, I related how I had been adopted by an Air Force chaplain and his wife, that they couldn't have children, how I was ridiculed in school because I spoke funny, that I became a U.S. citizen in Spokane and that I had studied in Munich, Germany for two years. I even shared what my dad told me: I was born of Norwegian parents but taken away from my mother at birth.

His eyes widened as he shifted his body to face me straight on.

I could feel a change in our relationship the instant he heard how I had been orphaned. His gruff demeanor slowly melted away. A melancholy mood filled our space and his dark eyes became sorrowful.

Like a father who has seen pain in the face of a son, he touched my arm and said, "Peter, what do you want from me?"

"I don't really know. Maybe I needed to tell a German who might understand me better than I know myself. Having you listen to me is all I really needed." I turned away from him to face the aisle and look at nothing of importance. I could feel emotions swelling up inside and I was afraid they'd escape into the open.

"I want you to work with me on my next film."

He stated it in such a matter - of - fact way. I couldn't say no, even if I'd wanted to. Initially, it had been a primary motive that had somehow melted away during the course of our conversation. I turned to face Mr. Preminger. "Me?"

"Yes, this summer in New York City. I want you there during the first week in June?"

"Yes . . . sure . . . if you really want me."

"I don't ask, I tell."

He slapped his meaty hand on my shoulder and rewarded me, once again, with a peek behind his rough exterior and into his heart. At that moment, I knew, he knew more about me than I did. The next instant, a calling card was shoved into my shirt pocket.

Head down, he informed me, "I'm busy and need to get some work done before we land in New York. I'm expecting you to call me; now get going." He shifted his legs and turned his attention to a script titled, *Such Good Friends*.

I stood and expressed my thanks.

He ignored me.

I'm not sure if I floated or stumbled back to my seat.

The summer of '71, Bonnie, and I rented an apartment on the west side on 79th Street in New York City. I was hired as a production assistant for Otto Preminger's new film, *Such Good Friends*; Bonnie enjoyed the local sights, museums and the ever - present energy of a city in perpetual motion. On a few occasions, she became a gawking tourist watching the commotion of an on - location outdoor shoot. By summer's end, when the movie was completed, Bonnie and I found an apartment in Flushing, Queens.

She taught on Long Island and I worked with a multi - media house on 42nd street and Madison Avenue. It was a production house. The primary objective was to put together an audio/visual presentation for the sales department of a major corporation. I spent most of my time finding pictures to match the aesthetic feel or energy of the creative presentation in the works. I definitely felt overqualified and began looking elsewhere.

During down times, I reflected on that airplane ride from Florida to New York, I'm certain Otto Preminger recognized the mystery I needed to uncover. I just couldn't read the signs or connect the dots to understand what it entailed. I wished I had had the courage to ask him.

In 1973, as spring proclaimed its presence with budding flowers and warmer days, the idea of becoming a parish minister began percolating inside me like a fresh pot of hot coffee. Film and production work were too unstable. I wasn't prepared to spend the better part of every week away from Bonnie. We decided to look for new opportunities in our neighboring states north of the city and refocus our sights toward starting a family.

During the summer, even though I wasn't official ordained yet, I accepted some preaching engagements and managed to perform a wedding and two funerals. More significantly for our future, I attended some regional clergy gatherings.

The National Association of Congregational Churches held its spring meeting at South Congregational Church in Hartford, Connecticut. I attended and met, to my surprise, an adjunct professor from Hartford Seminary. I had taken two classes taught by Dr. Elmore, never realizing he was the senior minister of South Church. We had a nice chat and I expressed my interest in parish ministry and mentioned, "I'm beginning to test the waters." He, in turn, wanted to add a new person to his staff - an Assistant Minister of Youth and Education.

On the drive back to New York City, Bonnie informed me that Dr. Elmore had extended a veiled invitation for me to explore the position opening at his church.

In disbelief I asked, "Really?"

"Peter, he was dropping all kinds of hints about the open position. I think he was asking you to explore the possibility," Bonnie insisted.

"It won't hurt to try."

That same night, I sat at the desk and typed out a response. Early the next morning, my epistle was in the mail.

Bonnie was right with her assumption. A member of South Church's search committee contacted me. A succession of interviews followed, culminating in a "Call" to serve as the new assistant minister of South Congregational Church, Hartford, Connecticut. My center of responsibility focused in the areas of Christian education, youth work and mass communication. If I'd tried, I couldn't have scripted a better job description myself.

The "Call" initiated the necessary steps for Ordination. I had to select a place for the celebration, present a paper stating my faith journey and pass an ecclesiastical board of review by area clergy. I elected to have the Service of Ordination held at my father's church in Glenolden, Pennsylvania - a few miles northwest of Philadelphia; my statement of faith was well received and the gathered board of ministers approved my credentials'

It was April 26, 1973, and I was officially ready to be a parish minister. I started work and, within the week, Bonnie was hired as the music teacher at Central Elementary School, Simsbury, Connecticut. We rented an apartment in West Hartford just off of I84. The obstacles had been cleared and we were now ready to face the challenges of establishing our new careers. The highlight of my five - years at South Church, Hartford, Connecticut was a four - week Odyssey with our high school students. Bonnie, an advisor and I began our journey. Our first stop was Athens, Greece. Pastor Zikas met us at the airport and became our personal guide for the entire week. We first drove to his Youth Camp located north of Athens and alongside the shores of the Aegean, Sea. We began our tour of antiquity gawking at ruins thousand of years old. We toured a full day in Istanbul, Turkey; and later in the week sailed through the straits of Corinth. The second and third week of the tour found us roaming the historic sites of our Christian roots: The city of Jerusalem, the Sea of Galilee, Nazareth, the Garden of Gethsemane and the Mount of Olive. Each location was breathtaking as our evening scripture readings came to life the next day. The final week we flew to Paris, France. Most of our time was spent touring historic cathedrals (which became a blur for most of the teenagers), walking the streets of Paris, taking in shows and filling our stomachs with delectable food from corner bistros. We came back to America with a greater appreciation of our faith, the youthfulness of our country and the excitement of a bustling European city.

It is important to recognize that ministry has its own pecking order for attaining a Senior Ministry's position of a large church. That was, in part, one of my intended goals. The opportunity to serve as the youth minister of South Church, Hartford, Connecticut was a critical step in my attaining that objective. It may appear business like but it's grounded in the precept of a call for ministry.

In 1973, I also tried to get commissioned into one of the branches of the Armed Forces. It was a lot harder than I thought it would be. The Coast Guard wouldn't consider me; my amblyopic (lazy - eye) eyesight disqualified me for the Air Force; the Army was trying to fill chaplain quotas with women or minority candidates; finally the Navy yielded to my persistence and accepted me.

In May of 1974, I went to Philadelphia to be commissioned a Naval Reserve Chaplain with the rank of Lieutenant Junior Grade (Lt. J.G.). My father served as my witnessing officer as I held up my hand in a Philadelphia courtroom and pledged my allegiance to God and Country. It was a proud moment for my dad and me.

I knew fusing together God's presence in my life with my love for America was an important aspect of being commissioned as a Naval officer. If I wanted to oppose the impact of an unjust war, I felt I could be more effective serving within the system. I reasoned that I would better serve the troops, who were sacrificing for our country, as a chaplain rather than by carrying derogatory posters and screaming into a megaphone. I also admired the work my father accomplished as a chaplain and felt it had great value. Over time, it made sense for me to follow in my father's footsteps as a Chaplain and a commissioned officer in the Armed Forces. I knew my military service would vary from his, but the commitment would still have meaning and make its own distinctive footprints.

My first reserve unit was located in Hartford, Connecticut. As a Reservist, my obligations were straightforward. I would "drill" with my assigned unit one weekend per month - hence the affectionate term "week - end warrior." An additional obligation for every reservist required an on location, two - week commitment of active duty. Balancing my responsibilities, as the assistant minister at South Congregational Church of Hartford with drilling requirements, as well as being a new husband, took some adjustment. I felt fortunate that the church council was very supportive of my military obligations; plus, the reserve center wasn't too far away.

In 1975, Bonnie and I experienced a miracle together, the birth of our first child. We named him Erik Stephen Kalk Brenner. His first name had the Norwegian spelling - Erik with a k; Stephen was taken from his grandfather on Bonnie's side of the family; and Kalk was the prefix of my dad's full German name, Kalkbrenner. Erik was healthy, active and the joy of our life.

During the ensuing year, I entertained the prospect of exploring active military service as a full - time career. It appeared a reasonable idea to have Bonnie and our infant son, Erik, accompany me to the U.S. Naval Station, Virginia Beach. I reasoned that the time together on a large, active naval base would serve for an excellent introduction to the lifestyle of a Navy chaplain. Hesitantly, Bonnie agreed to test the waters.

When we arrived, I checked into the Navy Lodge. The accommodations were a little tight, but doable - one large room, two beds, a television, bathroom and two chairs, cornering a coffee table, partnered a matching couch. The facilities included a pleasant pool area with an adjacent playground rounding out the primary amenities. At first glance, it appeared to be more than adequate for our needs.

The next morning, after we had breakfast, I drove to the base chapel and met with my supervising chaplain. After preliminary introductions, he handed me a folder outlining the responsibilities during my stay. I couldn't have planned it better myself. I would be assisting with their summer Vacation Bible School program, visit the brig when necessary, be available for family counseling, prepare an order of worship and preach a sermon for the coming Sunday. It would be an eight to five job with two days off for each of my two weeks. I was so excited to tell Bonnie the good news: evenings together, eating at the Officers' Club, going to the shore, exploring historic Virginia Beach and socializing with some of the area chaplains and their families.

Early the next morning, I greeted the receptionist with a hearty, "hello."

With only a hint of a smile, she said, "The chaplain would like to see you."

I entered the office, saluted smartly and snapped out an energetic, "Good morning, Sir."

With a slight wave of his hand, the commander directed me toward a seat. I sat and he forced out a smile.

"We have a change in plans, for you. The X.O. on the C.G. Yarnell has need of a chaplain. I assure you it will be an outstanding opportunity and a unique experience for you to engage in dynamic ministry while at sea." He measured me with an encompassing stare. "You are to conduct two services this coming Sunday, one mid-week, Bible study group, visits with the personnel in their workspaces and be available for possible counseling." He paused, assessing my paper-white complection. "Most importantly, you'll be conducting a burial at sea. It's a ceremonial service which chaplains have rarely been privileged to conduct." The base chaplain gave a warm smile. "You might not realize it at this moment, but you are one blessed reservist to have this unique opportunity drop into your lap." He paused before continuing, "Have you ever seen a burial at sea?"

"Only in the movies."

His robust laugh strengthened my weak smile. "Here is my issue of *The Chaplain's Service Manual*." He handed it over to me. "Don't lose it. It's my only copy. It has an answers for every conceivable question running around in your head."

Eventually, I felt the flow of warm blood returning to my cold fingers and toes. "May I ask two questions?"

"Fire away."

"When and how long will I be deployed?"

"Plan on twelve to fourteen days. It depends on when the mail run returns stateside." He stood. "You'll be deploying at 1800 hours today. It will give you enough time to get things in order and have lunch at the Officers' Club as my guest. And please assure your wife everything will be just fine."

I rose. I'm certain he noticed the Adams apple bob in my throat.

"We'll take good care of your lovely wife and baby. Don't you bother your head one single second about them."

"Thank you Sir."

"Drop off your son here on the way to the club. My secretary will handle all the details, paperwork plus any questions Bonnie might have." He extended his hand and I accepted his reassuring handshake. "I'll see you here at noon for lunch."

"Yes Sir."

Holy - Helo

Once at sea, I learned that Bonnie asked her mother to join her while I was gone. Nothing was going as I'd envisioned.

The base chaplain was right: I couldn't have scripted a better first - time experience. I visited the troops at their work spaces in an effort to build an immediate connection with them: the boiler room, mess hall, kitchen, brig, command post, library and every other conceivable corner of the ship. In a relatively short period of time, I got to know the men and they became better acquainted with me. Preparing and conducting the burial - at - sea service, I knew this was an extra special privilege that I would never be called upon to do again. The Navy was phasing out this honored tradition. The ceremony was to be conducted in memory of a decorated, retired Master Chief who had served during WWII. I felt so privileged to have been entrusted with such a sacred ritual.

It wasn't until Sunday that I learned how harrowing being at sea could be for a circuit chaplain - one who visits two or more ships - scheduled to hold Sunday services. A helicopter was my means of transport between the ships. Whenever a chaplain is hoisted up to a hovering helicopter, it is referred to as the Holy - Helo. Once I concluded the service on the C.G. Yarnell, I was escorted to the deck, where a steel cable to the Holy - Helo would crank me up. I felt uncertain and on the edge of fear when a young, inexperienced seaman fumbled with my harness in an effort to properly secure my straps. Once off the firm footing of the deck, I felt a tremendous down - thrust of wind created by the helicopter's swirling propellers. Once airborne, the force of the wind ripped me partially loose from my harness. I instinctively pressed the straps against my body and gripped the bands so hard they began to cut the palms of my hand. Every time I looked down, my hold would weaken and the prospect of being smashed onto the deck filled my eyes. The wind blew me from side to side and on occasion set me spinning in a circle. With my hands weakening, I countered by pressing my arms even tighter against my side - trapping the harness. About halfway, I decided to look up and concentrated on a sailor yelling instructions. I couldn't hear a word but somehow felt stronger and encouraged as I moved closer. I was still more than an arm's length from the opening when the Marine leaned over the side, stretched and bent down to grab me. I could finally hear him.

"Hang on Padre, I've got you. Don't let go, you'll be safe in a moment." He grasped my flight jacket and threw me into the helicopter like a bag of grain.

I could hear him yelling, "You're in, sir. You can relax now and let go of the harness."

I released my grip, stretched my cramped, aching fingers and took my first full breath. Slowly the pounding of my heart stopped its effort to escape from my chest. I had survived.

"Well done, Padre. You're safe now."

Somehow, I sputtered out, "Thanks."

The rest of the day was busy, but anticlimactic, compared to my earlier activities. The burial at sea, although dramatic, followed strict navy regulations. The casket slipping into the tossing sea sent shivers down my spine. It is an image I'll never forget. Two days later, I returned to my home ship. I was struck at how secure and comfortable my other Holy - Helo transports had gone. When I placed my foot on solid ground the sailors all started to cheer. I waved and plastered an awkward grin on my face that stayed with me all the way to my stateroom. There sitting on my bunk was a note. It was addressed; Chaplain Brenner and simply stated "The Skipper would like you to immediately report to his quarters." I tossed my belongings onto the bunk and headed for my rendezvous with the ship's captain. I knocked and heard an invitation from behind the iron - door. I entered, saluted and asked, "You wanted to speak to me, sir?"

"Relax, Peter. Inside my quarters you can call me Bob. Have a seat." He gestured and I eased myself onto a chair. "I need to inform you about an incident we had onboard this ship about three weeks ago. We had a tragic accident due to either negligence or faulty equipment. One of our personnel was harnessed during a helicopter exercise and died when he was dashed to the deck. It was my decision to withhold all unnecessary helicopter exercises until we could get a chaplain onboard.

"I don't understand."

"It doesn't make much operational sense, but I think you might appreciate what I'm going to say. I am a strong man of faith. I prayed and knew that a Padre needed to be the next person to be hoisted up and into our helicopter. I needed that helicopter to be a Holy - Helo."

I chuckled. "I like that."

"I agree, especially this time. I know you're a young reservist, but I also knew a chaplain had to be the next person on that pulley. Your harness appeared to be properly attached. Suddenly, you began twirling around. You reacted perfectly: Your grip was strong, you pressed the straps against your side and you looked up. I never once saw you panic, maybe fear, but not panic. It saved your life and exposed the problem. One set of straps was deficient."

"I don't know what to say except I was relieved when me feet hit the deck." Within an instant he switched onto another topic".

"I've got a surprise for you. Later this week, you will be granted a two - day visit with the admiral on the aircraft carrier USS Kennedy. I'm sure the chaplains there will scare up some work for you. Mostly, you'll be lingering around until the mail run heads back to the mainland. It's been a pleasure knowing you and if you want another couple weeks on this bucket, give me a call."

"Thank you sir. I appreciate the offer."

We rose and shook hands. I said "goodbye" and he gave a slight nod of his head.

I didn't know what to think. Had I almost been killed by the military in a test of equipment or personnel procedures - based on faith? I was Certain of one thing in Navy, you say "Thank you, sir", don't ask questions and briskly move forward.

The years in Hartford became a balancing act - among family time, youth work at South Congregational Church and the Navy Reserve. A pattern developed which I wasn't able to understand. Whenever our son Erik persisted with his crying, I found excuses to leave the room or do more work away from the home. Bonnie was wonderful. I knew it bothered her, but she seldom complained. I struggled to understand why my son's crying bothered me so intensely. It felt similar to my inner conflict when, I visited the children's ward at Hartford Hospital during my second year as a seminarian. Intellectually, I made the connection that crying babies were a problem born out of my past. Emotionally my logic remained floating in the air, like a wind - blown balloon, without direction. I was battling to control or make sense of my confusion. However, I wanted to shove everything surfacing back into my battered heart and then ignore the feelings on my way out.

I knew there was something wrong with me. During quiet evenings, I wondered if the Navy Reserve and youth activities served as my safety net and a means of running away from a past haunting me. The conflict inside was at once inviting and at the same time repulsive.

Wedding Scene
Bjorg being married to Hunter by my Dad,
Chaplain A.E.K. Brenner

Solo Shot of me
Peter at the age of 5 (1949).

Bjorg
My biological mother as a 17 year old teenager close to the time
she bore me.

Nurse with baby
Lebensborn Nurse in Nordrach holding me two weeks after my
birth (1944) at the Children's Home (1st orphanage).

Family Picture
An early Brenner family with adoptive parents
Chaplain and Mrs. Brenner plus me

Outside of trailer
Art and Trudy showing me my new home.

Family in car
Parents in NYC with me in my new red shoes and new outfit.

Mom with me
Adoptive mother (Trudy) holding me at the age of 3 (1947) at
Prien (my third orphanage).

Tanta with Peter
Director of my 3rd orphanage located in Prien, Germany.

Nordrach Children's Home
My first orphanage (1944 - 45).

Peter in Munich
On Sabbatical in Munich, Germany (2006). Picture that prompted
the title for the memoir

Steinhoring Complex
Headquarters for Himmler's/Hitler's Lebensborn Project.
My 2nd orphanage (1945-47)

Korean War
Chaplain Brenner standing with orphans in front of their tent and
the start of The Brenner Onyang Orphanage.

Navy Retirement
My retirement ceremony from the Navy Reserve Program after 21
Years of service with Bonnie at my side.

Portrait of me
Professional picture from Busath Photography (Don Busath 1988).

Brenner Family
Peter, Bonnie, Erik and Tim

CHAPTER V

Changing Times

"Do not let Sunday be taken from you. If your soul has no Sunday, it becomes an orphan."

Albert Schweitzer

During the fall of 1978, I accepted a position as Associate Minister for First Congregational Church of Wauwatosa, Wisconsin. It was a fantastic ministry for me. I was the minister of youth, young families and program development.

Bonnie was already pregnant with our second child. We recognized the importance of our children and decided Bonnie teaching full time was secondary to our newest miracle. We both agreed that her being a stay-home mom would be best for the entire family. Timothy Peter Kalk Brenner was born on March 15, 1979. His name, like Erik's, held great significance for us. Timothy is a great biblical figure in the New Testament. We agreed it would also be meaningful to have Tim carry forth with one of my names - Peter. With two very active boys in hand, Bonnie's days and nights were busier than any full-time job. Tim's birth was the second time I was blessed to be present and an active participant in the birthing experience of our son.

I still was absent from my boys more often than either of us desired. My excuse was work, navy reserve obligations and studies toward my Doctor of Ministry degree from Chicago Theological Seminary. The birth of our second son - and his inevitable crying - brought clarity to my anxiety of being around crying babies: Somehow, it reminded me of a roomful of screaming children. I knew I had to be involved with my sons if I didn't want to risk losing them.

Into my eighth year as a clergyman, I was still questioning the authenticity of my "Call." Was it a response to my dad's successful career as an Air Force chaplain; or my lingering aversion to political leaders, who in our national interest deemed it appropriate to continue placing our sons and daughters in harm's way? Proclaiming peace or protesting war was the battle within me. This prompted me to attend a workshop entitled, "Grounding the Ordained Clergy."

The purpose of my "Call" crystallized during an introspective, extemporaneous writing assignment designed to tap into the writer's subconscious. Students were given 15 minutes to sketch out, on one sheet of paper, their feelings about the topic, "Clarifying A Call?" The following flowed forth from my pen:

The Call

His stature was long and supple, like a birch tree bending on a windy day. He looked like Ichabod Crane being chased by the headless horseman.

It made all the difference.

His features were angular with more edges than smooth surfaces. Sunken deep within his eye sockets were glowing coals - like burning embers staring out from a campfire. On occasion, they flickered like sparkling gems reaching out from a brooding darkness.

And that was important.

Everything about him appeared mysterious and distant except his eyes. His gaze had a varying brightness that must have been fueled or energized by memorable and imagined experiences. They were beacons guiding the uninformed, the lost and the reluctant on a path toward fulfillment.

And that was a revelation.

If I could muster the courage to look behind the rough exterior, I'd recognize a hardness caused by trying times indelibly etched within the creases of his craggy face. Therein would lay the attainable secrets for enlightenment. This bearer of light had the power to set the seeker on a path leading from nowhere to a place called somewhere.

And that would be life changing.

I asked him, with a tremor in my voice; "what is a Call?"

He smiled. In an instant, his entire countenance changed. The body straightened and coal - colored eyes brightened, as the embers flickered again and lit up the vacant space within my own soul. With wisdom beyond my understanding, he questioned me, the seeker, with a rumbling sound resonating deep from within him.

"What is Ministry? Only you can authenticate that answer."
With the simple answer the conversation bloomed.
"I hear," I answered.
"Now it's time to discover your answers," was the response.

I realized a "Call" wasn't some magical power bestowed upon an individual during a service of ordination. Doing ministry defines the nature of a "Call." Ministry is helping others in need and showing how God's nonjudgmental love needs to be a part of our lives. Being reminded of what I already knew cleared my mind of nagging obstacles obstructing my view of God's handiwork materializing all around me - feeding the hungry, clothing the cold, providing shelter for the homeless and reaching out a hand to the rejected. The last piece resonated with me; it sounded like something an orphan would want to have included on a list of needs to be met.

However, I needed to do more work on myself. Only when I could be strong and feel confident in my abilities would I have any hope of being a conduit for helping others. I needed a cleansing experience.

I decided to act. During the autumn of 1980, I enrolled in a Doctor of Ministry program at Chicago Theological Seminary. CTS captured the same feel and atmosphere as Hartford Seminary Foundation (HSF) - only on a larger scale. Both institutions had catacombs where a seminarian could figuratively escape from the 20th Century; each had small, gothic chapels providing quiet space for meditation, reflection and private conversation with God; the professors were outstanding and the campus setting inspired and informed a student's quest for theological enlightenment. It was a heady place to learn how to do ministry.

For the second time in my life, an instructor emerged as an instrumental guide in my ongoing quest for inner peace. Dr. Phil Anderson, a tenured professor at Chicago Theological Seminary during 1981, served a similar role for me as Ken Canaday had at HSF in 1969. As a clinical psychologist, Ken gave me the courage to open doors I'd slammed shut. I had never imagined the similar impact of Dr. Phil Anderson's skills.

An advocate of Gestalt psychology, Dr. Phil Anderson tapped into the primordial importance of experiencing inner feelings. Dr. Anderson created a setting challenging me to unlock buried conflicts still struggling to be set free. During one of his classes, he introduced the question, "how does it feel to be orphaned?" I felt like Thornton Burgess' Peter Cottontail running into the brier patch. It was a necessary place to run into, but the decision would invariably result in emotional cuts and bruises.

The class included seven participants - the professor, four women and three men. Our shared stories bonded us together. We dealt with family deaths, the loss of a baby, an ugly divorce, physical abuse, lost jobs, new careers, betrayed trust, and being orphaned. Every personal account moved the teller of the tale and touched each listener. In this class, I learned to appreciate the person behind the smile.

As the classes progressed and the weeks slipped into months, I'd managed to minimize the impact of my being orphaned during World War II. Dr. Anderson, however, astutely observed our every action - body language, eye contact or lack of, the positioning of each student within the classroom, tone of voice and pattern of participation. When an opportunity surfaced, he'd turn and single out a particular person for group focus. One blustery day, late in the semester, the prevailing wind blew my way. The professor directed his attention toward me, drawing the stare of my colleagues. I fidgeted in my chair trying to avoid eye contact, while nervously running my dry tongue across sandpaper lips. Phil persisted; I resisted. His steady stare finally reeled me in like a hooked fish still hoping to wiggle free. My eyes stopped shifting around and settled on his face.

"What? Why are you looking at me?"

Phil silently checked out the group before returning to me. Looking only at me, he addressed the class.

"In this class, we have experienced how anger empowers our basic need for survival. When we trace scared feelings back to their origin, people often respond directly toward the group or person who has been the betrayer. It's an issue of broken promises. Some of it is real, some of it is perceived but all of it is painful." He paused for a moment before centering his focus directly toward me. "Is that true . . . Peter?"

"I guess."

"You guess? Would you agree that truth telling helps to remove barriers?"

"Sure . . . sometimes . . . it depends," I stammered.

"Class, I have a quick exercise I would like all of you to do. Get out a piece of paper and write down your first impression of the following three statements. I'll give you sixty seconds between each."

We rustled around to retrieve a pencil and paper. When everyone was ready, we faced Phil. I was relieved he'd gotten off my case.

"First, write down things I like about myself. Remember, you have only sixty seconds, (pause); Second, things I dislike in others, (pause); Third, what I dislike about myself, (pause). Okay, now hand in your paper."

My anxiety resurfaced when Phil selected my paper and began to silently read what I'd written. Everyone in the room knew Dr. Anderson had an ulterior motive to the exercise and it pertained to me.

"Peter, your answer to the first was 'I care about people and am respectful of other's opinions'. The next question, you say 'you dislike people who are deceitful and hurtful.' Is that true?"

"Yes."

"Finally, you refer to yourself as abandoned and shallow." Dr. Anderson placed the sheet on the floor beside his chair and looked at me. "Do you value yourself?"

"I think so; most of the time."

"Does your past make a difference to you?"

I could feel an uneasiness creeping into the room and anger mounting within me. I trusted Phil and the group, but was afraid of myself. I felt he was navigating into murky waters and I didn't like it, especially in front of my classmates.

"No . . . Not really . . . I don't know."

"Do you want to know the truth about who you are?"

"Sure. Who doesn't," I snapped.

Phil softened his voice to the point I had to strain to hear the words. "We all know you were adopted. Does that bother you?"

"So what, I don't care."

"That it was in Germany during World War Two?"

"That's nobody's business, but mine." I barked.

Phil edged forward with added emphasis. "Do you know your mother?"

"Of course, her name is Trudy," I said sarcastically.

"I mean your natural mother, not your mom."

"Sort of, I've met her twice, once as a kid and again when I graduated from college." A hush fell throughout the room.

"Do you care?"

"Not really. I'm not even certain if she is my mother." I shifted in my chair and threw quick glances toward the rest of the group. With a glare, I faced Phil.

"Peter, do you want to know who you are?"

My volume ratcheted upward a notch as the muscles of my neck tightened. I barked, "I'm fine. What part of the sentence don't you understand?"

"Peter, don't be afraid; we're here for you." Phil rose from his seat, cautiously moving toward me. He knelt at my feet and touched my hand. "Do you want to know who you are?"

Suddenly, a stranger from within me screamed, "Fuck you, who wouldn't?" I felt my whole body shake and tremble as I tried to restrain the sound of an unfamiliar voice striking out. "Why should I? . . . She abandoned me . . . She's got her own family . . . I'm illegitimate . . . Are you satisfied? I'm a bastard and full of shit. Is that the truth what you wanted to hear?"

The battle continued for several minutes as Phil and the beast within me fought. Suddenly, I collapsed into a circle of arms and wept uncontrollably. I felt ashamed, dirty, and worthless, out of control and humiliated. Grasping for breath, I struggled to see beyond my curtain of tears. A clear voice penetrated through my weakened defense.

"Peter, you're loved, but you won't understand it this way. Look at me and tell us what you feel." The group assisted me to a soft chair and gathered around me. I felt hands calming my tremor; I could hear their breathing, as they exhaled and inhaled with the rhythm and dependability of a metronome; it gave me an inner strength.

I looked up into their faces and pleaded, "I'm not illegitimate; wars are, parents might be, but I'm not. I didn't ask to be born. It's not my fault. All of my life, I have felt like an infected sore filled with a poison spreading, unseen, inside of me. Behind my smile lie shame, anger and pain."

Phil cupped my face in his hands and looked directly into my eyes. "Peter, do you want to know who you are?"

"I know. I'm a World War II baby, born in Germany of Norwegian parents. I know nothing of my father; I'm not sure about my natural mother and I have no clue where I was born or the places I lived, except the one I was adopted from. I know so little of my past, but all the pain; it comes from a time I know nothing about. I feel empty, soiled and worthless."

The next instant, I was being lifted into the air facing the ceiling. My body was stretched out to its fullest; slowly the group raised me higher and higher. I heard a chorus of voices chanting in unison, "You are a child of God and worthy of His love." Over and over the melodic words floated up to me like a chant, "You are a child of God and worthy of His Love." I have no recollection how long I was suspended in the air. I only felt relief.

When I was lowered, each person hugged me and told me how much they cared for me. My meltdown diminished as I realized what was being said about me - I wasn't illegitimate, I had a name, parents who loved me, friends who cared and valued me just the way I was and I was a child of God.

I looked at Phil. "Why do I feel so empty?"

He smiled and asked, "Why do you think so?"

"I still needed to know more about myself."

"And what else?"

"Talk to my mother and find out what really happened."

"Peter, I believe that's the source of your pain and unrest. We're here to give you unqualified, loving support. But for whatever reason, that's not quite enough. Who you are, in part, is still tied to those five lost years."

I pressed my face in the sofa as one - by - one the classroom emptied in silence. I felt their presence even as I remained to silently address my thoughts.

The class concluded two weeks later. During the last session, we all received gifts representing our journey and new discoveries. Mine was an olivewood carving of a woman holding her child. I made a promise to always keep the gift as a reminder of who I was - A child of God.

My time at Chicago Theological Seminary and, more specifically, my last class with Dr. Phil Anderson, was an epiphany. In short, I realized my public persona didn't match my private agony. My life wasn't balanced. Behind my smile hid a little boy afraid to face his past: explosive sounds made me quiver; sirens continued to frighten me; a room filled with crying babies always unsettled my nerves and movies of abandoned children regularly brought me to tears. I was living a lie, trying to connect a life separated from a past buried within the ugliness of a war.

I had to face my past if I had any hope for the future.

Even so, I decided to move forward and ignore the feeling of shame and disgust that repeatedly wiped away any smile trying to linger on my face. It was time to blot out the ugly past, whatever it was, and concentrate on the present. I wanted to be positive, happy and helpful. Dwelling on the negative seemed counterproductive to my personality and who I wanted to be.

As a middle-aged man, memories and new discoveries about my past heightened my sense of guilt. I felt like Jenna Blum's character in *Those Who Save Us*, who says, "Finding out about me is like reaching under a rock and touching something covered with slime. And now, I too am coated with it, always have been; it can't be washed off; it comes from somewhere within."

Maybe I should abandon my efforts altogether? Why invite additional rejection, punishment, and ridicule. Perhaps it would be best not to stir this nest of snakes slithering around my thoughts. To leave well enough alone sounded safe.

Yet my headaches persisted: I closed my eyes in an effort to blot out the images I saw; I tried to imagine being a different person; and I learned to wear a smile in public to divert inquisitive questions that might point to past iniquities. If I were Roman Catholic, I'd be a regular visitor to the confessional, but always in disguise. I sought cleanliness, but never understood why I felt dirty; I organized my life in an orderly fashion by hanging up my clothes, picking up around the house, folding my clothes neatly and perfectly aligning them in the dresser drawer. It was necessary to disguise the messiness I felt inside me. I looked in the mirror and identified all of my imperfections fearful that each would be obvious in broad daylight to all those people who were staring at me out of the corners of their eyes. I moved quietly behind drawn blinds, turned off lights when I left a room and locked doors to insure my safety. At night, I flopped on the bed, closed my eyes and lay perfectly still hoping, praying I'd awaken a different person. I decided to stay up late, until exhaustion forced my eyelids closed and restless comfort introduced itself into my weary body. The unknown filled me with shame and I didn't know the hell why.

I continued to ask, why these feelings? What had I done to feel this way? How can stories of World War II impact so dramatically upon my life? I was just a baby. It wasn't my fault that I was born. The time to start finding answers was now. Damn, I'm only 38 years old, already.

I decided to revisit Sigmund Freud. Surely he'd hold some of the keys necessary to unlock closed doors of the mind. I was aware that Dr. Freud was a prominent thinker; he was far ahead of his time with some ideas, but dead wrong on others. I was hoping some of his insights might be on target with what was causing my headaches.

I suspect every seminarian has had to delve into the legacy, right or wrong, of the founder of psychoanalysis, Sigmund Freud. The lectures, papers and stacks of books to read should have informed me of what was happening in my unconscious. I ignored it all until my past started disrupting my present. I began exploring. Marilyn Elias of USA Today wrote an article entitled, "Freud: So wrong and yet so right." It helped me to verify why I struggled so long to stop running away from my past and how my past haunted me throughout my life. I began at the beginning and worked forward.

My clinical therapy work at Hartford Hospital had led me to focus on what Freud's greatest ideas were and which ones pertained to me. He advanced the concept of the unconscious, his most important idea to stand the test of time. Drew Westen, a psychologist at Emory University noted, "Before him, nobody realized that our conscious mind is the tip of the mental iceberg." The notion that people act from unconscious motives that may reveal themselves in dreams stems from the mental iceberg image. "The research is crystal clear that we look the other way not to see what makes us uncomfortable," says Westen.

Another key Freudian notion that has held up well is ambivalence, adds psychiatrist Peter Kramer. "Freud knew people were very conflicted - they had mixed emotions, even about those they loved, and that was a revolutionary thought in his era."

Some pioneering ideas advanced by Freud are so widely accepted now that many do not realize who created them. Westen noted, for example, it's common knowledge that childhood experiences shape how we think of ourselves. They also affect how we develop adult relationships. Freud was the first to see this key influence.

I believe Freud's major contribution and the one most germane to my mental balance was the idea that a therapist could help ease emotional pain. "He invented psychotherapy," says David Baker, director of the Archives of the History of American Psychology, based at the University of Akron, Ohio.

I feel badly that the supportive environment that spawned the heyday of psychoanalysis after World War II, " . . . will not be seen again" predicted Sander Abend, training and supervising analyst at the New York Psychoanalytic Institute. Too many people shy away from the benefits of psychotherapy. Either we do not have the money to pay for expensive sessions or we are afraid people will discover we are seeing a "Shrink." In both seminaries I attended, I was fortunate to have trained psychologists guide me through my discombobulated thoughts. The insights gave me the courage to enter the troubled times of my early years.

In psychology classes, we learn that people often act from unconscious motives or emotions that may reveal themselves in dreams. That idea resonated with me. It made me feel as though I might not be as strange as I sometimes felt. During my explorations, I uncovered an unsettling behavior: A Fugue State - when one blocks out bad memories. I had to figure out how to release this logjam that was impeding my efforts to understand myself.

SALT LAKE CITY, UTAH

In 1983, we left First Congregational Church Wauwatosa, Wisconsin and I accepted my first call to serve in my very own parish. I turned down the Congregational Church of Forest Hills, New York and accepted a smaller Congregational church in Salt Lake City, Utah. I threw myself into my work, family and Navy Reserve obligations.

Serving a church in the heart of Mormon country presented its own unique challenges. Even though conservative Mormons thought clergy to be a "tool of the devil," I wasn't going to be distracted. Both of our boys were old enough to play baseball, moving me to coach Erik's team and assist with Tim's. Bonnie also organized a Tiger Cub patrol for Tim. That same summer I had the unique opportunity to take a backpacking trip with Erik, who was active in the church - sponsored Boy Scout troop, over the Saw Tooth mountain range, in Idaho.

My church supported my Navy Reserve work allowing me the time to drill weekends and 17 days during the summer. My monthly drills were held at Treasure Island, just outside of San Francisco. Twenty - nine Palms was the most challenging of my summer training exercises. It was desert warfare with live fire to keep us sharp.

My salary was meager, but the church's ministerial benefit package provided me a one-week continuing education experience. This afforded me a wonderful opportunity to attend leadership conferences in San Diego. It was in this setting I was able to enhance my professional development, meet colleagues and hear outstanding speakers. It also gave me an added and much - appreciated perk: Every two years, I registered and attended a leadership workshop located an easy drive from my birth mother's home. On each occasion, I made it a point to tack on an overnight stay with her and the family. I was confident that our time together would provide opportunities for her to relate stories and bring added light to my own circumstances. I knew patience would have to be one of my strengths.

Everything was moving along just fine. As a family, we enjoyed excursions to the various national parks, kept ahead of our bills, supported Bonnie during her graduate studies at the University of Utah. We stayed involved with school activities and kept the programs at the church alive and well. There were financial challenges - but nothing we couldn't face together.

In September of 1986 my world fractured.

Dad was diagnosed with an aggressive cancer. Due to finances, the Brenner family had only one opportunity to fly east to Cape Cod and celebrate Thanksgiving together. We arrived at my parents' home in Chatham only to find my dad a shadow of the vibrant man he'd always been. The long weekend together afforded each of us an opportunity to express our love and appreciation. My conversations with Dad were long. Several times he let me know how proud he was of me and how important it was for me to continue my relationship with B.J.

As we returned to Salt Lake City, I knew I'd seen my dad alive for the last time. During his final four weeks, Mom - with the help of Hospice - took care of him in their beloved Cape home. It's where they needed to be during his final days.

On December 23rd Dad died.

I mustered enough strength and spirit to preach and make it through the church's Christmas Eve services. The next day, I flew back to Massachusetts to help Mom with the necessary funeral arrangements.

The memorial service was held in a small Methodist church in Harwich. The church's minister, a close friend and fellow mission-project helper, officiated at the service. Only twenty or so people attended. A cousin came from my mom's side of the family and a close friend of dad's, from Philadelphia, sat next to Mom and me. Everything felt so inadequate.

Dad had accomplished so much for orphans during the Korean War; he retired a full colonel; worked on mission efforts in South Africa and devoted his energy to helping the less fortunate and disadvantaged. In a virtually empty sanctuary, he was being honored in front of a handful of people who actually knew what a great person he'd been. My heart ached and it took almost more will power than I had to restrain an angry scream struggling to explode toward the empty pews that should have been filled. I took some solace in the knowledge that Dad would receive full military honors during his burial at Arlington Cemetery the coming summer. The irony of the occasion was that the empty pews would not have bothered Dad. He knew whom he was and that he had honored his profession and "Call" by doing God's work.

For the next two years - as people heard about his death through publications, Christmas letters, and word of mouth - we began receiving letters, photos, post cards and phone calls extolling the admiration and love people held for him. Ultimately, his family acknowledged him and friends and associates from around the globe remembered him.

Dad's death had an unusual effect on me. He had been the one who insisted that B.J. (Bjorg) was my natural mother. Repeatedly, he encouraged me to consider getting to know her, to speak with her, to have her tell me about my Norwegian heritage. He felt it important for me to find out about my past and to learn more than what little he knew. With his passing, I felt freer to reopen my quest to understand my past. I knew it would benefit me to visit Bjorg and coax out answers to the questions gnawing inside me.

During the summer of 1987, I registered for another leadership workshop near B.J's home in Riverside, California. I made certain I'd have two nights to be with her and the family.

I had a good relationship with my half-sister Sandra and her father Hunter. My connection with my birth mother was lukewarm, but getting warmer after each visit and ensuing conversations. She was a private person and annoyingly secretive about her childhood and World War II experiences.

It was the first night of one of my visits, and I felt it imperative to get her to share some of her deepest feelings. I waited until the rest of the family went to bed. This particular evening, with drinks in hand, we went to the living room and sat down. We talked first about our families, her golf game, and my job until the evening extended well into the early morning hours of a new day. During this quiet time of the night, she gave me a glimpse into her wartime experiences: not much, just a little taste. I sensed the moment was right. I mustered the necessary courage and asked the first of many questions. My patience was rewarded.

"Mom, when was the last time you saw me?"

She looked at me for a long time. I could see her weighing the importance of what I had asked. The struggle for the right words deepened the lines keeping watch over the pain evident within her eyes. As she began, the story cautiously slipped out in the form of a whisper, and in the third person.

*   *   *

"It was a dark and dangerous night. A teenage girl hurriedly traveled alongside the road, occasionally ducking behind twisted trees and gnarled bushes for cover. Planes darkened the once clear sky above her. She knew the consequences of being out after curfew, but it made no difference. Her baby was in danger. The concussion of bursting bombs shook the ground beneath her aching feet. In anticipation, she dropped down to cup her hands over her ears in an attempt to lessen the deafening impact. As she neared her destination, she could see and almost feel the flames flickering upward lighting the night sky. After several hours on the road, the girl, tired and worn, entered the

town where she first held her infant. The Children's Home that loomed like a monolith at the north end of the town was an old Victorian building that stood out like a sore in the quaint village - just as she felt misplaced as a Norwegian in Germany. People were running in all directions, trying to find a basement or a protective wall to hide behind from the incoming artillery fire and oncoming soldiers. Safety was the least of her concerns. A man tried to grab her arm in an effort to pull her toward a makeshift bomb shelter. She struggled and broke away, determined in her resolve to reach the towering facility.

At the hospital, nurses, clad in white, were carrying crying babies bundled in their arms. The teenager stopped each one, rushing down the stone steps, imploring them to listen. Her plea was always the same, "Where is my baby boy?" She ran into the building, shoving against the oncoming rush of nurses, attendants, doctors and wailing babies. The bombs in the distance still had the forceful power and impact to shake the foundation. She ran to the room where her son's crib would be. They had taken the baby from her at birth, but this night it would be different. Tonight, more than a year later, she would take him back from them. For months, she had secretly paid off a nurse, granting her precious moments to touch and kiss her infant son. She wasn't going to lose him now. She ran to the crib where he was supposed to be. Only the ghastly sight of bloodstained sheets in an empty crib filled her eyes. Her son's torn nametag dangled at the foot of the bed. He was gone.

Frantic, she grabbed the nurse passing by the crib, "Where is my son, my baby?" The woman looked at her, acknowledging what she feared to be true; her child was dead. The cause of his death was ruptured eardrums - created by the concussion of exploding bombs. Distraught; the young mother stumbled back from the bed, rushed out of the room, through the door, down the staircase and onto the rubble - filled street. Her only thought was to get away, anywhere, as long as it was far away from the hell all around her. She ran and stumbled in an attempt to create distance from the place where sorrow filled her heart. Not until she saw a dark, empty house silhouetted atop a hill on the other side of a stream did she dare stop. Breathless and exhausted, she splashed across the freezing stream, scrambled up the steep hillside and entered the building, dripping wet and shivering from the cold. The young woman lowered her aching, bruised body onto the cold splintered floor. The sound of war was in the distance. Lacking the energy to take one more step, she fell in a heap as sleep captured her and the world slowly darkened. The next day a farmer hid her under a pile of hay spread out behind the carriage bed of his wagon. The war was winding down but not the pain and guilt brooding inside her.

I didn't know what to say or do. B.J. looked so frail and worn slumped on the sofa. I was too shocked to cry and too lost to find words worthy to be spoken. Slowly, B.J. raised her tearstained face and looked into my eyes. Her strong voice filled our space.

"Peter, they took you from me when you were born. I never imagined anyone could be so cruel. The war stole you from me until this moment." She rested her slender body against mine and closed her eyes. Silence enveloped us and it was all right; I knew then, for the first time, B.J. was my mother. The quietness within me felt calm and reassuring.

That night changed my relationship with B.J. I realized the most meaningful moments of my discoveries would emanate from the oral tradition; stories told to me by those who were an essential piece of my history. I cherished this sacred moment. It helped me to begin clarifying the roadmap that still lay before me. It was a hidden past that would only be revealed if I made the effort.

The hell and horror that was my mother's lot, I can't begin to imagine. The events surrounding our separation, however, afforded me a peek into her ordeal and unbearable sorrow and deep love for her baby - I still wondered, why her? Why me? Why us? The story emphasized the level of her determination to protect me and save face for her family in Norway. I will never forget that night and the look of sadness on her face.

That same visit, during the second night, she added to the story.

After the war, she returned to the town where she had last seen me. She stood before a dirt - filled mound where all the dead, orphaned babies were tossed into a shallow, mass grave. The babies had been a blot and an embarrassment to the German people. In a rush to cover the sins of their past, the children were left to lie unidentified and forgotten. Falling on her knees, my mother said "goodbye" and wept.

Now, we held each other knowing, somehow, we had survived for this singular moment.

CHARLOTTE, MICHIGAN

The family remained in Salt Lake City for another four years. The urge to move eastward began tugging at my elbow and I knew I had to start looking to relocate. The time with B.J. was important, but my mom was living by herself in Chatham, her health was poor and I sensed the need to be closer. In 1988, I began the search process for a new church.

It took over two years before I accepted a "Call" to serve as the Senior Minister of First Congregational Church, Charlotte, Michigan. The match was great for the Brenner family. Tim would complete his junior and senior high school years in the same town. It also provided Erik with his own four - year high school experience in the same school district. Bonnie and I felt stability and continuity for the boys was an important factor to prepare them for college.

Bonnie also wanted an opportunity to get back into the classroom setting as an elementary music educator. In the event of an emergency, I was closer to Mom; we could make the trip to Chatham, Massachusetts within a tiring but manageable 12+ hours.

My fear was borne out: In August of 1990, we moved to Charlotte, Michigan; in 1992, the day before Valentine's Day, mom died. During the ensuing summer, we held a family service for Mom at Arlington Cemetery. After five years, she once again was reunited with my dad. When Mom passed away, her mother, Grandma Pauline, lost the will to live. In 1993, at the age of 99, she passed away and was buried on a hillside of a local cemetery overlooking her beloved childhood town of Westminster, Vermont.

I was so fortunate to have an understanding congregation that responded to my various concerns. First, as their new minister, I received outstanding support in the church's major effort to successfully raise monies to help renovate and improve its facilities. Our success served as a spark for the community to embark on a town wide renaissance - a beautification program to enhance the image of Main Street. I also wasn't begrudged time to be active with my son's activities - I regularly attended our boys' basketball, baseball and scouting activities. My Navy Reserve obligations never became a bone of contention during the once - a - month drill dates or the two - week summer training exercise. In particular, I took an active role in the church's scout troop activities. The highlight of one summer program was being one of the three adult leaders to lead a dozen scouts - via Amtrak - on a high adventure trip to Philmont, New Mexico - the Cadillac version of any scouting experience. Tim completed his requirements to earn his rank of Eagle Scout, joining Erik and me in that honor. The ten years at First Congregational Church of Charlotte became a time of fulfillment for the Brenner family and my ministry.

There was another very critical component to my life. Every couple of years, my summer drilling requirements for the Navy Reserve (and the opportunity to attend clergy continuing education workshops) took me to the San Diego area. Whenever possible, I grabbed the occasion to visit Bjorg, Hunter and the older of my two half-sisters, Sandra. On the surface, everything was outstanding - except for one thing: emptiness I could no longer ignore. My urge to uncover the mystery of my past was consuming my thoughts. I needed to know the what, where, when, why and how of my early childhood. I owed it to my boys and I craved it for myself.

My mind kept returning to this task like a compass needle. I was determined to locate where I was born and to discover the whereabouts of my years as an orphan in Germany. That would require one last move. After ten wonderful years in Charlotte, we decided to return to the northeast sector of the United States. Moving to the east coast would position us nearer to our Chatham home on Cape Cod, rekindle our dearest relationship with close friends, and be an easy drive to Boston and New York City - where our sons were studying and working. I felt that New England would be a safe haven. For me, it would provide a setting where I would draw strength for the challenging task laying before me - uncovering the mystery of my past.

However, I still had one major agenda item on my to do list. I was scheduled to lead a tour of church members to see the dramatic presentation of The Passion Play - performed once every decade by the residents who lived in the small Bavarian town of Oberammergau.

The week of July 4, 2000, Bonnie, seven members and I flew across the Atlantic, headed for Munich, Germany. Once safely on the ground, we met our tour guide. In an efficient manner but peppy spirit, she directed us toward a minivan. We piled into a tour bus, luggage in hand, before being immediately whisked out of the terminal area heading south for two nights of lodging at a quaint Bavarian Inn. The next day, we were off for Oberammergau to experience the drama of The Passion Play. We were duly impressed. The following few days included a scheduled day-trip to visit the spectacular and most picturesque of King Ludwig's castles, Neuschwanstein, with another full day devoted to exploring the city of Munich. The famous Hoffbrau House was a pub filled with laughter, lots of band music and extemporaneous dancing whereever space opened up. Halfway into our ten-day tour, I was walking on the manicured grounds of King Ludwig's magnificent castle, Schloss Herrenchiemsee. It is perched on the highest point of an island, hidden from the mainland behind a forest of trees except for one swathe permitting viewers to have an unobstructed view of the pristine lake.

For some inexplicable reason, I suddenly turned to Bonnie and said, "We need to try and find my orphanage."

"Now?" Bonnie exclaimed with an astonished look.

"Yes, now. Prien is the town where my parents first found me and we're here. I'd never forgive myself if I let this opportunity slip through my fingers."

"What about the group?"

"I'll explain it to them. I'm certain they'll understand."

Trying to be supportive of my decision, Bonnie answered, "We're all doing our own thing anyway . . . you've already visited the castle . . . I've seen enough to get the feel of the place . . . Let's do it."

I gathered the scattered members of our tour group together and explained my urgent need to locate the last orphanage where I'd lived for over two years. I knew the children's home was located somewhere in Prien. They were supportive and graciously encouraged Bonnie and me to be on our way. We agreed on a two - hour and thirty - minute window before reuniting with them at the landing dock of Prien am Chiemsee. Momentarily freed of my tour - director responsibilities, Bonnie and I rushed to the docking area and caught the next shuttle back to the mainland.

It was midday as the ferryboat splashed through the wind - swept waves rocking the passengers as it churned westward back toward the shoreline. Under dark, ominous clouds, Bonnie and I took a final look at the tiny island disappearing amidst the misty fog. As the waves slapped against the side of the boat, the spray splashed against my face. I felt refreshed at the prospect of our pending adventure. I wasn't going to be deterred no matter how improbable the task appeared.

By the time we'd docked, intermittent showers had become a deluge of huge, pelting raindrops soaking us from the crowns of our heads to the soles of our feet. The outline of the castle Schloss Herrenchiemsee had already been washed away from our line of vision, but not its memorable history.

Ludwig II, known to historians as the "Mad King of Bavaria," had built a private, elegant and exquisite, smaller replica of the magnificent French castle, Versailles. Ludwig's gem was partially hidden amongst a forest of trees concealing it from curious onlookers. The one opening he created, when seen from the mainland, offered only the most ardent commoner a tiny peek at the King's palatial quarters. Stories confirm that the young 16th century king had spent a total of only 40 days on the grounds of his extravagant obsession.

Once on firm ground, we located a rental car agency and secured the only car available - a Mercedes. We stared at each other and chuckled.

I grinned and declared, "Mercedes, not too shabby for a starter car."

Bonnie smiled. "Well, Sherlock, where to now?"

I glanced at my watch. "It's 3:00pm; we don't have much time before we're supposed to be back here."

"Well, let's get going."

"When my dad was stationed in France, I remember the family took a weekend getaway to visit the castle. We stayed at a military resort situated on the southern tip of the lake and near the Autobahn. I recall seeing a sign for the installation when we turned off the highway."

"It's been over 50 years!!" Bonnie exclaimed. "Do you think they'd have records?"

"Maybe, if they still have a personnel department and we get lucky. It's only a ten - minute drive; I think it's worth a try."

Bonnie unfolded an area map and spread it across her lap. As I roared out of the parking lot, we began strategizing. First, we'd check out the resort area; if nothing materialized, we'd hustle back to town and try our fortune with some of the local folks. Satisfied, we sped down the road encouraged by our recent success.

The resort, a vacation spot for military personnel, turned out to be a dead end. On the way back to town, I impulsively swerved onto a driveway of a farmhouse. On a hunch, I decided to ask some questions of the woman I spotted sweeping the porch. The robust, middle-aged women stopped what she was doing as I rumbled up the driveway. I jumped out with the intent of asking one question. Fortunately, my German had improved enough over the past several days. I asked her if she knew anything about an orphanage located in town during the late 1940s. She apologized for not knowing, but volunteered a suggestion. She was confident a good starting point would be at the Bahnhof (train station).

"Go and talk to the taxi drivers. They're all old-timers. If anybody would know anything, it would be them." She gave a broad satisfying smile as I backed out of the driveway. I thanked her with a wave of my hand and hurried down the country road, my heart quickening with the promise of new leads to follow.

The Bahnhof was small and old. There was a strange familiarity attached to the station from which the trains chugged in and out on their appointed runs. I couldn't quite put my finger on the memory gnawing to come out. I redirected my attention to the taxi drivers.

They looked like clones of each other. I took a deep breath to steady myself, opened the car door and stepped out onto the dusty parking lot. Their beer bellies were constrained by decorative lederhosen straps; baggy wool socks, clinging precariously just below their knobby knees, covered stumpy legs; and worn, alpine fedoras rested atop wrinkly faces with tired eyes at half mast. None of them moved quickly and all gave toothy smiles at the arrival of another prospective tourist. I headed straight for the oldest and the most weathered looking veteran stationed at his post.

Bonnie wished me luck with a wink but opted to remain in the Benz.

I ventured forward. "Hello. I would like to ask you a couple of questions," I said in my best German.

Motionless, the taxi driver's worn, gravely voice moaned, "Where do you want to go? I will give you a first-class tour if you want. How long will you be here?"

"Have you lived here long?" I continued.

"Yes, since 1924. For a little extra, I can give you some history."

"Do you know anything about an orphanage that was here in 1947?"

He hesitated for just a split moment before answering, "I know nothing of such a place. I can tell you about the castle. I also point out interesting sights to see." He walked to the other side of the car.

"Have you heard of a person named Tante Marie?"

"Do you need a ride? If not, I no talk." He looked away.

"I'm trying to locate a place that took care of orphans. Do you recall any place like that?"

"I need to go. Try someone else." And just like that, he turned and walked away.

I tried two other taxi cab drivers, to no avail.

I returned to the car - discouraged but not defeated. The old codgers hadn't shared a morsel of revealing information. I couldn't help ruminating over how they had reacted toward my questions regarding World War II. Without exception, each of them knew something, but wasn't telling. I sensed a taste of embarrassment coating the words that spilled out from between their cracked lips. They were avoiding the truth. It strengthened my resolve to continue with the search.

"Well? What did they say? Bonnie inquired, poking her head out the car's side window.

"Nothing, not even tidbits to munch over," I declared in a somber tone. "It's as though nothing happened here during the war years."

"Not even a little clue?" Bonnie's eyebrows rose in astonishment.

"They just brushed me off. They didn't want to say anything, so they disguise the truth with forgetfulness and 'I don't recall' statements. They know something, but what can I do if they won't cooperate?" I walked to the driver's side of the car, opened the door to get in, and continued to wrestle with their reactions to my questions.

Bonnie ignored my frowning face. With a quizzical look she asked, "Isn't a Rathaus the same as a courthouse or city government building?"

"Yes. It's the same as a town hall."

"As we were driving in, I noticed a road sign pointing toward the Rathaus." Bonnie pointed to her left. "It's two blocks that way."

I leaned over and smacked a noisy kiss on her forehead. "You're a great co-pilot, but we better hurry, it's almost four o'clock and I'm afraid they might close soon."

We hurried out of the lot and steered our way back toward the center of town. Within minutes, I had the car squeezed into the first available slot, across the street from the Rathaus. I had no idea if I was legally parked - and I didn't care. We sprinted across the street, whisked through the tiny courtyard and pushed past heavy oak doors leading into the foyer area of an ornate stone building. From the train station to the courthouse, I'd been piecing together the best German phrases I could recall. We found the clerk's office and swirled in like a Nebraska "dust buster." Before I could utter a word, the receptionist greeted us with a disarming smile and the dreaded phrase, "Wir sind geschlossen."

"Guten Tag, konnen Sie mir helfen?" Ten minutes was all I needed to get the urgency of my story across to the kind - faced woman sitting on the other side of the counter. I started talking before she could respond.

She listened.

When I finally stopped, she slowly shook her head. "I'm sorry but I don't know of any orphanage that was here after the war. You must be mistaken."

I stared into her eyes and spoke with an inner strength. "I know it was here, because I was one of the orphans."

Silence enveloped the room, but understanding peeked out from under her eyelids. The following seconds seemed interminable before the older woman snapped the silence. "Wait just one minute, maybe Eva would know." She turned and called out her name.

An attractive, slender lady in her late twenties, with shoulder-length hair, emerged from a back office. She approached the receptionist, who looked up from her chair, rose and murmured a few words to the sandy-haired blonde.

Before speaking, Eva paused a moment, taking us in with a caring look. "You're right," she said in a firm, clear voice. "I know of the place you refer to."

I released the breath I'd been holding in.

In perfect English, she began explaining her background and interest in my search. "I was a history major at the university. I know of the place you seek." Eva came out from behind the counter.

I was speechless. I struggled to dam back swelling tears. Bonnie, touching my elbow, helped to steady my nerves.

I'll never forget Eva. Here stood a young woman, not much older than my oldest son, who was about to open a chapter in my life that had been closed for more than fifty years. I started to shake. Her voice and Bonnie's closeness held me together. Standing in anticipation before this stranger, I felt both fear and relief as both feelings wound together in a tight ball at the center of my stomach.

Her story unfolded. "The building you seek is no longer an orphanage; it's now a daycare center and located only minutes from here."

"Can you show us how to get there?" Bonnie asked. She unfolded our tattered map and spread it across the counter. Eva circled the spot in red ink. With the care of an illustrator, she traced the roads leading to our destination. I felt like she was uncovering a hidden treasure and X marked the spot.

Bonnie pointed toward the large round wall clock. "Peter, we've got to run. It's getting late."

We both stretched across the counter to hug the receptionist, and then turned to embrace Eva. I said, "Danke," as we headed for the door.

"Wait," Eva called.

We stopped and turned toward the angelic face of the woman who had given us new hope. Again, she spoke words that shook me.

"I wasn't certain if I should give you this information, but I believe you need to be prepared for one more important item."

"Which is?"

"The woman who started the school for orphans in 1947 is still alive."

"Alive!" I blurted out.

"Yes. And she lives on the grounds of the center. Because of her faithful service to the center and willingness to relinquish control of the operations to the city, she was given quarters where she could live out the rest of her life. We all know her as Tante Marella. Her place is now a private Kinderheim and goes by the name of Haus Marquette. It's a very small sign so keep a sharp lookout." To this day, I can still see Eva's eyes twinkling and the smile on her face.

I left energized.

How I managed to navigate the car through the narrow streets remains a mystery to me. My thoughts were years removed from the moment. I seemed to instinctively know where to guide the vehicle, even before Bonnie's directions reached my ears. Within five minutes, we were turning onto a dirt-packed driveway that opened onto a small but manageable parking area. A colorful set of playground equipment was located at the short end of an L - shaped, two storied building. I eased the car up against the grassy lawn, stopped and turned off the engine.

"I've been here before, Bonnie. The building looks so familiar, yet different. I've lived here." Silence enveloped us as I surveyed the grounds before me.

The property stretched gently down a gradual slope, easing its way toward the lake's rocky shoreline. The view was breathtaking. The shimmering blue hews of the water lay still, only to be intermittently disturbed by jumping fish or a bird swooping down in search of dinner. The view of Herrenchiemsee beckoned me now as it had some fifty - seven years ago. Across the lake was King Ludwig's majestic castle, peeking through an opening in the forest. It was as I had remembered . . . except for the playground equipment, taller trees and expanded facility.

I stepped out and walked to the edge of the lawn. I had a powerful urge to take off my shoes so the wet grass could tickle my toes and my soul could connect with the soft earth. The panoramic scene hadn't changed that much - only the little boy looking on.

I turned, as if in slow motion, to my left. The multi-colored playground structure featured slides, a pair of ladders positioned at 45-degree angles, others stretched horizontally between two vertical climbs and one that looked like a corkscrew rising up into the sky; two sets of swings patiently waiting for children to set them in motion; and a huge sandbox, large enough to hold a horde of children still waiting to be wanted. The play center nestled against the base of a small hill topped off by a row of tall trees swaying gently side to side.

It was a brief walk from the playground of Tante's orphanage to the edge of the lake. As an adult, I now stood between the home and the castle; I could clearly comprehend the collateral damage wrought by two madmen. One, whose obsessive need to build castles "mired his beautiful Bavaria in bankruptcy" and; the other's demented effort to "breed a perfect race" dishonored a nation and tore apart families. I felt the gnawing urge to stand on the soiled shore of my childhood and scream until my anger no longer had a voice. Other voices, however, were pulling me in another direction.

I turned to look at the house and felt a warm feeling as scenes out of my past swept into view. My thoughts transported me deeper into my past.

The emotions running through me were a mixture of joy, curiosity and nervousness. It was here where I was introduced to love, became acquainted with other orphans as friends, learned my ABCs, tasted warm meals and - for the first time slept in a room with less than a crowd of crying children. Where I now stood was not a briar patch fraught with the elements of fear and the unknown; here the narrow path of despair and hopelessness opened up onto a road that led to new adventures. I knew this little house to be a place where the positive always outweighed the negative and where I was accepted and loved. Here, I knew I'd be safe.

I could hear a distant voice calling me back to the present and away from April of 1947. I blinked and quickly wiped at a runaway tear slipping down my cheek. Before me lay a lawn much farther from the lake than I had remembered; more houses were pressing in from both sides and the building on the property was a colorful, two-story facility. For a moment, I wasn't sure where I was.

Bonnie stepped alongside me and linked her arm with mine. "Are you okay?"

I nodded.

"Peter, I hear someone coming our way." She pressed her hand into mine. Together, we turned to face the approaching footsteps.

I don't know how much time transpired before I heard a voice. I, who was always conscious of time and place, could not fit together where I had been to where I was now. Thoughts continued tumbling through my mind as an elderly woman stood before us. She was short, gray - haired, pleasantly round and displayed a natural smile. It was obvious that her remaining years would soon be a closing chapter of the time she'd already devoted to the care of orphaned children. The vitality of her movements, however, assured me that the timepiece ticking off her years would have to wait awhile longer. Stretched to her fullest, she'd still be a tad less than five feet tall; her hair was short but full as it framed her beaming face and warm smile. We might have been strangers to her, but she greeted us like family with outstretched arms inviting us to follow her toward the house.

We were standing before a white, two-story Bavarian home with shuttered windows, a second-story porch and glorious flowers adorning flower boxes artfully decorated to provide a welcoming feel for visitors. The longer left side of the daycare center featured an older, but still sturdy, building. A newer section had been added to create the L - shape design of the building and a second story. I thought I recognized the older section. Bonnie interrupted my curiosity.

She began tugging frantically at my trousers. "Peter, say something, she's speaking German."

I gave a sheepish grin. "Sorry, I was daydreaming."

I looked at the woman looking up at us. She stared into my eyes and smiled as though she had just read my thoughts. When she spoke, however, the melody of her voice was the magical key that unlocked my lost memories. The words seemed to rise out from within a deep well. I couldn't believe how rich and mellow words could be coming from such a small person. As surprising as the sound seemed, it was the spirit of her tone I recognized. The Bavarian accent, accompanied by her genuine laugh, spilled over me, once again, with a feeling of warmth and acceptance.

Without hesitation, I extended my right hand and introduced myself. "Ich bin Herr Brenner" - I gestured with my hand - "und meine Frau, Bonnie."

She invited us into her parlor like a mother hen leading her chicks toward a place of comfort and safety. The quaint but functional room became the setting of a string of questions. To my amazement, I comprehended their intent. I also knew, without a doubt, it was my Tante Marie sitting across from me.

I managed to string together a few coherent phrases. It felt like a game of Scrabble; all the words were in my head, it just took a little time to figure out how to arrange them.

Tante understood my plight and often slipped in a supportive smile.

I managed to compose myself while she scurried off to the kitchen to prepare some refreshments. She took her time, sensing my need to gather together my thoughts. Soon a tray of frosted glasses filled with iced tea and surrounded by cookies was set before us. I started by telling her who I was.

"I already know. You are Kleine Pater," she said with a genuine smile.

For the next hour, she shared stories in response to my litany of questions. She talked about how I cried and she would rock me to sleep; how every child called her Tante; and the times the staff chased frantically after me as I scampered toward the lake. She shared snippets about other children who had been my playmates and friends. She told us the children from the late 1940s were just now, after all these years, beginning to stop by and say hello. Tante was certain my favorite friend was now a doctor practicing somewhere in the city of Munich. I shared family news, what I was doing and how important this time had become for us. I gave her golden nuggets about my dad's career and Mom's variety of interests. She confirmed that they were the couple who had been on the field trip with us when I was three years old.

Throughout the rest of our conversation, Tante confirmed so many of my memories as she related the exciting stories we'd lived together.

Our shared time became one of the most revealing and significant segments of my journey toward understanding. I knew what she revealed would serve as the underpinnings of stories yet to be understood, experiences still to be uncovered and revelations still making themselves known.

We never ventured beyond the warmth of the parlor. I wish I'd figured out a way to return that night for a tour of the home and more stories. But I didn't. I had a group of people waiting for me to guide them to our next destination.

During our goodbye, I wondered if I'd ever see Tante Marie again. I promised I'd write and hoped to return someday in the near future. She made it clear her doors would always be open for us.

It was a huge emotional leap from our time with Tante to reuniting in the parking lot with my church group. I parceled out bits and pieces of our adventure with the members - locating the orphanage and talking with two women who were familiar with the early history of the children's home. I was too drained to spill out any more particulars of my specific relationship with Tante. I knew probing questions would crumble my defenses like a cracked pillar of stone. I was relieved when Bonnie picked up the conversation and elaborated on our miracle story of stumbling across the home from which I'd been adopted. Nobody in our entourage was pushy or intrusive, only happy for our good fortune. I was so thankful.

It wasn't long before we hurried off to our next destination - a rendezvous at the farm of Ernst & Ermgart. They were the parents of a Rotarian I'd met a year earlier, during an international luncheon/workshop. He offered his parents' farm as a unique opportunity to mingle with Germans in an unvarnished setting, away from the hectic tourist centers. I was fortunate my German had improved enough that I could serve as a translator between Ermgart and our entourage. The highlight of our stay was when Bonnie played the piano, accompanied by Ernst on his violin. I would never have guessed his gift on such a delicate instrument. He was a farmer/hunter with huge hands, thick fingers and broad shoulders. His appearance suggested he'd be more comfortable in the forest than playing a violin in the parlor.

It was a glorious evening with beautiful music, singing, a wonderful meal and lots of laughter. It was the perfect ointment to soothe my emotional state while redirecting my focus back to being a tour guide.

We expressed our delight in seeing The Passion Play in Oberammergau and visiting King Ludwig's two castles - Neuschwanstein and Schloss

Herrenchiemsee. I even managed to explain how our next destination was Salzburg to see the home where Mozart was born. I elaborated about the side excursion that would take us atop Hitler's Eagle's Nest in Austria. My tour members listened intently to every story and always made me feel as though I was being an excellent interpreter.

Interwoven within the 10-day trip was my exchange of pertinent information, via email, with the pulpit committee of First Congregational Church of Vernon, Connecticut. I tried to convey the importance of relocating ourselves closer to our summer home on Cape Cod and having closer access to our two sons - one who lived/worked in New York City, and the other, a transfer student enrolled at Emerson College in Boston. Over the years, the importance of family easily attained the top rung of my priority list. Not knowing anything about my natural father, very little about my natural mother and growing up as an only child reinforced my will to forge and maintain a deep relationship with Bonnie and our sons.

The European trip seemed to mirror my life: Never in one place for very long, hiding my past from people I valued and wondering who I really was. It was during this trip I came to the conclusion that any "call" I received would require another stipulation - time to uncovering the secrets hidden behind my quest for discovering who I really was.

VERNON, CONNECTICUT

From the pulpit committee's response, I sensed that First Congregational Church of Vernon could become a partner in launching a meaningful ministry. First, they knew it was imperative that I be granted a three - month sabbatical that there would be teaching opportunities for Bonnie and that, together, we would work in partnership toward a healthy ministry.

It all fell into place by the time we returned stateside. During my contract negotiations with the pulpit committee, I was granted sabbatical time for the summer of 2006.

Erik and Tim eventually landed jobs in the Boston area; Bonnie was hired as a music educator (K - 6) in Simsbury, Connecticut and I loved my new ministry in Vernon, Connecticut. We bought a beautiful, moderately sized split-level home and my ministry included a large church, an active membership, plus challenges that matched the needs facing the church and the strength of my leadership

CHAPTER VI

Divine Intervention

" . . . for I rescued the poor who cried out for help, and the orphan
who had no one to assist him;."

Job 29:12

By 2002 inexplicable forces began intervening, like a pebble interrupting the
surface of a still pond. It began in front of my computer. Armed with newly
developed ability, I began scanning my Hotmail messages. My first task was
to delete the dozen advertisements and untold junk mail; but something in the
subject line of an email caught my attention. The fingers of my right hand
hesitated over the keyboard. I stared, debating if yet another virus was poised
to weasel its disruptive chaos into my world. I dismissed my apprehension and
darted for the keys with a degree of anticipation that had no explanation. The
following message took me completely by surprise.

Dear Rev. Brenner,

I have had in my possession for several years now several rolls
of 8mm film from Rev. Brenner's family. He seemed to have served
as a military chaplain. To the best I can tell some of the footage
shows information, such as a church in Bennington, Vermont, a
gravestone with the name Fenn on it, a Camp Judson sign and even
an old license plate on their Vermont car from 1947. The films are of

the family's travels all over the world, to some of the most common tourist spots that people went to in the 30s and 40s.

I acquired these films at a thrift shop outside of Philadelphia in the late 90s, where they do large - scale estate clean outs. I felt terrible that such rich family history was possibly doomed to rot in a corner or end up in a dumpster.

If you are of any relation to this family or have any way of finding any further leads to return this treasure to some appreciative descendent, please let me know.

Respectfully, Barry
February 12, 2003

Each time I read the message, my eyes settled on the sentence, "I acquired these films at a thrift shop outside of Philadelphia in the late '90s, where they do large scale estate clean outs." I could hardly believe what I was reading. Some unknown person, out of nowhere, was referring to my father by name, career and location, beginning from as early as the 1940s. Without a doubt, I knew the originator of the email had in his possession home videos filmed by my dad. Suddenly it struck me: If this "historic footage" was authentic, it might reveal footage from my earliest years as an orphan. I immediately started the process to contact Barry. My hands quivered with excitement. I could hardly scoot the pointer across the screen fast enough to match my enthusiasm. I settled the little critter into position, pressed reply and started typing:

Greetings Barry,

My name is Peter. I'm certain there aren't a handful of people who know what you shared in your email about my family. My father, an Army/Air Corp Chaplain, was stationed in Germany following WWII and during the occupation of Allied Forces. While there, he and his newly married wife were hoping to adopt an orphan. I was the fortunate orphan they adopted in 1949.

Rev. Peter R.K. Brenner

I leaned back in my chair still fixated on the message before me. Barry's reference to "rich family history" became an ongoing phrase looping over and over again through my mind. My dad enjoyed using his video camera and jumped at any opportunity to record family vacations or outings; but why the e - mail now, after so many years?

I shut down the computer and made a mental note to check it regularly for any response from Barry.

The wait wasn't long.

Barry indicated various ways of contacting him. I elected to telephone. For some reason, hearing his voice was a prerequisite necessary to my learning his side of the story. Breathing in deeply, I punched in the numbers staring back at me. After the fifth ring, I heard a voice. In a strange way it startled me because it was unexpected. I had convinced myself that nobody would be at the other end of the line; that I was on a wild goose chase; that I could never be as fortunate as to bump into an opportunity to get a peek into my mysterious past after so many years.

The "hello" was so soft it was barely discernable.

I paused to take another sigh, so I could pull together my thoughts and review what I'd rehearsed earlier in the day. "Hi. Barry? My name is Peter Brenner. I'm responding to an e - mail you sent out this morning." There was a brief pause before the silence was interrupted.

"Yes, go on," a voice answered.

"You made reference to some family films you had in your possession?"

"Why yes, hello," he said with a sudden surge of energy.

"May I call you Barry?"

"Yes, yes, please do. So my e - mail made sense to you!"

"Indeed and the message you sent blew me away. I'm certain those reels of film you have in your possession are about my family. I have so many questions to ask you." Without a break in my sentence, I rattled on for several minutes before uneasiness crept into my voice. I felt awkward about how much I'd shared in such a short period of time to a complete stranger. I slammed the breaks on my flow of information and blurted, "Am I making any sense?"

"What you've just related to me confirms, without a doubt, that you are the person I've been looking for. If you don't mind, however, I need to ask some questions. Is that alright?"

"If it would help," I said with an air of excitement.

"How old are you?"

"I'm 58," I responded.

"Are your parents alive?" Barry continued.

"No, they're both dead. My dad passed away in December of 1987 and my mom, just before Valentine's Day of 1992."

"I'm sorry to hear that." I could hear his disappointed in the tone of his voice. He proceeded, "When were you adopted?"

I responded, a bit surprised by the intrusive nature of the question. "May of 1949" was my clipped response. I felt my defenses springing up; he was treading on private ground and uncovering items reserved only for family.

"The questions are getting pretty personal, Barry." I felt bad even as the words tumbled out of my mouth.

"I'm sorry if I seem to be getting too detailed, but I've had some strange calls in response to my inquiry. People are very intent on procuring authentic film clips shot during the occupation of Germany. It has prompted me to be more cautious. You're actually the first person who sounds legit. I had no idea that the fragments of information I shared in my e - mail would generate such a response."

"It was enough for me," I insisted. "I'm confident the films in your possession are a result of my father's love for recording family events. He and my mother were in Germany looking to adopt a child. How did you know to look for Brenner?"

"The name was chiseled into a rock. I assumed nobody except someone with a connection to the name would be interested in filming an inscribed rock for the sake of posterity. I felt like a detective in my quest to identify and locate the people in the film. There was no question in my mind, that what I had in my possession never had been intended to leave the confines of your family home. However, to substantiate my belief, I have two final questions. Did you and your parents live in the Philadelphia area during the late 1980s and early '90s?"

"They did."

"What area?"

"My folks owned a home in the township of Haverford, located outside and northwest of Philadelphia on City Line Avenue.

"That seals it," Barry exclaimed. "I have so much more to share with you. I bought a metal container housing several reels of super - 8 film at an auction house. The place was located near your parent's home. We need to see each other."

"Where do you live?" I inquired.

"I'm in Manchester, New Hampshire. And you?"

"Vernon, Connecticut. Maybe we could meet in Boston. I often go into the city to see our boys or attend meetings at Emerson College."

"My business takes me to Lexington. It's a quaint little town nestled about twenty miles northwest of Boston. Do you know where it is?"

"I sure do. I went to high school in Concord. In sports, Lexington was our main rival. My dad was the Base Chaplain at Hanscom Field The Air Force base."

"Unbelievable. After previewing the film several times, I decided the officer behind the movie camera had to be a military chaplain."

"What clues confirmed that tidbit of information?" I pressed.

"There were a few frames featuring chapels . . . I can't believe we have actually connected after all these years."

"At the risk of sounding pushy, Barry; I think we need to meet sooner rather than later."

"Sounds great to me," he chimed. "I'll check my schedule tonight and e - mail you tomorrow."

Together we said, "Until later," and then hung up.

Within the month, I found myself driving northeast on I - 495, the outer loop of Boston, and then eastward toward Lexington. We had established the Town Green as our rendezvous point, next to "the Minute Man" statue.

It was a brisk autumn afternoon when I drove into historic Lexington. I arrived earlier than our appointed meeting time. It was my intent to engage in some reconnaissance work to locate an appropriate location for our meeting place. I wanted some degree of privacy during our conversation, plenty of coffee just a few paces away and the option of light snacks. Ten minutes into the search, I located a great coffee shop. Satisfied, I made my way to the famous Revolutionary War monument depicting a Minute Man poised for battle. I thought, how appropriate for the task at hand.

I crossed the street to get a closer look at the statue standing in the town square. I marveled at the strength and resolve, captured by the sculpture, of the solitary citizen standing ready for battle.

Lost in my thoughts, I heard a voice calling my name. I turned, looked across the street and spotted a fellow waving at me. Ignoring the blinking "Don't Walk" signal, I headed toward him. Barry was somewhat taller than I, of medium build, with brown hair and several years younger. With a handshake and introductory pleasantries completed, I suggested the coffee shop I had already located which was two blocks down and on the north side of the street.

Once inside, we ordered and made our way toward a table tucked into a nook with a window looking out onto Main Street. It was relatively private, out of the mainstream and away from the noisiest section of the cafe - perfect.

Over the next two hours, Barry unraveled the saga of the Super - 8 films. In a sense, it became an exercise in weaving together two stories: first, a well - traveled canister housing bits and pieces of my family history; secondly, how my mom and dad owned two homes - one in Haverford and one on Cape Cod.

I explained how my mom and dad loved both places equally; each parent had a unique and emotional tie to their favorite home. My mom was a New Englander and wanted the two of them to retire on the Cape. My dad was born and grew up in Germantown, northwest of downtown Philadelphia. It was the Haverford home, on the "Main Line" that housed our finest items from around the world. Also, it was only a two - hour drive from Wrightstown, New Jersey, where I lived the first three years following my adoption and arrival to the United States. My conversation seemed to settle in more on the Haverford home. I took another sip of my coffee.

Barry grinned. "I guess this is where I come in," he ventured.

"Wait just one moment." I held up my hand. Before he could say another word, I stood, grabbed his coffee cup and headed for the counter to refill our original orders. I returned with a grin on my face and more coffee to fuel our conversation. I sat down, leaned back and said; "Now we're ready to roll."

Barry tested the steaming drink before looking up to continue with his story. I sensed that he was trying to determine the most appropriate place to begin. "There was a little shop in Ardmore, Pennsylvania called The Browse Around Thrift Shop. They bought goods, did clean outs for area houses, sold off the good stuff at auctions and then put the rest of the items in their store in Ardmore. Several little old ladies, who were very nice, operated the store. All of the proceeds were used to benefit their sister convent in Africa. I don't remember exactly what, but it seemed to be going to a good cause. The items in the shop were usually given away at pennies on the dollar. I don't think I ever spent more than 5 or 10 dollars on an item."

"That would make sense," I added. "My dad was very mission oriented."

"The proceeds certainly went to a good cause. But anyway," Barry continued. "One day in the early '90s, I was looking through the shelf where they kept used cameras, odd film containers and various accessories. Some seemed very old. I often wondered if they were worth anything to collectors. Then, I came upon an aluminum container housing eight or 10 large 400 - foot rolls of 8mm movie film. I have an interest in old film containers and had never seen one quite like it. I opened the front cover, which was secured by a clip or buckle. It became even more intriguing when each slot revealed a finger lever on the bottom. The case was constructed with compartments capable of containing old film canisters. I was even more fascinated, when I pushed one of the buttons down and out popped one of the containers. Wow, this is neat, I thought. I opened the circular case to reveal what appeared to be about 8 rolls of 8mm home movies spliced together and put onto one 400 - foot spool. It even had a small piece of paper tucked inside that promptly fell out. I read it, plus all the notations on each container. They identified places in the world by date and location. It seemed odd to me, during such a time in history, how anyone could have actually traveled to so many places throughout the world. I ended up buying the case and all the films for $5.00."

"I remember the canister. It must have been tucked away where I couldn't easily see it. What did you do then?" I persisted.

"I took the films home and set up our family's old 8mm - film projector. I wanted to see what was on the tapes. I watched with amazement as a young military chaplain traveled the globe, taking movies of his attractive wife and little boy." A broad smile crossed Barry's face. It was great seeing the fun the family was having together."

"Did you see any footage of Japan, Greenland or stateside assignments?" I interjected. "My dad was also stationed in Korea during the Korean War and afterwards the family joined him in Japan," I elaborated, hoping to clarify why Barry was seeing so many locations.

He nodded, acknowledging my effort. "I now understand how someone could travel so extensively. I was watching the travels of a military family and became particularly fascinated by the 1940s segment. I felt privileged to see such a unique piece of history unfolding before my very eyes. It was phenomenal. However, what nagged at me the most was how this film found its way into a cramped little thrift shop." Barry looked at me, hoping for more answers.

"I can shed some light on that. When my dad passed away, Mom decided to keep both the Cape Cod home and the house north of Philadelphia, on City Line. She couldn't part with the memories and good times we had as a family in the Haverford home. After a year or so, she began spending more and more time at the Cape. The drive from Massachusetts to Pennsylvania was getting too tedious and being alone in the house accentuated her loneliness. The strain was too hard for her. Besides, Massachusetts was much closer to her aging mother, who lived at Avery Heights in Hartford, Connecticut. Plus, we lived in Farmington and only a ten-minute drive from my grandmother. She also didn't have the heart to sell the house on Main Line. It was that same spirit that possessed me, when my mom died in 1992. I didn't want to sell either home because of what each of them meant to me. I also knew I couldn't afford to maintain three homes on a minister's salary."

"So you felt you had to sell the Haverford home. What did you do then?"

"We laid my mom to rest beside my dad at Arlington Cemetery in Washington D.C. Following the quiet service, Bonnie and I drove to the Philadelphia area the next day and visited the home in Haverford with the intent of selling the house. I was unable to spend extended time in the house. Every time I stayed overnight, I could sense the strong presence of my mom and dad all around me. Even if I'd wanted to, I'd never been able to live in the house. I made the tough decision to sell the home and have professional auctioneers handle the furniture, plus all the items we couldn't pack into our U - Haul.

I thought I'd looked everywhere before we left, but I never saw the canister containing all the Super - 8 film my father had shot." I stood to stretch my legs. We'd already been at the coffee shop for almost 2 hours. I was pleased to hear Barry's interest to unfold his side of the story as it related to the super - 8 film. Besides, I still had questions to ask him regarding the reels from the 1940s. "How did you uncover the information?"

Barry shook his head. "I tried to write down every lead buried within the hundreds of little snippets. From the old and torn frames, I came up with a military post in the Midwest that was supposed to store personnel information. When I called, they claimed it had burned down. I called several other places but no one was around who could remember anything from that time period. Weeks and months went by and I lost interest in trying to pursue the film's mystery. I stopped searching but made every effort to keep the film in a dry but cool storage area in an effort to preserve it."

"I was wondering how you kept the film from falling apart."

"The film is in horrible condition. I had to look at the images frame by frame. I was careful when handling the actual film, but to really see the footage well, you need to have it professionally repaired. I don't have the equipment, time or skill to do that."

"When did you leave the Philadelphia area?"

"In late 2000, I moved to a small town in the lakes region of New Hampshire. The canister housing the reels of film was packed with care and placed onto a bookshelf where it would not get ruined. It sat there for years. One day, when my wife was cleaning up around the house, she discovered the metal case and inquired about it. As I relayed the story to her, it hit me: Since my first efforts to locate this military family, the Internet capabilities had exploded. Now there was so much information to be had, I felt certain a Chaplain Brenner, with an adopted son, could be located."

"Well you were right and here we sit. Like a sudden gust of wind, your story blows me away."

"I've got something for you. Let's go to my car." We stood and left the shop, filled with coffee and a new appreciation of the unexpected. At the car, Barry opened the door and handed me the canister. "The films are in here." He lifted the container and placed the treasure chest at my feet. "I'm glad it's finally in the hands of its rightful owner."

We both made promises to stay in touch.

As I headed back to Connecticut, my mind began playing around with various options for getting the film repaired well enough to preview. One question repeatedly tickled my thought: Did my dad capture me on film, when they visited the orphanage where they found me? Receiving my family home video and having it repaired for previewing was an act of Divine Intervention.

For me, Divine Intervention is when God participates in the activities of mankind. He places opportunities before the seeker, leaving it up to the person's faith to ignore or act upon the revelation set before an individual. Without faith in God's "loving power," the clues go unnoticed, ignored, or excused away with words like chance, fate, luck or coincidences. A person of faith however responds to possibilities or revelations and miraculous things happen. The repairing of my dad's film illustrates Divine Intervention.

Barry recommended a friend of his to do the repair work on the brittle and cracked film stored in the canister sitting beside me in the car. I thanked him for the offer, but wanted to try and find a place closer to home. My first choice was to seek advice from my younger son, Tim.

Tim, my younger son, was doing freelance work with his own company, T Squared Productions. One autumn he joined forces with an area contact, Lauren, who had her own company, The Write Track: Audio & Visual Productions. Tim and Lauren were actively involved producing video Christmas cards. Little did I realize how the family film would soon be embarking on another unusual journey.

The two quickly realized they didn't have the technical equipment or skill to tackle such an extensive project as the repair of my 8mm film. Lauren, however, recommended the delicate project to an associate of hers who lived in West Hartford, Connecticut. I agreed. With the referral, Tim and Lauren set in motion a new travel route for my dad's home videos.

Weeks rolled over into months and soon we were into the New Year of 2004, I'd not heard a word about the status of the family film project. I asked Tim, who inquired of Lauren and she called her West Hartford friend. Lauren explained that her friend had referred the work on to a third colleague, who lived in Boston.

Concerned about the status, location and yet another unknown individual handling historical footage that was of such importance to me, I wanted to know more about the individual and where he was doing the restoration work. When I heard the name of the Bostonian and the institution where the work was being handled, I almost fell out of my chair. It was another expression of Divine Intervention.

Paul Beck was a Phi Alpha Tau fraternity brother of mine working at Emerson College, where I'd received my undergraduate degree in '67. I couldn't have picked a better institution or person to handle the delicate repair work of my precious films.

I called Paul on the phone that very day. The news was an incredible revelation for the two of us. I briefly shared my story and expressed my confidence in his ability to do the work. He conveyed the honor he felt being responsible for such a personally significant piece of film. Being frat brothers from the same college allayed all my fears.

He e - mailed me the next day elaborating on the task at hand.

First, he thanked me for the telephone call and then reiterated how he had not seen enough of the film to connect the project to me. He had done some preliminary work, but more needed to be done. Time would be his greatest adversary, because all of the work would have to be squeezed in on his own time given the delicate nature of the repairs. The following explanation helped me to appreciate the nature of the work going into the repair of my brittle home video.

Dear Peter,

I am pleased to send a DVD of the first reel of 8mm film, which has been restored, and transferred to a digital videotape format.

The films all have aged significantly and each splice point has either warped or shrunk, such that the film will be damaged if projected. (This is a normal phenomenon for film of this vintage).

Those splices that have not been affected by shrinkage or warping have simply failed, and the film has separated from the splice points, even as it was being carefully touched by hand for cleaning.

In a word, it just takes time to service each reel correctly.

I spend most Saturday nights and Sunday afternoons on film re - mastering projects like yours. I am clearing the tracks for your work and hope to have the bulk of them done and in your hands shortly after Easter.

Thank you for the opportunity to assist your research in this wonderful effort.

Paul R. Beck

3/9/05

Paul kept his word and we received all the reels by the start of spring '06.

With a sense of excitement, like a child going into a candy store, we popped in the DVD with the oldest dates typed on the reference tab. In anticipation of what we hoped to find, Bonnie and I settled onto our couch in the comfort of our T.V. room.

It became a sobering afternoon as we viewed the grim reality of the destructive aftermath of war. The images were astonishing, as each frame reaffirmed my contention there are no just wars, only wars justified by leaders in pursuit of power and personal wealth. The collateral damage passing before our eyes served to press Bonnie and me closer together.

Sighing and shaking our heads in disbelief; we saw blown out buildings leaving nothing but a skeleton form silhouetted against a gray sky, leveled towns, disabled tanks and downed airplanes defining a landscape populated by people in dark garb shuffling slowly along the streets, two years after the war's end. Their misfortune, to live in a town where the effects of war demolished their homes and took their livelihoods, crushed their spirit and fractured their families. I felt the pain as it flickered before me - frame by frame.

Intermingled with the images was a brief segment with my parents. They were filming little children alongside a mountain trail. It was obvious they were interested in the children as they honed in on a little boy and girl. One would guess they might be brother and sister. Off to the side was a solitary 3-year old boy playing and running around. I reran that segment several times, showed it to Bonnie and then studied it some more.

It's a strange and surreal moment when you believe that you are seeing yourself for the first time, as a child. It felt like an empty outlined figure was being miraculously colored in. The idea of being abandoned and rejected was instantly replaced; I existed in a tangible and touchable way. Somebody wanted me. It validated my existence - both the nightmares and hopeful moments when I realized that somebody cared for me. As the images flicked before my eyes, I knew my life would never feel complete unless an effort was made to find out how that little boy survived. Somehow, I knew he had to be me and Bonnie agreed.

CHAPTER VII

The Quest

"We orphans, we lament to the world: World, why have you taken our soft mothers from us and the fathers who say: My child, you are like me! We orphans are like no one in this world any more! Oh world, we accuse you."

Nelly Sachs (1891 - 1970)

The search for uncovering my early past has repeatedly been assisted by individuals emerging unexpectedly in a variety of backgrounds and personalities. It felt similar to a room of unopened gifts; the major difference being party packages are bunched together in a corner, while people are sprinkled indiscriminately throughout one's life. Ruth was such an individual.

My wife, Bonnie, is a music educator (K - 6). Her classroom is the first room on the left as people enter through the main doors of Central Elementary School, Simsbury, Connecticut. In the corridor, across from the administrative offices and pressed against the wall just a few paces to the right of her room sits a wooden bench. It's a rest area for early arrivals waiting to pick up their childen at the end of the school day.

One afternoon, as Bonnie was arranging her instruments for her next class, she could hear German being spoken outside her room. Curious, she poked her head out and around the partially open doorway. She spotted a middle-aged woman reading a book to a little boy.

Stepping out into the hallway, Bonnie greeted the duo with a pleasant, "May I help you?"

The lady silently looked up and gave a warm smile.

Bonnie continued, "I'm the music teacher. Are you waiting for anyone in particular?"

"Yes, my older son, but we're early so don't hurry."

Bonnie stepped forward and extended her hand. "I'm Bonnie Brenner."

"I'm Ruth, pleased to meet you," she responded with a strong accent.

"If I'm not mistaken, I think I heard you speaking German?" Bonnie asked.

"I was. Whenever I have a little extra time, I like to read German fables or stories to my son." The two looked at each other. "I want to make sure he doesn't lose his understanding of our language."

"What a wonderful gift to give your son. I wish my parents had done that for me," Bonnie sighed.

One thing led to another and before long the two started exchanging their stories. Bonnie shared our wonderful trip to Germany and the miraculous circumstances surrounding our visit with Tante Marie. She elaborated for Ruth information about the town of Prien and the orphanage from which I had been adopted at the age of 5. Bonnie began sharing our plans to visit Germany, France and Norway.

Suddenly Ruth interjected, "I don't know why I was sent to this school. Usually my son goes to another elementary school for his instructions." Bonnie smiled, "You were sent here so we would meet. I have a favor to ask of you, Ruth. Would you be willing to help my husband translate an official document?"

"Of course. What sort of document?" she volunteered with a broad smile springing to her face.

"Peter, my husband, is fairly certain it's a Baptismal Certificate, but there are some phrases he's hesitant to translate based on the importance of the official document."

"I would be pleased to help. When do you need it completed?"

"We really need it before summer. My husband believes there is information that points to his earliest beginnings. He believes it will help us determine our itinerary, when we're traveling in Germany."

Bonnie gestured for Ruth to remain seated and said, "Please, don't move; I'll be back in a moment." She returned carrying a photocopy of the document that needed to be translated. She entrusted it to Ruth.

"I understand." Ruth tucked the paper into her purse and looked up at Bonnie, "I'll work on it this weekend and get right back to you."

The two exchanged e - mail addresses as a promise of keeping in touch.

As promised, Ruth returned the following Thursday with the translated document in hand. "Here's the document. I think you will find it very significant."

Bonnie sat down as Ruth read the following:

Certificate of Baptism

"In the year one thousand nine hundred and forty - three (1943), on October 11th was in Nordrach/Baden born and on December 14, 1945 in the House Church of the Children - and - Mothers home, Steinhoering after Catholic rites baptized, Stromnes, Dieter Rolf. This is certified due to the local church record volume, page 545 #72 Steinhoering, December 14th, 1945"

Catholic Ministry

That evening, I had my first opportunity to read the Baptismal certificate in English. I was astonished; typed before my very eyes lay a document I had glossed over for 55 years. Upon closer review the reason appeared obvious: The dates, name and place were all wrong. Bjorg insisted I was born on March 18, 1944 in the region of Baden Baden and Peder was my first name. My dad confirmed I was baptized Lutheran, not Catholic. He had insisted the catholic certificate wasn't authentic based on the testimony of two people, he believed would know.

I made two immediate assumptions: the document had to be a mistake; or it was referring to another orphan. Stromnes was a common last name for Norwegians, but I knew nothing about the first name, Dieter. I also didn't relish the idea of my birth having been a year earlier, aging me a week and five months. Research reveals that the name Dieter, in old German origin, means "Army of the People." I definitely didn't like the tone of that explanation. A little more digging exposed a plausible explanation. After the war the Catholic Church gathered hundreds of orphans and ascribed new names and birth dates in an effort to bring the children under the guidance and care of the Church. On one level this didn't bother me for the simple reason that the orphans of World War II had nobody to watch out for them. In a sense, we were the forgotten segment of society for several years. What irked me the most was that changing names and dates was unethical and would invariably make it harder for natural parents to locate their lost child.

My impulses to further explain away this seemingly bogus, disturbing information was hindered by reluctant feelings. I didn't want to have the document hinder my enthusiasm to delve further into my past. In the same mix, however, this singular document was the sole official record validating my birth.

Implausible as the baptismal card appeared, it made sense to unravel this mystery. I had been doing research and the findings were pulling me in different directions. Deep down, I was afraid of what I might uncover.

Like rapid fire, questions started popping up in my mind: (1) why impose additional pain and possible rejection on myself? (2) At this stage in my life, what difference does it make? (3) What would I uncover? It was the third question that was keeping me from pressing down on the accelerator and rushing forward. I knew little of my birth father other than his name was Frank, that he was tall and that I supposedly looked like him. I often wondered if he might be a German soldier who had raped my mother, even though I was assured otherwise. I recalled a brief dialogue I had with a clinical physiologist and close friend, Dr. Richard Horn.

"Peter, why wouldn't you want to uncover your past?"

"I'm afraid of what I'll uncover?"

"You told me it represented hidden treasures. Aren't they still golden nuggets to be unearthed and brought to light."

"Dick, I believe some things need to remain buried."

"Why? You've worked so hard to get to this point in your search. Why abandon your pursuit?"

"What if the information is ugly? What if it's shameful . . . tainted?" I struggled to say each word.

"You are not responsible for what happened to you as an infant or child, Peter. You are who you are because of what you have done. Let history inform you, but not determine you."

Dick's insight brought to mind the wonderful observations by the author Squire Rushnell in his book, *When God Winks*. He repeatedly poses the question, "Were you led to a moment to learn more about yourself and the mysterious guideposts, which cause you to meet certain people, propel you in new directions, and place you into situations you never anticipated? If so, you're about to confirm something you have suspected all along that coincidence - God Winks - are little messages to put you on your journey through life, nudging you along the grand path that has been designed especially for you." I really believe "When God Winks" is another way of talking about divine intervention.

I came to the conclusion that Bonnie meeting and talking to Ruth, who was sitting on the wooden bench just outside her classroom, was yet another "God Wink" to help me along my journey, as was Jenna Blum's book *Those Who Save Us* and Dick's insightful observations. They are not chance moments. Ruth appeared outside Bonnie's music room for a reason and it wasn't fate. Uncovering my past was bigger than facts and it wasn't coincidence. I was connecting dots so a recognizable picture might emerge. It wasn't a matter of wanting to do it; I had to.

The Church Council approved my three - month Sabbatical that would encompass an extended trip in Germany, France and Norway. I was compelled to use the time to replace questions with answers. I proceeded, knowing it was the right course of action. The baptismal document unearthed 5 important clues to explore:

The significance of a town called Steinhoering,

2) My birth date,
3) The Catholic Church's involvement,
4) The general area of my birthplace and
5) A different first name.

I knew Steinhoering would be my initial destination and a critical first step back into history.

Ruth remains a valuable person for translating technical language, taped conversations, written letters and important documents. She is a warm, kind and willing person, who materialized like a messenger one quiet afternoon outside Bonnie's music room. She is a clear definition of "worthy" and a glaring contrast to Hitler's distorted understanding of the word's meaning and content.

My research had already revealed the mental and wholesale deception advanced by Hitler. He established the backdrop and setting for the program of creating hereditarily "worthy children," a 'pure race' to be raised . . . in the spirit of National Socialism." He wanted a program designed with the explicit purpose of taking care of "social - and - genetic worthful mothers" and their children. Hitler wanted to produce a "superior race" for the Third Reich. I knew Steinhoering held the answers to Hitler's madness. I pulled out my research notes and began to review what I'd already uncovered about this insane, man.

Hitler did not dare to fully implement a large - scale extermination of the useless and "degenerate" citizens until he had the cover of war. At the 1929 Nazi Party rally in Nuremberg, he mused out loud that " . . . *if a million children a year are born in Germany and 700 - 800,000 of the weakest people are eliminated the end result might be an increase in strength."*

On August 18, 1939, Interior Ministry health professionals were ordered to register all newborns and children under age three who had specified handicaps. Eventually, there would be some thirty children's euthanasia wards scattered all over the country. The first one opened in 1939 at Gorden, a large hospital complex just outside Brandenburg that became the training ground for doctors sent to handle the euthanasia cases in other centers. By October of the same year, with the killings moving forward, those running the program had stopped worrying about emotions and had begun to be concerned about the possibility of being prosecuted for murder. Hitler was asked to provide a document, or something in writing that would alleviate their fears. He presented the following handwritten statement on a piece of paper:

"Reichsleiter Boulder and Dr. Brandt are charged with responsibility to extend the powers of specific doctors in such a way that patients suffering from illness considered to be incurable, may, in the best human judgment and after careful assessment of their condition, be granted a mercy death."

On the basis of this vague note the program began to accelerate. The initial justification for adult euthanasia resulted in some 100,000 lives being terminated.

The preferred method for killing the relatively small number of handicapped children was with drugs. This was not practical for the tens of thousands of adult patients targeted for elimination. After considerable discussion, carbon monoxide gas was chosen as the most efficient method. In the fall of 1939, as the German Army invaded Poland, construction and testing (with human beings) of gas chambers and crematoria were begun at the Brandenburg asylum. Four other centers would be used at various times during the war.

Under the cloak of World War II, Hitler began in earnest the purging of the "unfit." Included on this list were "gypsies, homosexuals, the mentally impaired, the physically handicapped, the entire Jewish community, plus others who fell below the strict guidelines of acceptability."

The other end of the spectrum involved the procreation of life.

In redefining the role of individuals, Germany passed a series of laws known as the Nuremberg laws. These laws put into place mechanisms to further the adherence to the redefined roles of individual "Non - Aryan" individuals. (Gilbert, 1979)

These laws, know as the "race laws," were put into place to also differentiate "Aryan" from "Non - Aryan" people. These laws had a profound effect on individual family members from both groups. The central theme to all social restructuring laws was to create a master race of German people and at the same time exterminate "THOSE THAT DID NOT MEET THE DEFINITION OF ARYAN." While the history of the Holocaust is well documented, the plight of orphaned children and the effects these laws had on them has been shrouded in secrecy, denial, doctored documents and destruction of any evidence casting light on their existence.

December of 2000, following our summer trip to Germany, I accepted a "Call" to be the Senior Minister of the First Congregational Church of Vernon. The move solidified my desire to uncover the secrets of my buried past - once and for all. Five years passed by quickly for us in Connecticut.

Quicker than a snap of ones fingers, we were planning our second trip to Germany and a visit to my Norwegian relatives. The itinerary would start with Steinhoering, another trip to Prien and then points unknown. Research encouraged me to believe that I might have been in an orphanage located somewhere in the vicinity of the resort town near Baden Baden. If not, we'd still make a visit into France and visit the little village of Spada - where my parents lived when my dad was stationed in France. Tim would join us for the trip through France and then on to Norway. I also planned to take a side trip to Verdun, France where I attended a boarding school during my senior year of high school. From there it would be a night in Luxembourg and then a short flight up to Oslo, Norway. I could barely contain my enthusiasm and excitement regarding the prospects lying before me.

It was amidst our planning that I received a surprise letter. It was in response to an earlier correspondence to Tante Marie dated June 21, 2005. The letter arrived at our Connecticut home July 15, 2005. The message was brief and disheartening.

Mr. Peter and Bonnie Brenner,

Via some detour I am in receipt of a letter. I am Erika the daughter of the one you refer to as Tanta Marie, and cannot answer the questions in your letter out of my own memory, because during 1947 - 1949 I attended a boarding school out of town and was not at home for this reason. My mother is still alive at the age of 93, but has lost practically all her memory. I am sorry for not being able to help you and remain sincerely yours . . .

Erika.

My response to Erika noted that Bonnie and I were planning to visit Germany sometime during the summer of 2006. I asked if we might get together for a conversation.

Her return e - mail was a curt and an emphatic NO.

I waited until we had finalized our itinerary for the European/Norway trip. I sent a short e - mail explaining how important her mother, had been during my stay with her the years immediately following the war. I was very specific with our planned visit to Prien - July 31st thru August 4th. I assured her, if she were available, I'd adjust our schedule to meet her time frame. There was no response.

The response, or no response, from Erika didn't dampen our spirits. It was exhilarating to study our map of Germany as we located the cities and discovered how close Steinhoering was to Prien.

SUMMER OF 2006

The phone rang; I picked up the receiver, placed it to my ear and quietly listened. It was my half - sister from California updating Bjorg's. health. I mumbled a response before returning the phone back into its cradle and silently stared at Bonnie.

"What?" she said with a puzzled expression. "Is everything alright?"

"It was Sandra. She says B.J is in the hospital."

"Is it serious?" Bonnie quickly replied as her concerned expression matched mine.

"She thinks we shouldn't come out because Bjorg will be laid up for some time. I think I know where she's coming from. Our visit is supposed to be a celebration of her parent's 60th wedding anniversary."

"What did you say?"

"That we should come out: The tickets are bought, the plans have been finalized and I need to be with her now as much as any other time."

"Renewing their wedding vows would have been so beautiful. You would be officiating for a wedding service similar to the one your dad performed for them sixty years ago in Germany. You must feel awful."

"I would have liked that, but it's not meant to be."

Bonnie flashed a supportive smile. "I guess we better get ready, we're leaving for LAX in two days."

The idea of visiting B.J. and her husband for their 60th wedding anniversary still pulled at me like the tug of an angler's line. My desire to be with B.J. consumed my thoughts, tickling nerves and raising the small hairs on the nape of my neck. Imagined conversations and vivid revelations interrupted my efforts for a restful night of sleep. Such was my state of mind as we drove toward Logan airport, in Boston.

Once inside the outer ring of terminal B, I decided to immerse myself in the minutia surrounding me. It was a way of distancing from what I knew was lying before me.

Bonnie and I approached an imposing bank of self-service, check-in computers. Uniting our efforts, we electronically punched in the pertinent numbers and personal information necessary to retrieve two sets of flimsy paper tickets for American Airlines, flight twenty - five. Passing through the security check consisted of flashing a picture I.D; emptying the contents of all our pockets onto a waiter like tray; taking off our shoes and placing them alongside our remaining items into huge, gray plastic bins, which reminded me of my busboy duties at Emerson College's cafeteria. By the time we had walked the full length of our terminal, we still had to wait another hour before queuing up to board. It was more than enough time for me to drain a large cup of regular coffee, explore the numerous eateries, shops and newsstands lining the inner zone of the waiting area. Boarding was also uneventful. I wheeled my carry - on down the aisle, hitting an occasional leg and, like a pinball out of control, bumping several protruding shoulders along the way. Our seats were located half a dozen rows in from the back of the plane. I hoisted our luggage, shoved both suitcases into the overhead bins and quickly plopped into the window seat. Bonnie graciously slipped into 32E, a middle seat. A thin Asian man, who slept through the greater portion of the six-hour flight, flanked her on her left. I was on her right, peering out the window, counting the pieces of luggage moving at a snail's pace up the conveyer belt. I always prefer the window seat. This way, once we are airborne, I can peer out the portal and watch the terrain magically change below me. I always enjoy identifying the various cities, rivers and natural wonders as they materialize.

I took in every detail around me to avoid addressing the bigger picture - the disappointment of not officiating for a Renewal of Vows ceremony for B.J. and Hunter. Our visit would precede the trip to Europe by only three weeks. The positioning of the two events seemed surreal.

We drove from the airport directly to Riverside Hospital. Hunter was kind enough to have e - mailed us explicit directions to the facilities. I wanted to spend as much time as possible with my B.J. before heading off to Banning and a couple of nights with Hunter. Bjorg was in a private room under close supervision. She recognized us the moment we entered the room and approached her bed. She reached for me; I took her extended hand. A genuine smile lit up her face and warmed our hearts.

"Come closer, Peter. I want to see your face."

I kissed her forehead; she squeezed my hand harder. "Hi. I'm glad to see you awake. How are you doing?"

She ignored my question and answered, "You didn't have to come. It's so far and expensive."

"We both wanted to be here, with you. This is where I need to be."

For the next half - hour or more we shared stories about our kids, work, golf, our pending trip to Europe and Norway. It was amazing how much information could be condensed into such a brief period of time. I even shared my dream of working on my memoir. I told her, "I need to uncover more of my hidden treasures." She wished me luck - accompanied with a pensive look, but no added information. Once again, I wondered what was churning around in her head. If only I could hear her thoughts.

Hunter recognized that his true love was getting tired. Nevertheless, he gave a handful of good reasons for Bonnie and him to slip out so the two of us could have some private time together. When they disappeared around the corner, she pulled me close to her. "Peter, I need to tell you something."

I focused on her face. I didn't want to miss one single word slipping out from between her lips.

"I know you're going to Norway for the family reunion. My sisters told me. I don't want you to be nervous; they all know you are my first - born." I struggled to dam the tears surfing at the corners of my eyes. "Son, you can ask them any question you want. They want to see you and welcome you into the family." I buried my face against her shoulder. She stroked my hair and continued, "I should have told you more, but I couldn't. The horror goes too deep and the pain is too unbearable. Please try to understand . . . I'm so sorry."

Teary eyed, I looked up. For the first time B.J. had referred to me as her son. It felt natural for me to refer to her in a more intimate manner. "Mom, I understand. I've been avoiding my past for a lifetime. I want you to know, I love you and that I have the courage to face what lies before me. That's all that matters." She pressed her face against mine. We lay silently together and it felt good. As I sat quietly beside the bed, I realized I had called her Mom. For the first time, I could see her as my Mom and not merely the biological mother. The smile on her face told me she knew what I was thinking. It was a sacred moment for both of us.

We looked toward the door. Hunter and Bonnie entered with a smile gracing their faces. I stood up and discreetly wiped my face. Simultaneously, we all smiled.

"Back already?" B.J. chuckled.

"I don't like being away from you too long," Hunter answered.

Bonnie came to my side and whispered in my ear, "Do you want to give them a blessing?" I nodded.

I stood, still holding on to mom's hand, and said, "Under the circumstances, it looks as though we'll not be having a Renewal of Vows today. However, if you would indulge me, I'd like to give a blessing for the sacred moments we've shared together. Would you mind?"

Without hesitation Hunter took B.J.'s hand and Bonnie stretched out her arms toward me and entwined her fingers with mine, while mom tightened her grip on my other hand. I can't remember exactly the words I uttered. I do know, I emphasized the sacredness of the moment, the love surging through all of us and the presence of God's Grace surrounding us. I believe it was a powerful moment for all of us.

We gave hugs and kisses before time nudged us toward the door. I turned and waved. Mom nodded flashing a tired, but warm smile. Experience told me she still had more time to give and that Hunter and she would continue together for a little time more. I also sensed this would be the last time I'd see her alive.

Due to B.J's unscheduled transfer to another facility, we weren't able to see her during our departure day. We, however, had two nights and a full day to visit with Hunter and Sandra. We managed just the one visit with B.J. The next day we were off for LAX knowing it would be the first leg of our trip to Europe/Norway and possibly the last time I'd speak to my birth mother.

GERMANY

Our plane landed at the Frankfurt airport early on the afternoon of July 29, 2006. We headed straight for the Bussbahnhof (shuttle bus terminal) and took a quick ride to terminal 1 where we followed signs to Fernbahnhof (long distance train) and rushed to Gist 4 (gate). We decided not to wait for our reserved afternoon seats on the 4:15 train, instead; we were fortunate to catch an earlier express (ICE 727) at 3:09. Our itinerary included two intermediate, overnight stops to include the town of Wurzburg and the city of Munich, before driving on to Steinhoering. At the time I had no idea how significant Wurzburg was in relationship to Bjorg.

For some reason, my parents never dwelled on the fact that Dad had been stationed at Kitzingen Army /Air Corps Base, Germany, located 17 kilometers south of the Bavarian city of Wurzburg. He was the base chaplain. It was during his time there that my parents eventually drove south past Munich and on to Prien. The area also played a significant role in Bjorg's travels during and after the war. The proximity of Wurzburg to Steinhoering, for whatever reason, got me to thinking about my conversations with my Norwegian Mom.

While living in Salt Lake City and during my visits with Bjorg, our late-night talks opened closed doors that led to our past. I carefully pieced together her story.

My natural mother's account begins as a seventeen-year old teenager in Norway. She had met a nice hometown boy by the name of Frank. They became very good friends and were involved in the Resistance movement when she became pregnant by Frank. She turned to her sisters for advice. They all had fears about what her father would do if he learned what happened. One of her older sisters suggested that she get out of the country to save embarrassment to the family and Bjorg's boyfriend. Out of fear and shame, she sought a way to leave Norway. Bjorg saw a posted notice of employment in Germany, decided to accept the offer and in late 1943, she and a friend named Anne were flown to Germany along with several young people. She recalls that her first job was in a Berlin munitions factory with other foreign workers. There was an explosion in the factory and the Germans suspected that the workers had caused it. Bjorg escaped to Wurzburg a tired, frightened and pregnant young girl. She felt fortunate to find employment as a housekeeper. When the lady of the house recognized that Bjorg was pregnant and close to delivery, she put the teenager on a train to go to a hospital/home where her baby would be born. Bjorg was told that the home was a safe place for unwed mothers to bear their child. Ten days after her arrival she gave birth to a son. Two weeks later, when she started to leave the home, her newborn son was immediately taken from her. A nurse, clad in white from head to foot, informed her that they kept the boys. If it had been a girl, she could have left with the child.

Not knowing what to do, Bjorg left the hospital and made her way back to Wurzburg. When the local authorities found out that she was Norwegian, she was told of a Nanny position and directed to contact a specific family. The husband was a German officer, his wife was Russian, and they had twin daughters. She remained with the family until the end of the war and in the region for another couple of years. The Germany officer was stationed in Wurzburg and walked the same narrow streets familiar to Bjorg and my parents.

My mother's story and our current location intermittently weaved its way through my thoughts like a roaring river.

Our first night in Wurzburg, Bonnie and I stood at the back of a Catholic church while the locals worshipped. All present in the sanctuary were surrounded by glorious art work and enveloped by the sounds of a magnificent organ as music filled the small church and spilled onto bowed heads. In the beauty and sanctity of the church, I prayed and wondered why there was an uncomfortable tightness in my shoulders. I think God was trying to tell me something, but I was so busy taking in everything surrounding me that I wasn't paying attention to a little voice within telling me to listen. The next day we hopped on a train for Munich and left behind a significant piece of history, to be discovered later on in my journey.

I was familiar with the city of Munich. My first two years of college were spent on the campus grounds of McGraw Kaserne, home of the University of Maryland, Munich branch. The fact that the city was the epicenter of Hitler's rise to power never became a part of the curriculum. Now, Bonnie and I enjoyed the sights, drank the Hoff Brau Haus beer and studied our map. Our next stop was Steinhoering.

Munich was overcast with threatening rain. By mid - morning, we were in a rented car and headed east on route 304. The car sped by farmland communities clustered against the rolling hills like little fiefdoms. The busy road narrowed every time we weaved through the tiny streets dotted with a Gasthof (guest house), restaurants, gas stations and stores necessary to sustain village life. On occasion the country road was guarded by groves of towering trees casting darkness on the road. The town of Edersberg came and went, while the knots in my stomach pulled tighter. The map affirmed our destination would be the next town.

STEINHOERING

We stopped the car at the outer edge of a tiny village to stare at the sign - STEINHOERING. We drove another 100 yards before I spotted a large sign, Betreuings Zentrum Steinhoering. We turned into the driveway and stared. Before me towered a three story, whitewashed stucco building. The blood running through my veins felt ice cold as my eyes started to water. We slowly coasted down the driveway and around to the back of the building. I took a deep breath, locked my eyes on the second story, my face paled and I started to shiver. I'd been here before and the feeling frightened me.

I looked at Bonnie and whispered, "This is where I lived." I was afraid to speak any louder; least I wake horrible memories.

"You remember, don't you?" Bonnie looked at me and began slowly to rub my arm. "Are you okay?"

I nodded, still hesitant to speak. Slowly, some words spilled out, "I think so . . . I can feel heaviness . . . darkness." I looked around. "The area is the same, but there are more buildings." I turned back to face the stucco structure and pointed to the second floor. "That's the same."

"What do you want to do?" Bonnie said in a soothing, almost healing tone. "Maybe we should leave and come back later."

"I spotted a sign when we drove in. Did you see it?"

"What did it say?"

"It was all in German."

"Could you read it?"

"Enough to know it's some kind of hospital or sanitarium. The institution is a clinic dedicated to the care of handicapped and mentally ill. It's bigger than I remember. Let's see if we can drive through the area and take a quick look - see. I released my foot from the brake pedal and allowed the car to slowly coast to a silent stop. We were parallel to the back of the main building. There were three stories with flowered balconies on every level.

"I slept on the second floor. I think we ate and did activities on the first floor. I can't remember anything about the top level. Maybe, mothers with infants stayed there." I remained motionless.

"Are you okay, hon?"

"I can't believe I'm here." I turned to face Bonnie. "We have to find someone who can show us through this place."

"Should we go to the entrance and find somebody who might help us?"

"No. Not yet . . . I need more time . . . Let's get going. I don't want to attract any more attention than we already have." Silently we drove on. We slipped through an area that looked like apartments. On occasion, I saw a gaunt face peering out from behind a curtain. Once off the grounds and sitting in a parking lot on the eastern outskirts of the village, we spied the road sign one would view when exiting the village. The name Steinhoering had a black line drawn through it. How appropriate I thought. Even the town's people are expressing their embarrassment of the town's connection with history. I later learned all the little towns had the same markings indicating that you were leaving the town.

I turned to Bonnie. "I'm certain this was the Lebensborn Center run by Heinrich Himmler. It was the headquarters where he, at the behest of Hitler, carried out their plan for the creation of an "Aryan Race". This is the very location where babies, taken away from their unwed mothers, or mothers having babies by German soldiers, were raised in the hope of furthering the Youth Movement of the Third Reich."

I rummaged through my briefcase until I located my folder on Hitler and the Lebensborn Project.

"Bonnie, I want you to know what I've uncovered about the programs perpetrated on unsuspecting mothers who were housed in the buildings we just passed. It's a horror story". We reviewed it together.

LEBENSBORN PROJECT

The Nazis were not interested in the traditional moral aspects of producing children. They were only focused on "purity of number." A large reservoir of "racially pure" individuals was vital to the support of Hitler's expansionist plan. Every possible avenue was used to promote large families. Birth control clinics were closed and penalties for abortion were toughened. Abortions could only be performed to protect the hereditary health of the race, in which case they were mandatory. By 1941 only those of "alien" race could have an abortion with impunity and indeed were encouraged to do so.

The state provided every feasible form of help to acceptable mothers. Existing welfare organizations were expanded and consolidated under the banner of the National Socialist Welfare Organization (NSV). None of this was altruistic. At the counseling centers the women and children were carefully observed for flaws and educated in Nazi family policy. In the maternity homes, often installed in villas confiscated from Jews, indoctrination classes filled a good part of the day. Before meals, grace was said to the Fuhrer. With hands raised in the Nazi salute, the mothers thanked him for their food and intoned, "To thee we devote all our powers, and to thee we dedicate our lives and those of our children." The center's objective was to mold the mother's mind and keep the children safe for Hitler until the schools could take them over at the age of six. Platoons of uniformed nurses made regular visits to the homes of young children, whom they expected to give the Nazi salute and encouraged to play war games so they could grow up to be " . . . fighters for the Fuhrer."

Nazi efforts to protect and encourage single mothers and remove the stigma of illegitimate birth were less successful. The NSV home did not discriminate against hereditarily correct unwed mothers or their so - called state children. They ran an adoption and foster home service for this special designation. A boy born of Norwegian parents would fall into this designated category. Nevertheless, unwed mothers did not fit in well with the concept of the Kinderreich family. Even Nazi race specialists were opposed to illegitimacy on the logical basis that one could not be sure of a child's "purity" if its father was unknown. Such children were also popularly thought to be less healthy as well as mentally unstable. Mainstream agencies did little more than give the single woman the polite title of "Frau," tax relief, and equal access to welfare.

Admission to the Lebensborn program for an unwed mother was not generally allowed. In addition to the already complex SS requirements, a candidate seeking admission, had to produce hand - written biographies, photographs, and a sworn statement that the listed father was the real one. If this were impossible, in selected circumstances the baby would be taken from the mother, after which she would be ejected from the program. Himmler himself had the final word on admissions.

"Bonnie, I think Bjorg fell into this category. They wanted me because she was a pure Norwegian woman."

"And they took you away from her because they didn't know anything about your father's health but that he was 100% Norwegian."

"Which was great, but not enough for her to keep me or stay in the Lebensborn Program," I elaborated.

"So she was kicked out of the program and you were kept."

"Right. Wait until you hear what's next. Let's continue reading." We turned back to my research.

Babies born in Lebensborn homes were not registered with the local civil authorities and therefore had no recognizable "place of birth." Those who were accepted became wards of the SS, which set up a special guardianship office for their support. This led to dreadful complications with the mainstream children's agencies. The normal routes to medical care, education, or welfare were closed to Lebensborn children, as they were not listed in any known jurisdiction. The SS went so far as to establish false identities and actively supported elaborate deceptions.

This mentality and wholesale deception by Hitler established the backdrop and setting for the program of creating hereditarily "worthy" children, a "pure race" to be raised " . . . in the spirit of National Socialism." He wanted a program designed with the explicit purpose of taking care of "racial - and - genetic worthful mothers" and their children. Hitler wanted to produce a "superior race" for the Third Reich.

In 1935, with the ostensible aim of promoting this policy a program was founded by Schutzstaffel Reich Commander, Heinrich Himmler with the explicit design, to produce a "superior race" of Germans. He set up a small organization within the SS (Secret Service): The Race and Settlement Main Office (RuSHA). This became known as the Lebensborn Society. It was referred to as "Source of Life" or "Well of Life." Its initial declared objective was to support SS families. But, it also promised to place and care for unwed expectant mothers, who were found upon examination to be racially and biologically sound and whose child would be "equally valuable," and to take care of the illegitimate child once born.

The first Lebensborn home opened in August 1936 at Steinhoering, near Munich. By 1939 there were five more centers in Germany and Austria. The homes, like the NSV ones, were discreetly located in former institutions or villas in suburban or country settings. The interiors of the facilities were better equipped and the emphasis on indoctrination far more important. A veil of secrecy hung over the inmates, who were addressed by their first names plus the prefix "Frau" even if they were unwed, which was the situation of approximately 50% of the residents. SS doctors responsible for admission were "bound by secrecy not only by their professional code but beyond that by special oath to the Reichsfuhrer SS." They were also expected to stand up for the honor of expectant mothers" and protect them "from social ostracism."

Secret dossiers were kept on each mother and child. The SS leader divided the families into four categories. Lebensborn or other SS agencies often employed the women in Group I, the most desirable listing. Those in Group IV were expelled. The criteria for retention in the program at this stage were even less scientific than those used for admission. "Worldview" and "character" were given the same weight as race and health.

Despite all the promotion of motherliness, it was the child that was important to Himmler. The babies were kept in nurseries separate from their mothers under the watchful eyes of teams of nurses. This was not just a matter of efficiency. Under the close supervision of the nurses an "unworthy" child could be immediately identified. If the defect was not too serious, mother and child were simply expelled. SS pediatric theory held that children did not remember anything up to the age of two and could be kept in "collective" situations without detriment to their well being. Enrollment remained low until the war was well under way. In most cases, the facilities were located far from the constant bombing; the inhabitants were provided adequately with food, given the assurance of secrecy and a place of safety for frightened and often desperate women. It was unnerving for me to realize I was one of these babies and that I had been taken away from my mother at birth.

By the end of WWII, it is estimated that about 5,000 "illegitimate" babies were born at Lebensborn homes in Germany. It was a far cry from the hundreds of thousands Himmler had envisioned.

(Cruel World, chap. 3, pp 40 - 65 by Lynn H. Nicholas)

"It's hard to believe we're here," Bonnie said.

"We need to find somebody who speaks English." I got out of the car and began pacing around, inhaling as much fresh air as my lungs could possibly handle. My heart felt like a pile driver banging away. A voice broke through the incessant pounding in my head.

"Peter, let's drive back through the village. I know we'll find a person who can help us."

I got back behind the wheel, started the car and drove toward the business area. There were only a couple of people milling around. I thought, who in the world is going to know any English in this sleepy little village? No wonder Himmler picked this place as his Lebensborn headquarters. It's in the middle of nowhere.

The next ten minutes, we gave ourselves an auto tour, driving up and down every alleyway and side street we could find. During the drive, we passed the Catholic Church. I wondered if it was the very sanctuary where I had been baptized. We passed the Rathaus, but it was closed, as was the school just a couple of blocks further down. The most promising establishment was the Sparkkasse (town bank). We reasoned that tellers in a bank would have more occasions to deal with the public and possibly be better educated; plus, it was open.

The village bank only had two tellers and a manager, who was working at her desk in the back office. The employees were standing behind small, round tables that looked like something you'd find in a coffee shop. A young female teller was busy tending to a middle - aged woman, who appeared to be with her father, an older gentleman standing quietly at her side. I approached an equally young man at the second table. In my best German, I introduced myself and asked when the Rathaus would be open.

Oliver Humel answered in perfect English. He was 25 years old, and our conversation never touched the topics of credit, interest, deposits or withdrawals. Our primary interest was depositing and withdrawing valuable information from each other. He was a gold mine. He knew of the Lebensborn Center and was fascinated with the prospect of helping me recover valuable facts pertaining to the facility located at the edge of their little town. He volunteered to make a few phone calls and see if there was anyone who would help. While he was on the phone, I was drawn to an elderly man standing behind his daughter. He was several years older than I was, definitely old enough to remember the war. He had overheard my conversation with Oliver and visually expressed an interest. He came over to me and said he remembered the Lebensborn Center. We had a nice chat until the daughter hurriedly whisked him away. I felt as though he would have liked to tell me more. I never even got his name. I felt it was a missed opportunity.

After finishing his phone calls, Oliver began talking to Bonnie. "Good news. The president of the town's historical society, Herr Preimesser, will be available to meet with you tomorrow morning. Can you make it?"

I joined their conversation and chimed in, "Absolutely. What time does he want to see us?"

"He would like to meet you in the morning at 9:30. If you would like, I could come as an interpreter. Herr Preimesser doesn't speak any English."

"If you would; I'd be so grateful. I don't trust my conversational German enough to handle technical words or understand colloquialisms." I gave a sheepish grin."

"You speak very fine," Oliver said in a complimentary tone. He turned to see what the manager was doing. "She is off the phone now. I will ask if she will grant me a couple of hours to be with you tomorrow morning. I'm certain she will once I explain the nature of our business." He went to the back office and began talking. She would often glance our way and smile. I could easily detect her willingness to be helpful. Oliver confirmed what I'd observed. "She's allowing me the time to be with you tomorrow morning. We need to leave here no later than 9:15."

"Should I drive?" I asked.

"No. Park your car in the lot and we can walk over together. If it rains, I have umbrellas for all of us. It's only a two minute walk from the bank to the Rathaus."

I wanted to talk some more, but Oliver had to get back to work. We said our goodbyes and at his suggestion checked out the two Gasthofs in the vicinity. We selected Hotel Gasthof Huber. It was located five kilometers west on a hill overlooking Steinhoering.

It was a picturesque hotel nestled at the center of a dorf one - fifth the size of Steinhoering - and Steinhoering is small. I was informed that a dorf was the German word for a very tiny village. From our porch, we saw a farmer tending his patch of ground. Soon it would be dark and another day of work completed. I wondered if his family had been tending the fields when a train full of orphans rolled by on their way into the village. I felt raindrops pelting my head. Looking up I noticed the black clouds hovering overhead. Was it an omen of things to come? When the rain stopped Bonnie joined me.

"Why are you standing out there in the rain?"

"It's only sprinkling. Did you notice the sky?"

"The rain cloud is directly over us," she noted.

We pulled two chairs under the eaves and sat down. "I wonder what we'll uncover tomorrow?"

"Is your stomach still knotted?"

"Not this very moment," I said with a sigh of relief.

"Oh look, a hummingbird," Bonnie pointed off to our left. It began to hover over the orange and white variation of geraniums. The potted flowers were expertly arranged in decorative flower boxes. Speaking as an expert in Native American culture and folklore, Bonnie related the importance of hummingbirds. "When a hummingbird appears it means one is on the right path of life." She looked at me and grinned. "I believe that with every fiber of my being that Tuesday will bring clarity for you, Peter." She stood with a smile and entered our room allowing me more quiet time to think.

A single, straight, active train track ran alongside the farmer's plot of ground and later curved to the left on its way toward Steinhoering. I could see the Center in the distance and wondered if that track had been the primary means for transporting little babies to the Lebensborn Center. I surmised I probably was one of those little children since the train tracks lead into the gated compound.

The other end of this spectrum involved the making of life. The Nazis were interested in purity of numbers. It was vital for them to produce a large reservoir of racially pure individuals to support their expansionist plans. Norwegian women were top on the list. Being born of a Norwegian made me a prime victim.

I felt a shiver run the length of my body. I now knew I fit into one of those horrible categories. The thoughts of shame and anger froze my ability to be relaxed or at ease. Only the knowledge of my being born in 1944 and not 1935, when Hitler commenced his insane plan of cultivating a "superior race," gave me a slight sense of peace. I offered a quick prayer of thanks as I looked across the quiet landscape and wondered; what if? The rain fell increasingly harder, forcing me to go inside. I glanced at my watch. It was time for supper and a nights rest.

The next morning, at the appointed time, we met Oliver at the bank and then walked to the Rathaus (City Hall). Herr Preimesser was already there. He greeted each of us with a firm handshake and joyful spirit. He ushered us into the building, where a kindly faced receptionist greeted us. Our local historian began speaking without a comma or period in his sentences. I was lost within the first two minutes of the monologue. I was thankful that Bonnie was taping every word and Oliver was shedding light on the flood of words coming from Herr Preimesser. On occasion, I got him to speak more slowly allowing me to engage in a limited conversation. The highlight of the stay was when the receptionist opened the registry. There, in legible print was my name. The registry recorded that on April 4, 1945 my name was Peter Rolf Stromnes. I had arrived in the village of Steinhoering one month before the end of WWII. A fascinating map was spread out before all of us to examine. Herr Preimesser pointed out eight major Lebensborn Homes. He pointed out Nordrach and then, with his finger, underscored Nordrach/Baden on my Certificate of Baptism.

He smiled, "Du bist heir geboren."

I didn't know how to respond to being shown the town where I'd been born. I think I said "Mich," with a tone of disbelief. I was speechless.

Nordrach was a Dorf located at the southwest corner of Germany's Black Forest, in the Baden Region.

Bonnie redirected everyone's attention to the Certificate of Baptism, provided by the Catholic Church. She pointed out that the certificate had my birth date as October 11, 1943, but the Baptismal Certificate recorded the date as December 14, 1945. "Why?"

Herr Priemesser elaborated on a common practice employed by the Catholic Church allowing it to gain ownership/control of the orphaned child. In all likelihood most of the babies had no birth certificates, no recorded parents and had been moved around. At the end of the war over 300 babies were transported to Steinhoering and the Lebensborn Center. They had no identities other than their own warm bodies. The church wanted control of the children, so it made up birth dates older than what the babies actually were, made minor name changes - in my case from Pater to Dieter - baptized the children, and then transported them to their orphanages and Catholic schools.

"I have another question. I know my final years in Germany were spent in the town of Prien in a children's home. Do the records indicate the specific date when I departed Steinhoering for Prien?"

His answer was given without any hesitation, "Nein." He then volunteered to make a call to the Rathaus in Prien and see if they might have any records. His guess was they wouldn't. I told him we were headed for the town later in the day. He said he'd alert them of our coming. He also promised to do some research about my birth and if there might be a way to secure a birth certificate from Nordrach.

"It is wrong for a person not to know their beginnings," he exclaimed.

"I agree. This is why you have been so helpful. Because of you, I now know where I was during my years in Germany."

"It is a start," he proclaimed. "It will feel even better when you have documentation of your birth - like finding the Baptismal Certificate."

My smile widened as I struggled to say, "At least I have discovered that I was born in Nordrach, spent two years at Steinhoering and was adopted from Prien. I knew none of that until this morning at the Rathaus."

"You are one of many who are beginning to have the courage to search and delve into a painful past. I wish you well, for you are a special person and God has smiled upon you for a reason."

Church bells began ringing at noon and Oliver knew he had to get back to work. We exchanged calling cards, took some pictures and made promises to keep in touch.

It was then we learned that Oliver was planning to come to the USA. He had an uncle who taught at Wesleyan University in Middletown, Conn. I couldn't help but think God was winking at us once again in the personhood of Oliver Humel. I asked Herr Priemesser if he had time to give us a tour of the Lebensborn Center. I volunteered the information that I believed I had lived in Steinhoering until the age of three or four. He wholeheartedly agreed to my request for a tour.

The visit struck me at two levels. First, I recognized the building and I felt the presence of crying children. Our guide, the village mayor, acknowledged that other orphans had been brought to the facility in large numbers after the war. He told us that in the past few years these babies, now adults like myself, were beginning to emerge out of their self - imposed silence, after all these years, to visit the Lebensborn Center of Steinhoering. Their reactions led him to believe that children three year old and even younger remember major experiences - such as a room full of crying babies. As I moved thru the rooms and down the halls I felt a darkness pressing down on me. When there was extended silence I could hear the cries of babies wherever I turned. I remember asking the mayor if we could walk the grounds. I think he sensed my uneasiness.

Primarily, I was amazed at what the people of this little town had done to transform the center into a place of healing - an institution formally identified with human experimentation, indoctrination of mothers, and perpetuation of a policy of genetically creating a superior race. Herr Priemesser was proud to point out that current programs were developed to aid the mentally impaired, the physically handicapped and the mentally disturbed. They were now doing what any sane person would deem ethical and moral. I was proud to see a facility, which I had learned to despise because of its history, reconcile with a past, which the people of this village abhorred. They didn't bury the place under a mound of dirt and try to deny what had happened. They built upon the very grounds Himmler paced, expanded upon the facilities, and added new programs that would heal, protect and assist the very segment of society Hitler had targeted to be purged.

PRIEN

The next morning, Bonnie and I were driving on our way to Prien. For the first time, in a long while, I had a good night's sleep. My aches, pains and knotted stomach were gone. I now knew where I was born and the location of the two other orphanages I'd lived in. The story was coming together in a way I'd never imagined. I could barely contain myself as we wound through the countryside. Maybe I would meet Tante Marie again or her daughter and uncover more information about my final stopping place before being adopted. Then it would be off to Nordrach where I was taken away from my mother after the second week of birth. What would I find? As Steinhoering disappeared behind me I pulled out and slowly reread the letter I'd written to my Tanta Marie. My mind fantasized a hundred possibilities as we sped by the countryside and its rolling hills. It wasn't long before we crossed the town line into Prien and the map in my mind noted the pinpoints for Steinhoering, Prien and Nordrach.

I quickly pulled out the letter I'd written to Tante and read it slowly.

Dear Tante Marie,

My name is Peter Brenner. In July of 2000, my wife (Bonnie) and I visited you in Prien. Our stay lasted a mere hour. In a miraculous way, the brief time together affected me dramatically. I felt as though, we had stepped back into the late 1940s. Our conversation continues to fill my thoughts with valuable memories.

I am embarrassed that it has taken me so long to get back to you. I pray you are still in good health. I hope this letter finds you in good spirits.

Here's what I recall from our visit. I was in your first group of seven orphaned children - frightened and alone. You mentioned that you were filled with the desire to care for children who had been separated from their parents. I was the youngest and smallest of the group, so you called me "kleine Pater." I still have the verbal picture you painted of my being held in your arms, crying myself to sleep.

Your early records might have me listed under the name of Dieter Rolf Stromnes, a Norwegian child just a few months over the age of three. Somehow, you gathered together a group of us who were of preschool age. In fact, you informed me that I was too young to be enrolled in your program. However, you elected to keep me - and I thank God for that good fortune. Your records indicated I was with you for approximately two years. During that span, an Air Force chaplain stationed in Germany and his wife visited your school looking to adopt a child.

I'm trying to make sense of my story. You are a valuable link to my early beginnings. I welcome your efforts to help fill in the blank spaces of an unknown story: how you discovered me; and why I came to live with you; and to recall stories about our time together and what eventually led to my adoption. More important, I'd like to learn more about you.

During the summer of 2006, I plan to visit Germany with my family. I would be honored if we could visit you once again.

With fondest memories,
Peter and Bonnie Brenner
June 21, 2005

The last few sentences of the above letter reminded me of my frenetic efforts to locate Tante Marie during our brief visit of Germany in the summer of 2000. For me it was another illustration of Divine Intervention.

My translated letter to Tante Maria dated June 21, 2005 arrived at our Connecticut home July 15, 2005. The message was brief and disheartening.

"Mr. Peter and Bonnie Brenner,

Via some detour I am in receipt of a letter. I am Erika her daughter and cannot answer the questions in your letter out of my own memory, because during 1947 to 1949 I attended a boarding school out of town and was not at home for this reason. My mother is still alive at the age of 93, but has lost practically all her memory. I am sorry for not being able to help you and remain sincerely yours.

Erika

A return letter to Erika noted that Bonnie and I were planning to visit Germany sometime during the summer of 2006. I asked if we might get together for a brief visit.

Her response was a curt and emphatic NO!

I waited with my reply until we had finalized our itinerary for the European/ Norway trip. In a brief email, I explained how important her mother had been during my stay with her during the years immediately following the war. I was very specific with our plans to visit Prien - July 31st thru August 4th. I assured her, if she were available, I'd adjust our schedule to meet her time frame. There was no response.

It was exhilarating to study our map of Germany and discover how close Steinhoering was to Prien. We traveled narrow back roads winding over and between rolling hills checkered with farmland crops and multicolored fields of wildflowers. The distance travled was less than 50 kilometers. Even in the driving rain, and with a couple of unscheduled stops, we made the trek in less than two hours. As we approached the outskirts of the town, we decided to drive straight to the home and delay our motel search until later. It was mid - day and plenty of time to find lodging for two nights.

We entered Prien from the west. Once again, I remembered the stops and turns to put us on the road toward Tante's Kinderheim. Bonnie focused on spotting the sign, Haus Marquette; I concentrated on recognizing the pencil - thin, dirt road leading to the preschool. Suddenly, my thoughts transported me back in time.

*   *   *

With white - hot anger, I recalled the place filled with crying children. Over time the orphans, in residence, dwindled. The once crowded three - storied children's center emptied. One - by - one our playmates mysteriously vanished. Any given afternoon we'd be together and the next morning, like a puff of smoke, they were gone.

When it was my turn to disappear, I was glad.

I didn't know why I was being placed in a car, or where I was going, or whom I would meet; I was alone but it didn't matter. I was more than ready to leave this wretched place. As the driver started the car and pulled out to drive away, I refused to look back. I wanted to escape the ugly memories still fresh and firmly embedded in my mind. The exodus began mid - afternoon and finished during that hour when day and night began negotiating the transformation of light to darkness. As the sun splashed its colors and painted the clouds skirting across the sky, the car bumped its way up a narrow, dirt driveway and stopped before a single storied, whitewashed building. There was nobody around. I suddenly felt fear crawling over me - a sense of abandonment.

I cautiously slid out of the car seat, grabbed the long pole attached to an oversized handkerchief containing all of my belongings, and walked tentatively toward the house. Before I reached the door it opened and out stepped a woman much smaller than the ones I'd just left. She stooped down to meet me at eye level.

With the kindest voice I'd ever heard, she declared, "You must be Pater. Welcome." She opened her arms and encouraged me to come closer.

I stood as still as a stone. Even if I had wanted to move it would have been impossible. My arms felt pinned to my side and I was certain my bare feet were cemented to the stone path. She leaned toward me, ever so slowly. My shoulder muscles tightened, preparing for the unexpected. Her next move astonished me. With a gentle stroke, Tante wiped my dirty feet with a soft cloth. I stared at the top of her head, which was covered by a shiny blanket of smooth, dark brown hair.

"The children here call me Tante Marie." She looked up. "I know I'm not your aunt, but I'd be pleased if you'd call me Tante".

In silence, I nodded in agreement. The tone and softness of her voice settled me. I later learned that she valued each of us as her own.

"Let's go into the house together. I have some friends I'd like you to meet. We've been waiting for days to meet you. Here, take my hand and we'll go in together and say hello" Tante reached out and I took hold. My sore, bare feet no longer hurt as the two of us went inside.

I was the youngest of seven children in Tante Marie's first class of preschoolers. She liked to refer to me as Kleine Pater.

For the longest time, late into the night, Tante would rock me as I cried myself to sleep. She never asked me why I cried. I'm glad, because telling her would have been too difficult to put into words. I didn't want her to know what I'd been through. What was important was that I always felt safe in her arms. Being preschoolers and orphans, we attracted a stream of active suitors. Early on in my stay, one couple showed continued interest in me. I think it was because I was adventurous and always happy. They were privy to my free spirit on several occasions. On more than one visit, they'd watch the assistants trying to catch me as I scurried around the lawn eluding their grasps or circling around the trees. For obvious safety reasons, we weren't allowed to wander off toward the lake. I, however, was always escaping and running toward the lake to explore the shoreline, watch the whitecaps or look for jumping fish.

Bonnie took my hand, bringing me back to the present.

The grounds looked as if they'd been rearranged since our previous visit in 2000. The playground had been moved across the lawn and there appeared to be construction work in progress. We climbed out of the car and scrutinized the area. Turning toward the facility, we observed a woman, in her late sixties. She made a beeline straight toward me, extended her hand and greeted me.

"Good morning, Herr Brenner. It is so good to see you." Her English was excellent.

"Thank you. We decided to stop by on our way to the hotel. What a change. The place looks so different."

"The new owners are making renovations. I come down to help supervise and be available for their questions and concerns."

"Did I hear you say new owners?"

"Yes. My mother had to sell the place when she went to the convalescent home. Her memory is pretty much gone."

"I'm so sorry. We were so fortunate to have visited her six years ago."

"I'm glad you did. She talked about you often. But things change; three years ago, she got so she couldn't take care of herself. I took care of her for as long as I could. We sold the place to the County Court with the assurance that they keep it as a daycare center." Erika gave a weak smile. It was her effort to show support for a difficult decision.

"What a wonderful tribute to her," Bonnie commented.

"It's what she wanted."

In a supportive tone, I responded, "I'm sorry we can't see her, but it's a special gift to have you here today."

"Thank you. As you can see, they are already redoing the place." Erika looked longingly toward the center. "I grew up here. This is my home, too."

"Where did you learn to speak English so well?" I asked.

"My son married an American and they live in Minnesota. I needed to learn the language so I could communicate with her and my grandchildren."

"Erika, would you mind giving us a tour?

"No. Follow me."

The next half hour we walked throughout the old and new sections of the building. I recognized the area where we all slept. It had been raised to become the second floor. The game room had been transformed into a large storage area; the kitchen was modernized; the new section replaced the dining area, and Tante's parlor, where we drank tea and coffee with her six years ago, was empty except for a few boxes tucked into the corners.

We pulled up three dusty chairs, sat and began talking about the 50 years Tante had dedicated toward taking care of orphans, and later, preschoolers. She was known and respected throughout the town. I was so proud of her work and of having been a part of her first years as a teacher. Soon the place would be different and nothing would be the same again. Erika promised she would try to uncover her mother's records and possibly some pictures she could send me. It was hard to believe this was the same Erika who ignored my earlier e - mail.

Within an instant the word "picture," conjured up my own set of mosaic images.

I found myself reliving my farewell from Haus Marquetta and seeing a five - year - old boy standing at the doorway - half in and half out. I remember Tante stooping down to address my sorrowful eyes.

"My Kleine Pater," she began. "You're going on another adventure more exciting and wonderful than anything you've ever dreamed of."

I nodded and shifted the pole with my belongings onto the other shoulder.

"I want you to know; I'll always love you and be thinking about you wherever you are. Do you believe me?" She tousled my blond hair and gave me a hug.

Tante placed her forefinger on my lips to slow down the torrential out pouring of words rushing forth from my lips. "Know that I honor and love you. That's what you need to remember from this day forward." She paused.

"I don't want to go! Why are you sending me away?" She cradled my face between her palms and stared deep into my eyes.

"Where am I going? Do I have to leave? When will I see you? Why?" I demanded.

"So you can be loved everyday by a Mother and Father who want you. I know this to be true. Do you trust me?"

I nodded and threw myself at Tante, dropping my belongings and hugging her with all the might of a little five - year old boy.

"Now, pick - up your things and I'll walk you to the buggy. We don't want you to miss your train. And remember, we'll see each other again. I promise."

I looked around the room and thought how fortunate Bonnie and I had been to find her that rainy day 6 years ago. It was a slice of time that validated my need for defining my past. Bonnie, our two sons and Tante provided the spark that gave me the courage to move forward to explore my history. I'm indebted to Tante Marie more than she could possible have fathomed. Or maybe she did. She said my trip to America would be an adventure and she was right.

Bonnie and I spent two nights at Hotel Neuer am See. It was located on the main road leading to the docking area. Its front porch overlooked the parking area for the tour boats heading out to Ludwig's island castle. We liked it because the start of the lakeside trail was just to the left and less than two minutes from the hotel. The walk back into town was in the opposite direction and only ten minutes from the hotel.

"There's our rendezvous point." I pointed toward the gate leading into the parking lot.

Bonnie tugged at my arm. "Peter look. That's our tour boat coming in right now, the one we took back from the castle."

"I love this hotel, Bonnie. It's located in the middle of all the action, and the perfect place to continue our search to uncover more clues about my past."

Holding hands, Bonnie and I watched the coming and goings of the people, cars, vendors and boats. It was a full fifteen minutes or more before we moved.

"We need to check in, love. It's getting late."

Our second day was busier than the first. Following breakfast, we took a stroll into town for our visit with Frau Rucker at the Rathaus. The people in the office were not the same twosome we spoke to during our visit in 2000. Like the first time, one spoke excellent English and the other barely a word. Frau Rucker was very helpful.

I began my questioning. "Do you think there might be any records listing all the orphans enrolled in Tante's orphanage, Kinder Marquette?"

"I don't believe there will be any records. Everything was pretty much lost or destroyed after the war . . . it was a long time ago."

"Wouldn't she be required to register all her orphans with city hall?"

"Not then. It was a private school. Does she have records?"

"She had them in 1947," Bonnie chimed in, "but her daughter claims they are lost."

Frau Rucker's face saddened. "We have another problem. All our records were saved on Microfilm."

"That's good," I declared. "You might have something from when I was here."

"One problem: the machine is very old and it has to be repaired before we can access the data."

"How long will that take?" Bonnie asked.

"Who knows? We don't have budgeted money to fix it or buy a new one. Maybe it will be working in four or five months." She raised her hands palms up, in a sign of futility.

"Here's the information we're looking for." I grabbed a piece of paper and proceeded to scratch a brief message along with my e - mail and home mailing address. I handed it to Frau Rucker with a hopeful look on my face.

"I will try." She took the sheet and placed it into a folder before stuffing it into her satchel.

The brief visit was of minor significance. Now it was a waiting game. We waved as we headed out the door.

Our backup plan included casual shopping and slipping into a tourist mode for a couple of days. We ambled up and down Main Street peering at window displays and popping in and out of the shops. It wasn't long before I settled onto a bench and promised Bonnie, I wouldn't move until she returned from her run through a few more stores. She wanted to look for sweaters, Christmas gifts and momento's of the trip.

I needed to organize my thoughts before we headed off for the orphanage where documents authenticated was my place of birth.

NORDRACH/BADEN

The trip to Nordrach proved to be more stressful than Bonnie and I had imagined.

We turned onto the German autobahn heading south from Baden Baden and paralleling the French border that was only fifteen minutes west of us. We talked about the weather, commented on the various car license plates zipping by us and marveled at the beautiful scenery.

An hour passed before we turned off the major highway and angled southeast toward Offenburg. There were no road signs noting our desired destination, only towns and small villages we'd become familiar with by name from endless hours of eye-aching work scrutinizing maps and atlases. Turning north at Biberach, I shifted my attention toward our specific goal of locating the precise coordinates of Nordrach.

"Bonnie, do you think Nordrach exists? I mean, do you think it's really a place, now?"

"Absolutely, we saw it on the map."

"Only one map, and none of the atlases showed the town," I persisted.

Sensing my anxiety, Bonnie reassured me. "It's waiting for you to find it. It's just up ahead."

"What if the town is there but the Children's Home is gone and we've driven all this way for nothing?"

"Peter, it's probably around the corner. Believe me."

"I don't know if I can handle an empty lot or a mound of dirt."

In silence, Bonnie gently massaged my knotted neck muscles.

A sign signaling the outskirts of Nordrach popped into view with the suddenness of a jackrabbit. I slammed on the brakes and reversed the car until the sign once again loomed before us. I pulled off to the side of the road and stared. It was a work of art. The detailed woodcarving, coupled with vibrant colors and intricate figures made me want to encourage the townsfolk to donate their road sign to some local museum.

Like Steinhoering, Nordrach was small enough in population and size to be considered a Dorf. The village was at the southern end of Germany's Baden region and nestled at the foot of the impressive Black Forest, renowned more for the folklore of Hansel and Gretel than its impressive trees. The Dorf's main street was the last stretch of a flat, gentle curving road before a precipitous incline, featuring several hairpin turns, snaked upward. Its unique location attracted mountain bikers, back - packers, hikers and river - water fishermen. It was a thriving tourist stop for people who enjoyed outdoor vacations. The villagers strived to make every one's holiday stay a memorable one. Our slow drive through the village revealed a church, senior - citizen center, two quaint eating establishments and a tourist center. A flowing stream paralleled the western side of the main street, with homes pressed firmly up against the mountainside.

I steered the car to a paved parking lot that separated the church grounds from the contemporary senior - citizen facility. I looked at the modern, single - story building with mounting dismay. It appeared to be the only sensible response to the embarrassment of a Lebensborn Home. The tourist bureau was situated across the street, a short block back from the highway.

"Let's go to the tourist center," Bonnie insisted. "Maybe they'll have some helpful information to offer."

"Let's hope so," I responded.

"The papers we reviewed, while visiting the Rathaus in Steinhoering, claimed Nordrach supported one of Hitler's Children Homes."

"It's here somewhere, we've just missed it," Bonnie chirped confidently.

I countered, "Maybe during the war, but what about now?" My negativity was out of character and it annoyed me. I began wondering whether I was hoping all evidence of the Home had been erased, or was I afraid we'd uncover something ugly.

"Don't get discouraged, Peter. We've been through too much to quit now. Let's keep looking until we find the building or what happened to it." Bonnie grabbed my arm and pulled me across the street.

The tourist center/store was a medium - size room: neatly organized with designated areas for memorabilia, maps, paintings, postcards, a variety of travel pamphlets and books highlighting the area. The older lady behind the counter looked up and over her eyeglasses to greet us. She was petite, gray haired, and projected an amicable, bubbly personality: the perfect antidote for my dampened spirit.

Her broken English intermingled nicely with my improved conversational German. I launched into my talk highlighting the major reasons for our visit to her village. When I mentioned the Lebensborn Children's Home, her countenance physically changed: I could see sadness surface in her eyes, a slight tremor disrupted the flow of her words and a degree of nervousness materialized in her movements. There was no doubt in my mind; she knew the explicit purpose for my being in Nordrach.

Her answers to my questions were brief; there was no malice in her tone, only a wish to be helpful.

"Yes, there was a Lebensborn Home here in 1942."

"Yes, it's still here - and only a two - minute walk from where we stand."

"Yes, we have information about the town's history and the Home."

"Yes, the original building is still intact. No, it wasn't damaged too badly." She ended my version of an inquisition by reaffirming, "The Children's Home is now an insane asylum for the mentally disturbed. You can see it, but it's closed to visitors for patient security."

I thanked her and began leafing through books and pamphlets she had spread across the countertop. One book had pictures and a brief description of a 1935 clinic that later became the Lebensborn Home. Bonnie ambled around the store before stopping at the postcard rack for a closer look.

The lady disappeared in the back room for a few minutes while we took our time to explore. She came back with a town map in hand and pointed out the location of the Home. "Please take the map," she insisted.

By the time we were ready to depart, she had gathered enough items to stuff a tote - bag with the town's name stitched across the top: It included a historical, pictorial book of Nordrach, a detailed map of the Dorf during the early 1940s and a couple of postcards. She wanted us to know they were a gift from the village to us. It was refreshing to see her demeanor rebound to its former perky state. We expressed our thanks - for her help plus the bulging bag of gifts - before heading out the door and on our way. As we rounded the corner, I could hear a call coming from behind us. We turned to see the lady frantically waving for us to return. She was talking to an older man, who looked to be in his late seventies. When he saw me, he immediately stepped forward and shook my hand and volunteered to be our guide. His granddaughter stared at me with wide - eyed curiosity.

Together, the four of us headed back toward the main street. When we turned the corner, I instantly saw the Lebensborn Home perched on a hill overlooking the north end of town. I couldn't fathom how I missed such an imposing building, unless I was blinded by the idea of the senior - citizen center being the location of the orphanage. The Children's Home was located on a hill overlooking the community. It seemed as out of place as it must have been during the war. The Victorian building had two round towers dominating the skyline. It was a mansion the size of a small hospital. The home itself was constructed of tan bricks topped by a reddish tiled roof. The first floor had a wrap - around porch occupied by slump shouldered men in clothes three sizes too big. Their stares met ours. I turned away first.

The Home for mothers and their children served as a breeding ground for Hitler's pursuit of an "Aryan Race". The majestic building and the serene beauty of the area didn't match the filth I felt clogging up my thoughts.

Old anger, lingering from my seminary days in Hartford, swelled up like bile that needed to be spat away. I was reminded of the embarrassment I felt toward my mother for having abandoned me and how my pain wasn't so deep that tears wouldn't find their way to the surface. The hurt was acute and I knew the feelings were still conflicted within me.

But now, the strength to hold back my tears was gone. The man understood without my saying a word. Taking his granddaughter's hand, they moved quickly ahead toward a gold - tinted, bronze plaque embedded within a large, gray stone. He stopped and they kept their backs to us, waiting for me to compose myself.

With Bonnie at my side, it took only a few moments before I was able to rejoin them. Somehow, I knew the next few moments would reveal much of my first year of life as an orphan. How would I feel? What would the information do to me?

I learned that Frau Von Rothschild built a private clinic on the north end of Nordrach. She lived there from 1936 to 1942. In 1942 the SS discovered her almost hidden clinic and sent members of the Gestapo to her door. Being Jewish, the entire family was taken to Auschwitz and, in all likelihood, exterminated. Her mansion, a clinic dedicated to healing, became a major Lebensborn Home for Mothers and Their Children until April of 1945.

Two hundred and twenty babies were born in the mansion that loomed before me - and I was one of them. Now it was an insane asylum. How appropriate, I thought.

I could hear a voice trying to break into my thoughts. The gentleman was telling his story of the night the village was destroyed. It ripped me away from the grip of self - pity. He shared the horror of a night when Allied Forces destroyed everything the town's people owned and cherished. His agony seemed as fresh and real as though the devastation had taken place only yesterday. I could see the broken bodies, feel his agony at seeing family members bleeding to death on the streets, and hear the thunder of artillery fire as homes were reduced to piles of stones and broken timber. Then, he told me about the babies in the Home. The first group to be evacuated made it out of town on carts, wagons and the backs of attendants and nurses. But the warnings came late and many of the babies left behind died, because the concussion from the exploding bombs burst their little eardrums. He hugged me and said, "You must have been in the first group of children. God smiled upon you."

We embraced each other and cried the same tears.

I was frozen in thought. I was born on March 18, 1944 in the very building towering before me. In April of 1945, by the Grace of God, some of us were evacuated to safety. I left Nordrach for Steinhoering, and the war would be over in a month.

This man and I were here at the same time, in the same town. Somehow, we both survived - he as a 10 - year - old boy and I as a one year - old baby. The language barrier evaporated. We felt the same emptiness, agony and inner pain - two men still grieving together some sixty - two years later.

It was time for me to stop being angry, to reevaluate my relationships and fill the empty spaces of the unknown. I felt different - weak and strong in the same body.

When the time seemed appropriate the two of us stepped back from our grief. We thanked each other for the sacred moment together. With a timid smile, he departed with granddaughter in hand. Intermittently, the little girl would steal a glance back.

I waved.

She smiled.

I'm confident we both felt better.

Bonnie captured our story on tape. I recorded it in my heart.

Under the pretense of taking pictures, Bonnie drifted away so I could be by myself. I grinned inside realizing Bonnie probably knows me better than I do. What a gift she has been to me. She was giving me private time. After 36 years of marriage, I still needed space to explore my options; like a prospector crouching alongside the bank of a running river, panning carefully through the silt for hidden treasures, I too wanted precious moments to patiently sift through my thoughts in the hope of discovering the hidden treasures waiting to be unearthed.

I stood at the bridge, watching the rush of fresh, pure, cleansing mountain water flowing below me. The imposing building where I was born was merely a shadow casting its secrets upon me.

I no longer felt anger toward my mother for giving birth to me in such a place or arranging for my adoption. I could finally affirm that she'd done what was best for me. As it turned out, Bjorg probably saved my life.

I lingered at the bridge a while longer. The man and his granddaughter were gone. I never even got his name. I crossed the street to be with Bonnie. Arm - in - arm, we headed for the car.

"Let's grab a bite to eat," I suggested. "I'm not ready to leave just yet."

"I saw a quaint eating place on our drive in. It might even have a gift store attached to it," Bonnie volunteered in a hopeful tone.

I nodded.

I remember the rustic restaurant as being clean and filled with locals peeking at us over their tall, slender beer steins. A young woman dressed in a decorative blouse, and flowery skirt greeted us with a warm smile and one menu. I ordered Wiener schnitzel with dumplings. Bonnie had sauerbraten smothered in sauerkraut. We washed down our meals with a cold glass of light beer.

When we finished our meal, Bonnie made her way toward the gift store. "Want to come?" she asked.

I shook my head and waved her on with encouraging words, "Why don't you go ahead and look around for a bit. I'll join you later. I'm going out onto the porch for some fresh air."

"Okay. I won't be long. I can already see some precious items that would be wonderful souvenirs." Bonnie disappeared quicker than a chipmunk scurrying toward new treasures.

Once on the porch, I closed my eyes and drew in a deep breath. My lungs felt refreshed by the mountain air, invigorated and more importantly clean. I turned my head in the direction of the town. And then it came to me. The journey required my standing before the place where it had all begun.

Before long, Bonnie was at my side.

"I have a souvenir of Nordrach." She held up a little wooden carving representing the spirit of the area. "It will be a great reminder of our trip."

For the first time, I smiled knowing what lay behind the smile of my public mask. I also thought the woodsman would be a great companion for Monk - my worn, but still cuddly Curious George that Mom and Dad gave me the day I arrived in America. It was so long ago and yet it seemed so near. I was finally ready to leave Nordrach.

I was excited by what we had learned but knew there was more to uncover. Our youngest son, Tim, joined us for the final leg of our summer journey - France, Luxembourg and a family reunion in Norway.

CHAPTER VIII

Norway & World War II

"A bond between a mother and her child is naturally sacred. It is physical, psychological and spiritual. It is very resilient and very flexibe. It can stretch very far - naturally. Any artificial or violent injury to this 'stretch' constitutes a serious psychic trauma to both mother and child - for all eternity. This means that children need their mothers and mothers need their children - whether or not, a mother is married or unmarried."

Phyllis Chesler

The final leg of the 2006 summer trip was our hopscotch flight to Oslo, Norway. I knew this would be a unique opportunity to experience the evolution of my life's journey from inception to a present day family reunion. I chuckled to myself when I realized I was backtracking into my past with visits - albeit a little bit out of order - to the three orphanages I lived in and now Norway. Bjorg's life and war experience set up my years as an orphan in Germany. It made sense to be visiting my Norwegian family and uncovering how Hitler influenced all our lives. He had specifically redirected Bjorg's future and the course of my life.

We landed on a sunny morning at Oslo's airport. I had no idea whom to look for. I was relieved when an attractive, slender, shorthaired woman started waving at us. In perfect English, the reddish haired lady, displaying an inviting smile, came up to greet us.

"Hello. My name is Elin."

Bonnie, Tim (who had joined us in Verdun, France) and I shook her hand and introduced us. I began a more extended conversation. "I'm so glad you recognized us. We have your telephone number but no description or picture."

Elin laughed. "At first I was concerned, but when I saw you coming out of the passage way, I knew it was you."

"You did? I didn't know you had a picture of me," I said in an astonished tone.

Elin grinned, "You're a Stromnes. You look like your mother. I had no problem picking you out of the crowd."

"I'm sure a group of wandering Americans didn't hurt the cause?" Tim chuckled.

"True, but mostly it was your Dad I spotted." Elin encouraged us to follow her. "My car isn't too far from here, so we can walk. Our son is still in school and Erik is at work, so I was the lucky one designated to be your driver."

We all thanked her and willingly trailed behind as she navigated through the crowd guiding us toward the baggage claim and then the parking lot. The hour ride to the northern outskirts of Oslo took longer than we had anticipated. We had been on the move via bus, shuttle and plane since 4am. It was a welcomed moment when we entered the Brodwall home: Elin showed us to our third - floor accommodations; the middle floor was where the kitchen, dining area, living room and porch were situated; and the three Brodwalls slept on the first floor. I can't begin to capture how hospitable and accommodating our hosts were. Except for a couple nights at Alf and May Einar's home - where the family reunion was housed - and two nights at Bergen; the rest of the evenings were with Erik, Elin and their only child, Even (8 years old).

Our first day, we learned how to navigate the excellent public transportation system. We rode the public bus with Erik to his ophthalmology clinic in downtown Oslo. He apologized for having to work, but directed us to a couple of sites that were a must for short - time visitors. The three of us wanted to see the center where the Nobel Peace Prize was awarded, plus Norway's Resistance Museum. The museum was our first stop. It was an eye - popping experience. It gave me a context to begin understanding why my mother felt compelled to make her difficult, life altering decisions.

First, the tour of Norway's Resistance Museum clearly dispels any held notion that Norwegians were neutral during World War II. The old museum was part of Akershus castle. It sits atop the fortress wall facing Oslo's Harbor. Its commanding presence consists of a house and two stone vaults built around 1650. The vaults house six cannons and a second battery positioned above the vaults, hence the name The Double Battery and The Frame House.

Hitler's mindset for Norway appears to have been twofold: German military interest to control Norway's ports - especially Trondheim and Narvik - dating back to October 1939; and Hitler's specific interest in the blonde - haired, blue - eyed women of Norway. The first was necessary to gain superiority of the North Sea; the second was to carry out his demented plan of perpetuating "a superior race" for the Third Reich.

Norway figures prominently in World War II. On September 1, 1939, Hitler invaded Poland and two days later, Britain and France declared war on Germany. On October 18th of the same year, Scandinavian heads of state met to confirm their countries neutrality. In late November, Russia invaded Finland.

Norwegians were surprised and unprepared when Nazi Germany, with its superior military strength, invaded Norway in April 1940. The public and their political leaders believed Norway would be able to stay out of the Second World War, just as the country had maintained its neutrality in World War One. They believed their country was strategically on the periphery, protected by British naval power.

Norway's history of neutrality proved to be of little consequence. Strategic interests led both Germany and England to be involved in violations of Norwegian waterways and in operations within their coastal borders. From mid - December 1939, both the German and Allied sides analyzed scenarios involving operations in Scandinavia.

More extensive and radical, Hitler's plan called for the complete occupation of both Denmark and Norway. One motive was Germany's desire for naval dominance of all Norwegian bases, thus positioning them for the pending war at sea.

On April 8, 1940, the British off the coast of Kristiansand torpedoed Blucher a German troop transport. The next day, the wounded ship sank in the narrows of the Oslo Fjord, south of the city's harbor. The sinking of the Blucher served as a signal of approaching danger, giving the king, government and members of the Storting (Parliament) additional time to make good their escape from the capital. A thirteen - point German ultimatum, handed to the Norwegian Government on the night of April 9, 1940, when the German invasion was already a fait d'accompli, received an uncompromising "NO" from King Haakon VII and the Norwegian Cabinet.

The German plan for the invasion of Norway had begun. Nearly the entire German navy, six army divisions and a large air force contingent took part in the attack on 9 April 1940. The historic battle lasted only 62 days, but resistance to the occupation lasted for another five years.

The day the Germans took Oslo, Vidkun Quisling, leader of the 4,000 member Nasjonal Samling (the Norwegian Nazi Party), declared himself Prime Minister. He immediately made a nationwide broadcast announcing his takeover of the reins of government and declaring resistance to German troops to be a crime. He ordered all officers of the armed forces to take their orders exclusively from the new government.

This was astonishing to all, not only because the king and government were still in the country and had not surrendered, but also because Ouisling had never managed to get himself or any member of his party elected to the Norwegian Parliament. His lack of support immediately became clear to the Germans. After six days, he was removed from office. (Cruel World, ch.10 p 279)

Thanks to the efforts of the Storting President, Mr. Hambro, King Haakon VII, Prime Minister Johan Nygaardsvold and his Cabinet and members of Parliament were able to escape Oslo on the morning of April 9th. An afternoon meeting was convened, first at Hamar and later at Elverum, where the so - called Elverum Authorization was formulated and put into operation.

This provided the constitutional basis for the exercise of Norwegian authority by the king and government in exile. At the last cabinet meeting held on Norwegian soil in Tromso on June 7, 1940, it was resolved that king and government continue to function abroad. The fighting in Norway ceased allowing German occupation to exist. Two months after the attack on Oslo and seven other towns and cities along the country's lengthy coast, Norway's' king and the Nygaardsvold government boarded the British cruiser, HMS Devonshire. The Norwegian government resumed its activities from London.

In the summer of 1940 the Germans contacted Norwegian political leaders with a view to negotiating a more permanent and national form of government, a "Council of the Realm." The King of Norway rejected all the demands set before him. Negotiations with the Germans broke off and on September 25, 1940, Reichskommissar Joseph Terboven, a German, declared the king and government deposed, dismissed the Administrative Council, dissolved all political parties and appointed a puppet government directly responsible to him. Now the only legal political party was the Nasjonal Samling, whose members were appointed to fill the highest government posts. Quisling was not yet one of them. His role for the time being would be to build up his party behind the scenes. (Cruel World by Lynn H. Nicholas, ch.10, p 279)

After the capitulation of Norway, Germany's iron grip became daily more oppressive. It was clearly seen in Germany's effort to control the press, containing information, appeals, official notices and promulgations. Resistance intensified bolstered by the knowledge that King Haakon and his government had resolutely stood their ground amidst mounting pressure from Germany's newly formed government.

What is important to note is how the negotiations of the Council of the Realm and the activities of the Norwegian Nazi Party (NS) stimulated Norwegian resistance. This is reflected in a newspaper cutting entitled "No Norwegians for Sale." This type of article usually led to newspapers becoming Nazified or production being stopped. The Nazi party's "Fritt Folk" (Free People) became the official mouthpiece. However, this only strengthened solidarity among "good Norwegians." To demonstrate their loyalty to king and government the people first waved flags, then they wore paper clips (symbol of unity) on their cuffs and collars. Red pixie hats combined with other white and blue garments were popular. Less obvious defiance came in the form of a red - tipped match worn on one's hat, which stood for "flaming hatred." Resistance brought the leaders together; and out of this cooperation was born, in the autumn of 1941, the Coordinating Committee (KK), which later directed civilian resistance against the enemy, and the NS.

To address the growing resistance movement, the Germans established several concentration camps and prisons in Norway. The better known were Grini on the outskirts of Oslo, Berg in Vestfold County, Arkivet (Kristiansand), Ulven (Bergen), Falstad (Trondheim) and Osen in Nordland. The Germans arrested approximately 50,000 Norwegians during the occupation. Of these, 9000 were consigned to prison camps in Germany.

At the beginning of the Second World War, Norway's merchant navy was the fourth largest in the world, and the modernized mmodernized. The country's greatest contribution to the Allied war effort abroad was the hazardous service of sailors in the merchant navy. The modern Norwegian merchant fleet carried oil, war material and food to soldiers and civilians all over the world and to all arenas of the Second World War. Both sides were aware of the Norwegian merchant navy's great importance and did their best to secure as many ships as possible. Quisling ordered all Norwegian ships to make for German, Italian or neutral ports. Captains of every Norwegian ship ignored the demand. They responded to the appeal by placing their services at the disposal of the Allies.

In the Resistance Museum at Akershus Castle pictures and articles depicted the campaign in northern Norway. On the one side, defeat and cessation of hostilities south of Trondheim; on the other side, pictures from the naval battles off Narvik, where the Norwegian Royal Navy scored a notable success by sinking 10 German destroyers and their supply ships. The battle marks the dividing line between Norway's struggling resistance in the south and organized warfare in the north.

Throughout the war, the underground press fulfilled an important role in spreading news and information and in maintaining a high standard of morale among Norwegians. The first underground newspaper appeared as early as the summer of 1940. By the autumn of 1943, there were some 60 in circulation. About 5,000 women and men assisted in their production and distribution.

My beginning starts amidst sketchy stories and patchwork speculations. Its genesis is located in Norway with the death of my mother's mother in 1939. Bjorg was only thirteen when a distraught and angry father dealt with the care of eight children. Later stories depict, at best, a sad and remorseful family situation. The father parceled out his children; some sent to relatives and others farmed out to labor in the fields. Like so many others, it was a fractured family brought about by the horrors of war.

Germany's occupation of the country, including my family's town of Fredrikstad, became a reality of life. At varying levels, the siblings participated in Norway's Resistance Movement. I learned at the family reunion that my mother and her boyfriend Frank were an active part of the resistance effort. She and her sisters became couriers. As young runners, in their mid and late teens, they were less conspicuous carrying information, publications, even supplies from one location to another. It was dangerous work; detection resulted in death, imprisonment or backbreaking work at an isolated labor camp. Underground military groups worked in conjunction with civilian resistance to assist the Allied and Norwegian intelligence operations. The groups were useful in reporting the movements of German vessels and the transport of troops and material.

The dangerous nature of their work came close to home for two of my aunts. Karin, an older sister to my mother, was caught passing information and placed in jail resulting in close surveillance of other members of the family. Klara, the oldest of the eight siblings was married to Leif. They bore two children, Wilhelm and Helen. During the occupation of Norway, Leif was a very active participant in the Resistance effort. During a family reunion in 2006, Wilhelm shared a story with many of us regarding the lengths his father would go to assist the movement against Germany. As the story goes, it was approaching nightfall when, acting on urgent instructions, Lief devised a plan to smuggle ammunition across town to assist fellow fighters. Patrolling soldiers were closely scrutinizing everyone on the streets. Time was of the essence. Lief carefully laid his two children in a baby carriage before starting his critical stroll across town. Unbeknownst to the passing soldiers, the two infants (including Wilhelm the story - teller) were lying atop cases of explosives.

To resist the Nazification of society, the people protested at every turn, especially in the schools and most of the churches. Thus, Quisling's NS party only got a modest grip on the "people's soul" and could only exist under the protection of the German armed forces.

The Nazi Party endeavored in February 1942 to "organize" all teachers. Schools and young people were generally the Nazis' primary targets, toward which the Nazis made every effort to infiltrate their propaganda and ideology. Outraged by the resistance in the schools, Quisling, having been granted greater authority, ordered obligatory membership for teachers in a "Teachers' Front," described by a pro-Quisling newspaper as "a strait jacket for all those who are unwilling to do their duty to the State and to Norwegian Youth."

The teachers, like those in other professions, had long since set up an underground communication system. Following instructions sent through this network, 1200 teachers refused to accept the restrictions. The teachers had refused to sign the declaration of loyalty to the Nazi authorities, promising to instruct their pupils "in the new spirit". Over a thousand teachers were arrested. A hundred thousand parents supported them. Thirteen hundred more teachers were then arrested, and nearly half were sent through a series of brutal camps to the Arctic. A museum showcase contains a model of the S/S Skjaerstad, in which 500 teachers, crammed in the holds, were transported from Trondheim to Kirkenes for hard labor. Photos depict the arrested teachers in concentration camps and in railway wagons on their way to internment in the far north. In protest, the schools remained closed for two months.

Efforts to centralize sports and youth activities were no more successful. The young simply boycotted the Nazi competitions. Church leaders ignored the German hierarchy and declared unacceptable "the forced mobilization of all children from the age of nine or ten upward." Church leaders also resisted Nazification. Their efforts surfaced with the posting of a pastoral letter of February 1941 on the Church and the Constitution. All Christian denominations joined forces against the Nazis.

In the spring of 1942 the struggle between the Church and the Nazi authorities came to a head. On February 24th the bishops resigned their offices. Shortly thereafter the pastoral letter, "The Church's Foundation," was read from the pulpit in practically every church in the country. Of a total of 858 incumbent clergy, 797 resigned their positions, and they had the support of their congregations. Many leading churchmen of various denominations were arrested. The bishops and 55 other clergy were interned and an additional 127 banished from their parishes. One showcase in the Resistance Museum contains a wooden cross, made of three separate parts that were kept hidden by three prisoners in the Bardufoss concentration camp and assembled whenever they had an opportunity of coming together for worship. The resistance shown by the Church and the schools in 1942 proved a powerful stimulus to morale, and told the outside world just where Norway stood.

But darker days were yet to come, again impacting the Stromnes family and the decisions Bjorg would feel forced to take.

When the German campaign in Russia developed into a protracted winter war, German supply shortages intensified and as a result there was wholesale requisitioning from the Norwegian population. A public proclamation was issued ordering people to hand in blankets, gum, boots, tents, rucksacks and "windcheaters". The penalty for failure to comply was three years in prison or, in extenuating circumstances, a fine of up to 100,000 Norwegian crowns. The lack of food and other supplies during the occupation years defined daily life in all the towns and villages. In normal times, its low degree of self-sufficiency in food production forced Norway to rely on imports and supplies. The 400,000 Germans on Norwegian soil compounded the problems. Per capita, more Germans occupied Norway than any other country during the war.

The food situation during the occupation worsened. There was extensive rationing and the amount of food available for distribution diminished. Leather goods disappeared totally and were replaced by paper shoes with wooden soles; paper handbags, blankets and sleeping bags of paper were substitutions for the real thing.

There was a special emphasis directed toward the underground press, which reached a peak in the difficult year of 1943. By February 1, 1944, this important resistance activity suffered a severe blow with the arrest of 203 persons, resulting in the closing down of 13 underground papers.

In June 1944, the Allied Supreme Commander, General Dwight D. Eisenhower, directed that the Norwegian Resistance be trained and equipped to serve as an offensive reserve force. Sabotage of shipping and other selected targets would continue and would intensify when the time was ripe. The Supreme Command were determined to utilize the skills and dedication of the Norwegian Resistance force as a factor for defeating the German military. The British committed to providing the Resistance with 40,000 uniforms, while the Americans supplied winter equipment for 30,000.

The war would continue for another year, but on June 7, 1945, five years to the day following the king's departure from Tromso, Norway welcomed back King Haakon VII, the very symbol of national resistance. The occupation was now at an end, and constitutionally established law and order could now function for the first time since the occupation. The Norwegian people could now tackle the task of rebuilding their country.

However, it wasn't just the country that needed rebuilding. Broken families, separated by the ravages of the war and its consequences struggled to piece together their lives. In the Fall of 1943, Bjorg's distraught father was frightened by the family situation; brothers and sisters were being parceled out to various relatives; food supplies were sparse; danger and death reigned all around; clothing was wanting and although he did not know about it, his teenage daughter, Bjorg, was pregnant and no doubt, overwhelmed by her circumstances. In this grim, convoluted setting, tension and stress must have weighed heavy on my mother's shoulders. What should she do?

The pregnant, seventeen-year old girl felt compelled to leave her homeland, so that her unborn child might have food, be sheltered and survive the chaotic world surrounding her. She left her family behind to avoid the shame of being an unwed mother in Norway, to hide her secret from a childhood boyfriend, and to find a safe haven for herself and her child in some foreign country. She departed toward an unknown future, collateral damage; in a war that filled her with pain and anguish. Her pact with herself was to keep silent about her past.

I inherited that attribute more than I would have imagined.

Norway was of primary interest to Adolph Hitler. He anticipated the access to Norwegians as a valuable source of good Nordic blood. The Lebensborn Project started in Norway during the spring of 1941. The acting Reichskommisariat, rather than Heinrich Himmler's SS (Secret Service), was primarily responsible for the content and emphasis of the new program. This shifted the primary focus of the Lebensborn objective in Norway. Unlike in Germany, the primary purpose of the "Race Policy" program was to prevent abortions, increase birth rates and help women giving birth to these children. The program acted as a German public institution for welfare and Mother Child Care Centers. The United Nation (UN) in 1948 registered 626 children delivered by Norwegian mothers in Germany. One can only conjecture what drove so many Norwegian women to Germany. Bjorg was one of those women noted by the United Nations. I was one of those 626 children born of Norwegian parents, in Germany.

Norway's involvement throughout World War II was far from neutral. A country known for its spectacular fjords and great Olympic skiers played an integral role in Hitler's quest for military dominance. Hitler was obsessed with the use of Norwegian women to procreate boys as a means for perpetuating his diabolical plan for an "Aryan Race." It's the closest example of an "antichrist" I can imagine.

Our visit to Norway helped me clarify the sickening circumstances influencing my mother and compelling her to flee Norway. I began to better understand how she must have agonized to make the choice of sparing her family and boyfriend the added shame and ridicule of being a pregnant, teenager. The idea of escaping to Germany, to conceive her unwed child, was the only sensible decision - protecting the honor of her family and finding a safe place to bare her baby was the lesser of two evils.

That piece of history certainly charged the atmosphere of my pending family reunion. What would my first cousins, aunts and uncles think of me? When I walked into their midst, what would they say to me? What had only been a story, prior to the moment I entered the scene, would suddenly be flesh and blood. I was filled with questions. Did B.J. really tell them enough about me? . . . What did she say? . . . Will they be angry, disappointed, curious, indifferent or all of the above? I wondered if I'd look like any of them? . . . Would there be a language barrier? . . . Would I really look like a Stromnes, which Elin said I did? . . . Would I carry the stench of being perceived as an illegitimate child? The scroll of unending questions continued to unroll in my mind as Bonnie, Tim and I entered Alf and May Einar's home located alongside the Oslo Fjord in the town of Tonsberg.

I was such a fool to doubt. I should have realized that if Bjorg's siblings were one iota as accepting as the Brodwall family the reunion would be a warm and accepting experience. It was. The host family received us with open arms and with a graciousness that immediately put me at ease. I think I did more staring and asking of questions than the gathered family members. There were moments around the dinner table, when I became the center of attention. I realized everybody was trying to fill in the blank spaces of the family tree. The general consensus was that I carried the physical traits of the Stromnes branch of the family. Both Bonnie and Tim felt I looked like my first cousin Kare Mathison.

The family reunion was a resounding success and the highlight of my week in Norway. It was more awe inspiring than the train ride across the mountain tops from Oslo to Bergen; our numerous stories matched the melodic tones of Norway's famous composer Edvard Grieg's Piano Concerto, Varinen; and the family homestead of Fredrikstad gave me a firmer grounding than any boat anchored in Oslo's harbor. The earlier time spent with Erik, Elin and Even Brodwall began the process of untying the knots of doubts that I'd accumulated wondering if I would be accepted as a family member.

I finally know that the Norwegian blood coursing through my veins is real. I have no doubt that the loving spirit and strength of my Nordic family is also mine. A week earlier, I found where I was born. By the time I left Norway for America, I uncovered my roots and became part of a new family, which had accepted me with open arms. At the gathering I saw, tasted and felt my roots. The family setting reaffirmed for me that no orphan should be denied the knowledge of his or her beginnings. Feeling my past and sitting among the branches of my family tree gave me purpose and new meaning for the future.

CHAPTER IX

In Pursuit of Clarity

"What we have done for ourselves alone dies with us. What we have done for others and the world remains and is immortal."

Albert Pine (English author, d1851)

It was a fall day one year and five months after my summer family reunion in Norway. I was in fellowship hall of my church in Vernon, Connecticut helping to lead a Confirmation Class overnighter.

The sound of the church's kitchen phone barely disrupted the attention of the 15 teenagers. Linda, the church's Minister of Christian Education, rose from her seat and quickly moved to silence the intrusion.

"Hello, this is First Congregational Church, can I help you?"

I turned to check out what was happening. A concerned expression began to form on Linda's face; her wrinkled brow was a sure sign that something was terribly wrong. I first thought it might be an emergency call from a parent - a car accident, an illness or a sudden need to come to the church and take their child away from our abbreviated youth retreat. Linda hooked the receiver back onto the cradle and beckoned me over.

Never taking my eyes off her, I pushed myself up from the floor. Linda's slumped shoulders, quiet demeanor and tentative movements aroused my suspicion. The fact that she replaced the phone heightened my anxiety.

"It's for you, Peter." 7

"Is everything alright?"

Linda shrugged in response. "Bonnie didn't elaborate, only that it was serious and she needed to talk to you as soon as possible."

"I'll telephone her from my office . . . it'll be quieter there."

As class teachers, Linda and I were supervising the Fall Retreat for our confirmation class - consisting of boys and girls who were in the ninth grade. We were about halfway through Mel Gibson's emotional movie, *The Passion of The Christ*.

"I hope everything is going to be alright," Linda said in a worried tone.

She turned to look at the teenagers, sprawled all over the floor, eating junk food, their eyes riveted to the movie screen. Jesus' trial, a miscarriage of justice, was unfolding before them. The scene was filled with a raucous mob screaming, " . . . release Barabbas to us . . . Crucify him! Crucify Jesus!"

"I think they're pretty occupied for the moment."

I gave a weak smile and whispered, "If you need anything, come and get me." I turned and headed down the hall. I doubt any of the boys and girls even noticed my departure.

Once in the office, I called Bonnie from my cell phone. "Hi love, what's up?"

"Peter, I'm in the church parking lot sitting in my car. I called earlier, but you didn't answer your cell phone."

"I never heard it. We're watching the movie and it gets pretty intense."

"I guessed as much, but I can't get into the church because all the doors are locked. That's when I decided to call the church number."

"Come to the office side of the church and I'll let you in." I went to the door, opened it and was immediately embraced by Bonnie.

"It concerns B.J. Your sister, Sandra, called and wants to speak to you . . ."

"Okay, let's go inside where it's warmer and you can tell me everything you know."

We clasped hands, stepped back inside and headed for my office. I knew the news was bad, so I lowered the blinds for added privacy.

"Peter, I had to tell you the news in person." Bonnie gave me another kiss and a reassuring hug before leading me to the couch. "Let's sit down."

A sickening feeling came over me. I knew what was coming and was already fighting back tears. Just a few days before I spoke with Sandra and she forewarned me of our mother's failing condition, " . . . it's about Mom. We're going to pull her tubes and start making funeral arrangements. You know, stuff like that." And there were e - mails from B.J.' husband that redirected my thoughts to what Bonnie was telling me.

"Hunter called earlier and told me your mother had passed away only a few hours ago."

Before another word could be uttered, in one motion, I fell against Bonnie and began to weep. All I could think about was Hunter's most recent e - mail and how I had wished I could have been with B.J at the hospital. His message left no doubt; her final days with us were coming to a close. I had the note in my wallet. As soon as I could see beyond the tears, I pulled out the single sheet of paper and slowly - out loud - read the message to Bonnie.

Hunter wrote, "It's not good here because I'm losing Bjorg. The doctor at the hospital tells us her time is short. In addition to her emphysema, she also had a stroke and a hemorrhage on the left side of her brain. This left her right side immobile. With breathing and feeding tubes in her throat, she couldn't talk to us but she could open her eyes and look at us. She squeezed my hand."

Two days later Hunter had sent another email updating my mother's condition. I couldn't see through my tears to read it, so Bonnie read it for me.

"We all gave her kisses (including a big one from you) and verbal goodbyes . . . I hate typing this but felt you should know her status. Now we wait together for that final moment."

I have no clue how long Bonnie and I embraced. By the time the tears dried up, my sore chest, aching eyes and pounding headache told me it was time to move on to the next step.

I asked Bonnie, "Did Sandra say anything else?"

"She wants you to call her tonight or tomorrow morning."

"I'll call her tomorrow. They're probably busy making decisions and a slew of arrangements for the memorial service. It makes more sense for me to wait until I can clear my mind and be coherent."

Bonnie squeezed my hand. "Do you want to come home tonight? I know Linda would understand."

"I need to stay. It's our annual retreat for the class and I don't want to disrupt the retreat anymore than necessary. Later tonight, I'm leading a discussion about major symbols woven throughout the story. Besides, we need a male presence to handle curfew and I'm in charge of tomorrow morning's closing circle. I'll be fine; besides, I know the kids will be good for me. They always give off positive energy and that will help."

"Are you sure?"

"Yes, I'm certain."

"If I can do anything to help, let me know - promise?" Bonnie rubbed my back as she spoke.

Her touch was already helping to bolster my spirit and settle my nerves. "You came when I needed you most; go get some sleep and I'll be fine." I hugged her tightly which helped to hold back my tears. I took a deep breath; it was time to be strong.

As Bonnie drove away, my thoughts took me back to my dad's death. We were in Salt Lake City and he died the day before the church's big Christmas

Eve service. I managed in 1986 and knew I needed to do the same, now. The agony of my thoughts kept me awake all night.

It seemed too soon before Bonnie and I boarded a plane to start our flight cross-country to Los Angeles, California. It was deja vu as we walked down the terminal with luggage in tow; we located the rental section of the airport, completed the necessary paperwork for a car and headed for the nearest exit. Once again, we were speeding eastward on an expressway, heading toward Banning - a small town thirty minutes west of Palm Springs.

When we arrived, Hunter greeted us at the door. He was the only one at home. It was late and Sandra had already gone back to her apartment. He looked worn, but graciously greeted us with a warm, "Hello," on a cool evening.

"Peter . . . Bonnie . . . I'm glad to see you two arrived safe and sound. It's so nice that you took the time to come. I know Bjorg would have been pleased."

As always, he was attentive to our needs. "Would you two like something to drink . . . a bite to eat?"

"Water is fine for me," Bonnie said.

"The regular for me," I grinned.

Hunter motioned for us to find a seat. He went to the kitchen, opened the refrigerator and remembering, from so many of my previous visits, pulled out an ice - cold can of root beer. He plopped some ice - cubes into a tall glass of water for Bonnie.

With drinks in hand, Hunter began outlining our itinerary for the next few days. "I've reserved a motel room not too far from the funeral home. It's centrally located and a short walk from a couple of popular restaurants." He pulled out an area map to help orientate us for the coming days.

"Oh my, look at the time. You folks must be exhausted and here I am keeping you up! It's late and we all need our rest."

"It's way past my bedtime," Bonnie joked. "During the school year, I get up at 5:30a.m and am ready for bed by 9:30p.m."

"Then you two need to get going. I'll see you tomorrow. Can you meet up with us at 10 in the morning? Sandra will be with me and we can make some final decisions and arrangements for the memorial service . . . this is all new to me."

"We'll be there," I said reassuringly.

By the time we were checked into our room, it was past midnight.

The activities of the next couple of days became secondary to the feelings tumbling around in my mind. I was moved that Hunter and Sandra wanted my help with the planning of intimate elements of the memorial service: selecting the best pictures to be displayed, arranging the flowers, discussion of the proper etiquette for family seating and being introduced to the Scandinavian minister who would be officiating for the service.

The memorial service was a wonderful tribute to my mom - her strength, courage and sacrifice were all weaved expertly through the minister's message. On several occasions, I swallowed back private emotions in an effort to remain calm and composed in public.

The funeral home had a tribute page available for anyone who wanted to write parting words in memory of B.J. I wrote the following:

"I remember Mom sitting at the end of the kitchen table, as we stole quick glances toward each other. Over time the looks evolved into chats and eventually insightful conversations. Most importantly, I learned that her love for family included me. Now, my love for Mom continues to grow as I recall her relaxing on her seat listening to all the chatter spilling throughout the room. I'll never forget our times together; it made all the difference in the world. I'll always love you, now and forevermore."

Hunter, Sandra and the rest of the family all made me feel needed and appreciated. At the time, I wasn't completely sure why this was so important to me. During the service and at the reception back at the house, I felt welcome. For the first time all of Mom's children were mingling, talking and eating together in the same room. For the first time, I didn't feel like a half - brother.

On Sunday, Hunter treated the immediate family to brunch at the condo association's clubhouse. As I looked around the table, I reflected on the uniqueness of the situation with my two sisters and three brothers - Sandra, Karin, Bruce and Brian at the table, plus Erik who had returned to Texas for work. I could feel Bjorg's presence amidst the gathered family plus Erik. I gave a private prayer for Hunter. He loves her deeply. Since it was Sunday, my thoughts naturally recalled a text from the Book of Revelation:

"And I heard a great voice from the throne saying, 'Behold, the dwelling of God is with all people . . . He will wipe away every tear from their eyes, and death shall be no more, neither shall there be mourning, nor crying, nor pain anymore, for the former things have passed away . . . Write this, for these words are trustworthy and true . . . It is done. I am the Alpha and the Omega, the beginning and the end."

I know we are all God's children. The very thought satisfied my insides like savoring comfort food during stressful times. I smiled, fully aware that for one weekend I'd come full circle into the center of another family - which had suddenly become exceedingly important to me.

I have no idea what the future will bring, but the morning was filled with acceptance, kindness and a love that revealed itself among people who respected and accepted each other. I felt the presence of Bjorg - my Norwegian mom who bore me, sacrificed much so that I might survive a war, and then later accepted me as a part of her new American family. All of us had finally come home to pay our respect and love to our mom. I knew she was still with us that day.

My oldest sister Sandra wrote a wonderful, poetic tribute to our Mother.

POEM OF OUR MOTHER

MOTHER WAS A FIGHTER
HER COURAGE OUTWEIGHED HER FEARS,
NEVER WALLOWING IN SELF PITY,
WHEN OTHERS FOUGHT THEIR TEARS.

TODAY WE HONOR HER VALIANT SPIRIT,
THAT COMES FROM DEEP WITHIN,
SUBMISSION WAS NOT CONSIDERED
HER GOAL HAD ALWAYS BEEN, "TRY, TRY, AGAIN."

MOTHER FOUGHT HARD TO STAY WITH US,
THE POWER OF LOVE WAS STRONG,
LETTING GO WAS NOT AN EASY TASK,
THE BREAK WAS HARD AND LONG.
SO WHEN YOU SEE A STARLIT NIGHT,
THE BRIGHTEST STAR YOU'LL SEE,
SHE ALWAYS SAYS, WE'RE BOUND IN LOVE,
OUR FRIENDSHIP, BROTHERS, SISTER AND ME,
I KNOW THE BRIGHTEST STAR WILL SHINE, BEFORE THE NIGHT IS THRU;
FOR RIGHT NOW I FEEL ALONE, THAT STAR WILL BRING ME THROUGH;

HEAVEN WAS MISSING AN ANGEL.
OUR MOM HAS BEEN CALLED BACK HOME.
REMEMBER, WE ALL ARE BOUND IN LOVE
SHE'LL NEVER REALLY BE FAR AWAY.

The smile never left my face that day, and it always returns when I think of what my mom did for me. I've been blessed, and now I give thanks for every day of life God has granted me. My journey for self-discovery began with Bjorg and continues as I move forward with her in my thoughts.

CHAPTER X

Variation of a Story

"Compassion is the basis of all morality".

Arthur Schopenhaue (German philosopher)

The month following B.J.'s memorial service, I was preoccupied with the mental task of connecting broken links from my past. The collected information stored in my head felt like a desk strewn with papers. Each piece needed to be assembled in an organized fashion, to provide some semblance of clarity for my thoughts.

But how could I tackle such an impossible task?

I elected to address the "organized chaos" spilling out of the darkness of my first five years. The central characters in my convoluted melodrama were Hitler, Bjorg and Hunter, my adoptive parents and me. A thumbnail sketch, scratched in some orderly fashion in my mind, gave direction to my thoughts.

The primary culprit of my early suffering was Hitler's madness. He was the architect and engine of an unjust war. He held the delusional thought that a "Superior Aryan Master Race" existed and could be further developed by "breeding superior ethnic groups," that "inferior social elements of society," should be eradicated, and "elimination of the entire Jewish population" be a critical component of the master plan. He worked to do this by developing a "military force second to none." All in an effort to make sure his world order would prevail. His demented madness permeated every aspect of my childhood: he dismantled my mother's teenage years and drove her to flee her native Norway; and then took her away from me at birth; moreover, he scarred my mind for decades and set into motion a sequence of events that profoundly changed the direction of four lives.

There's no easy way to put it. German soldiers who policed the country with an iron hand occupied Norway. Society judged Bjorg harshly for being unwed and pregnant. To avoid shame and ridicule to her family and her boyfriend, she fled Norway, keeping the birth of her son a secret. As I noted in an earlier chapter, a friend accompanied Bjorg when she fled from Norway to work at a munitions factory outside of Berlin, Germany. While there, a German officer - married with twin daughters - befriended her. When the munitions facility was bombed, they took the pregnant Bjorg to be the nanny for his daughters. Their home was in Kitzingen, Germany.

I believe it was there she was made aware of a German assistance program for pregnant women. Bjorg, I'm certain, recalled how the program in Norway was focused on helping any unwed mother give birth to her child. The Norway program acted through a German public institution for welfare and a Mother Child Care Center. However, the Lebensborn Program in Germany was a mere shadow of the welfare design enacted in Norway.

Being frightened, young and naive, she was unaware of the evil implications of Himmler's version of the Lebensborn Project. Bjorg was initially accepted and enrolled as a category 4 participant - A Norwegian mother with unknown specifics of the father. Bjorg was shocked when her newborn son, Peder Rolf Stromnes, at birth, was immediately taken away from her. I truly believe she never imagined that this would happen to her. Her baby was pure but she was soiled. My mother had become an unwitting victim of Hitler's demented plan, under the supervision of Heinrich Himmler, for perpetuating a "superior race."

And so life begins. Beneath the surface lay a story about fractured lives and a mended soul. It is my story of self - discovery because of Hitler's maddness.

As far as I knew, I was a Norwegian baby, father unknown, born in the Nordrach Nazi Children's Home. The facility was one of eight similar centers, hidden away in secluded places, throughout the German countryside. The plan was for the stolen children to become a major resource for Hitler's youth movement and ultimately his elite fighting force of the future.

During the war's final year, I lived in Nordrach. In October of 1945, Allied Forces bombed the surrounding area and assumed control of this small, mountain village. Only a few orphans survived the attack and escaped. The babies who died were buried in a mass grave - a vain attempt to hide the numbers enrolled at the Children's Home. I survived the bombing and was part of a small contingent transported by train to the farming community of Steinhoering - Himmler's primary headquarters for implementing Hitler's Lebensborn project.

As the war came to a close, all of the Children's Homes in Germany transported their children to this primary center. Within weeks, there were 300 orphans crammed into a three-story building nestled on the outskirts of a small village located approximately 30 minutes southeast of Munich. I lived there for a little more than two years.

History substantiates my feelings and inner pain; the years following the war were not good years for Hitler's babies. As offspring of the Lebensborn Project we were unwanted, neglected, mistreated and scorned by all who remembered the intentions of the program. Every orphan, I believe, felt the wrath of an angry society.

After my third birthday, I was relocated to Prien. I was the youngest of seven children at the pre-school center for orphans. It was there I learned how it felt to be loved for the first time and how to appreciate Tante Maria. It was here where my future mom and dad would first see me - Chaplain and Mrs. A.E.K. Brenner.

A year later, after my arrival at Prien, Chaplain Brenner and his attractive wife began their search to adopt an orphan they could take back to the States. Their search took them to the tiny orphanage at Prien, where they met its director, Tante Marie. They saw Peter, a little boy just a few months over 3 years old. They immediately knew he was the child they could not conceive. Complications immediately emerged. The boy the couple sought was of Norwegian parents, born in Germany and trying to be brought to America. The red tape was horrendous.

The German officials finally declared that the only way this adoption would take place was if they found the Norwegian mother and convinced her to sign a consent form assigning the child into their care.

I couldn't help but recall the conversation I had with Hunter following the memorial service. With a smile on his face, Hunter Johnson recalled how he first met Bjorg. He centered on the first meeting of my Dad, a teenage girl and himself - a young army officer. The three had met in Kitzingen during the Allied Occupation of Germany.

He began piecing the story together.

There was a time during the post - war period, when all non - German residents were required to report to the American Embassy in Wurzburg. There, Bjorg met Joanne, an American Red Cross girl, who befriended her and gave her a job at nearby Kitzingen Air Base. Bjorg was in the sewing room helping to repair clothing. Later she was put to work as a waitress in the Officer's Mess Hall at the base. She did her job well but disliked the insulting comments and improper advances by some of the officers. Bjorg complained to the officer in charge, Lt. Al, a good friend of hers, and a bit later she was given the job of managing the doughnut and coffee shop in the hanger at the flight line.

Bjorg became attracted to Hunter, who liked chocolate doughnuts; she always saved one for him. Over time they grew closer. One day, Hunter was encouraged to attend a dance at the Officer's Club in downtown Kitzingen. His roommate took him to the club insisting that he had someone he should meet. Bjorg didn't speak much English and he didn't know any Norwegian but they danced and got along very well. From that night on, they regularly met at the club. It was love at first sight.

Hunter received notification that his time in the military was growing short; he would soon be going home to California. Realizing that he could not leave without Bjorg, he insisted they be married immediately. Bjorg was concerned; if she agreed to get married so soon, she might never get back to Norway to see her family. Hunter promised that someday, he'd take her back home.

For the marriage to take place both had to have official approval by the base chaplain and the base commander. This was accomplished with just a few meetings. Once the official documents were signed, Hunter and Bjorg were ready to get married. The wedding was consummated on July 1st as a required civil ceremony at the burgermeister's office on July 6 and then at a small, local church on July 8, 1946.

*   *   *

Dad also had a version of the couple's wedding. He was certain Bjorg was my biological mother. His wedding records noted that the boy they wanted to adopt was of Norwegian descent. During the pre-wedding consultation, Bjorg had told him she had fled Norway for family reasons. Also, the birth date of March 18, 1944 coincided with Bjorg's story of how she had born a child, out of wedlock while working in Germany. She lost him a year later during a bombing. Following the war, publications were circulated throughout Europe listing the names of orphans. It was an effort of connecting children with parents from whom they had been separated during the war. While stationed in Germany, Dad came across this list and recalled my name - Peder Rolf Stromnes. A review of his notes on Bjorg and Hunter's wedding and the wedding certificate verified that Bjorg was Norwegian and carried the same last name as the orphan listed in the article. My dad was confused by the names noted on the certificate: Bjorg and Hunter were referred to as Monica and Johnny. The records showed they had moved to Riverside, California.

He decided to call the couple and lay out the enormous, procedural difficulty confronting him and how Bjorg was the only person, who could help him. Following some chitchat, the spirit of the telephone conversation went as follows:

"Monica, I think Trudy and I have found your son?"

"That's impossible. I visited the mass grave in Nordrach; where he's buried," she answered.

"Are you positive?" my Dad continued.

"Absolutely. I've already prayed and said my goodbye."

He decided to shift the subject to a different, less painful area.

"The information on my wedding form shows that you have a different first name. Why?"

"Actually, my name is Bjorg. Nobody could pronounce it, so Hunter helped me pick out an easier one that I liked."

"Hunter?"

She laughed. "Hunter is Johnny. Everybody thought his first name sounded like a last name so they started calling him Johnny."

"Well, whatever your names are, I have an important request to make. Would you willing agree to fill out a form stating that the boy we want to adopt is yours? Signing the papers will allow us to adopt Peter as our own? It's the only way we can bring him back to the States."

There was an awkward silence at the other end of the line. A few moments later, Bjorg was back on line. "Chaplain Brenner . . . In my heart, I know my son is dead. I prayed at his graveside. You need to understand that Stromnes is a very common Norwegian name. Because you were so kind to give us a church wedding, I would be honored to do anything I can to help you adopt this child. I will say he is mine and sign whatever papers are necessary to help you two adopt him."

"Bjorg, I don't think you can begin to imagine how much this means to us. I promise, we will keep in touch with you and take great care of this little boy."

"I know you will and I thank you for all that you have done for us. We would like to have your family visit us if you're ever in California."

"I promise, we will."

Two years later the paper work was completed and I was riding on a train from Prien to Munich to catch a flight to New York City and meet my adopted parents - Chaplain and Mrs. A.E. K. Brenner.

My dad promised Monica and Johnny, now living with their real names B.J. and Hunter, that he would keep them informed on my whereabouts plus my development through the years. B.J. said it was fine with her if that was what they wanted to do. Still insisting her son was dead; my biological mother signed the adoption papers.

May 14, 1949, I flew to America.

Fortunately, the child within each of us is never completely lost to the mishandling of adults. That which defines us, however, takes its form from our earliest experiences and contacts. I wasn't responsible for my beginnings. I was only an expression of the turbulent times. I learned that orphans, like me, are not illegitimate children. I was the collateral damage of a madman and not the architect of my own beginning. I was frightened, so I tried on several masks to find one that would hide the shame, anger, pain, abandonment and rejection swirling throughout me. I was only five and didn't know any better. Now, I'm in my late 60's and understand that I'm the author of who I am now.

CHAPTER XI

Korea

"When a needy person stands at your door, God himself stands at his side".

Hebrew Proverb

I was informed an author should know the ending of his book before laying pen to paper. But what if the ending is a mystery that whets the appetite only to start a journey with no clear beginning? I believe memoirs fit into such a category. I didn't recognize or see the ending of my story until I had the courage to face it.

I addressed my past during a two-week visit to South Korea. The clues were as rewarding as the dawning of a new day.

During the winter of 2006, Mia Kang, a piano accompanist for Bonnie's select choir at Central Elementary School, Simsbury, Connecticut, invited us to participate in her Friends of Music in Korea, an International Music Camp.

We said no, explaining that, "Our summer vacation will be a three - week trip to Germany, France and Norway. My purpose is to locate the orphanages I'd lived in and visit Norwegian relatives." We declined again in 2007, on the premise that "I'm feverishly working on my memoir and need more time to write and do research."

In 2006, Mia insisted once again, "Both of you have to come to Korea."

I hesitated before answering, "My book is almost complete and I need a dedicated block of time to organize my chapters, rewrite and formulate the ending. Maybe we can make it next year?" I said in an apologetic tone.

Mia, who lost her sister in 2007 "None of us know how much time we have left. You must come this year." I heard her take a deep breath before continuing, "I will help you contact the Onyang Brenner Orphanage and arrange for our musicians to give the children a concert."

I relented some and said, "We'll think on it." I already knew Bonnie wouldn't go to Korea without me and our sons couldn't fathom why we weren't jumping like rabbits at the opportunity to go.

Earlier in the week, Tim declared, "You can't afford not to go. If you don't go to Korea, you'll regret it for the rest of your lives."

Our thoughts, however, remained steeped in the excitement of Erik's earlier graduation ceremony. He earned a Masters of Administration degree from the University of Massachusetts. Later that evening, Bonnie and I were driving west on the Mass Pike. Her cell phone rang. It was Mia.

"Hi," she chimed. "The deadline for buying your airline tickets for Korea is tonight. In three hours, I will be purchasing our seats. It's not too late to join us for the music festival."

Silence surrounded us. The idea of actually flying to Korea had been barely a blip on our radar screen. We looked at each other and in that instant said, "Yes, we want to go." Bonnie transacted the necessary information over the phone and before we crossed the border into Connecticut our tickets for Korea were confirmed.

On July 4, 2007, Mia, Bonnie and I were in flight on Asiana Air, headed for Chung - Kang College, Eachun, South Korea. Mia arranged for us to be seated in the business class section of the airplane. The accommodations were a welcome upgrade for a 13 - hour flight. In a strange way, it felt familiar to my flight from Germany to New York City - I was being well cared for.

I knew then, we'd made the right decision.

"Friends of Music in Korea" was a dream being realized by Mia Kang and her husband, Shin. The music festival was held at a site tucked between two mountains, near a ski resort and on a college campus one hour south of Seoul.

The formula was simple but meaningful in its implementation. During the morning and afternoon, six skilled musicians shared their expertise and dedication to instruct talented youth striving to better their musical skills. In the evenings, we played games, had talent shows, visited area sites, tasted wonderful Korean food and presented concerts (at two hospitals, one for the college community and a final performance for the parents and friends of the music camp). Bonnie was bubbling with excitement for the opportunity to teach voice and choral technique to such motivated boys and girls.

I was honored when Mia invited Bonnie to take students, instructors and some parents to perform a classical concert at the orphanage my father established during the Korean Conflict. The facility is located in Asan.

Thirty-seven children, between the ages of 5 and 18, greeted us when our bus rolled onto the grounds. There were twenty - one girls and sixteen boys plus a smattering of staff.

Paul Kim, the grandson of Rev. Donald Chau, was the current executive director and only person who spoke English. That certainly helped the six instructors and me. Our students were Korean and immediately began to talk, relate and play games with the children - basketball, soccer, dancing and, of course, music. I thought what a great bonding experience among the children.

We gathered in the community room that also served as the dining room and activity center. The facility is now a home and a part of the government's Social Services Department. Paul Kim and the board of directors were instructed, within the past few years, to change the name of the orphanage to better reflect the new era. They were instructed to drop the name Brenner from the title. The program is now known as "Joyful Orphanage." I sensed that Paul felt awkward that, after all these years, the name of the orphanage no longer displayed the name Brenner in the title. I assured him, "You selected a wonderful name. It captures the spirit of the children."

Paul went on to explain, "The enrollment has a different make up from when your father and my grandfather took the children off the war - torn streets of Onyang."

"How is it different?" I interjected.

"Why, the children are brought to us. Of the 37 enrolled, six were abandoned. They were left at stores, shopping malls and doorsteps just days after their birth. They have no knowledge of where or who their parents might be. In the narrowest sense, these six are the only orphans in our program. The rest of the children came from abusive homes or neglectful parents. Some single parents have visitation rights, allowing the mother to stay overnight with her child in the guest room."

Despite their difficult situation, we felt the joyful spirit of the children as they performed for us and then settled down to listen to a classical concert. I'm certain that every child who experienced the music felt privileged. Currently, a piano is their one and only instrument, a gift of a generous donor. I couldn't help but see the joy in the face of the young girl as she played a selection from the Phantom of the Opera, which she taught herself to play and for the rest of us to enjoy. It brought to mind the statement, "Teach an orphan a tune on an instrument and the instrument will become a friend for life."

It is a truism; I know it to be accurate because of my own experience as an orphan. As a child of five, my Mom and Dad bought me a fuzzy and cuddly stuffed animal - Curious George. Sixty + years later, I still have my buddy perched next to my side of the bed watching over me with a watchful eye. It sounds silly until one understands that this stuffed character was the first item that I could call my own. It has been a lifetime friend through out our travels around the world. And so it will be for any orphan who is given his or her own instrument to make music. It will be a friend for life.

At the end of the presentations, I gave Paul a framed picture of his grandfather and my dad standing before the tent that housed the original 55 orphans taken off the streets of Onyang in 1951; he promised that the story of how the orphanage was started would never be lost to the children under their care and guidance. I felt reassured to hear him make the promise. In turn, I received an inscribed plate with the following Korean text:

In appreciation of Brenners

You have shown us the love and the
care to our children and made them
feel welcome at the site you have established.
The love of our children to you
will be in there hearts forever.

By 8:30pm the concert contingent had boarded the bus and started their two-hour ride back to the college campus. Bonnie and I elected to stay an extra night. We wanted more time with the children.

The next day, after breakfast, we hung around with the younger children, as the older ones, in uniform, scattered from the premises and headed off to public school. My attention focused on a five-year old boy, the youngest and smallest of the 37 children. His stature reminded me of when I was five and about to leave Germany. I taught him how to high five, cluck his tongue and say my name. He taught me how to make funny faces. There wasn't much communication, but we both understood how to laugh and smile a lot. By the time we left, he was waving and clucking his tongue. I gave him thumbs up as our car pulled out of the driveway; he mimicked me and then flashed a huge smile. I wondered how many times he'd seen a friend leave. It was a good morning for both of us.

Paul showed us around Asan. My thoughts, however, brought me back to my new buddy.

I saw myself in him: He was tiny; his mind was inquisitive; he liked being around people - even if they were strangers; and his smile although partially hidden was ready to surface with a little encouragement. My hope for him was that he'd be wanted by loving parents who adored him; that he'd find friends who would value him for who he was; and that he'd not be afraid to discover his whole life - from beginning to end.

After a quick tour of the area and before we needed to leave, Paul Kim presented me a framed set of Korean masks. I looked up the meaning of the Tal - nori (Ha noe village) to see if it might have any significance to my journey. It did.

Korea adopted Chinese characters prior to the invention of their own unique alphabet under King - Se - jong (1397 - 1450); they still use Chinese characters extensively. Therefore, the original meaning of the Tal - nori (Tal play), or Tal - chum (Tal dance), is a play or dance that helps shed one's stress and grief. During the Koryo Dynasty, there was a considerable amount of social tension and the lower classes found a way to relieve not only their everyday stresses, but also tensions, which existed among the many social classes in Korea through the Tal - nori. I learned that my mask was designed to disguise and shield me from another person's judgment. My mask is a warm smile, conversational chitchat and quick humor. I'm like a smooth stone skipping across water, touching lots of people and places but not for any extended stay. It's how I wanted to protect myself. Experience tells me that perception is reality, even if we try to convince people otherwise. I wanted to control how much the outside world would know about my inner life. Like my mother, I kept it a secret for over 60 years. It's a form of self-preservation and the most basic instinct of mankind. I understand why B.J. did what she needed to do. That knowledge gives me permission to love and forgive her in the same breath.

Believe my Dad built a lasting orphanage so I might see and feel the part of my history I was afraid to face. He knew, one day, I would visit Onyang Brenner Orphanage (JOYFUL ORPHANAGE): a difficult world filled with challenges; a place where a child thirsts for acceptance, even as others turn there shoulders and walk the other way. He knew I would see children struggling to be valued; and recognize why we try on masks, and discover a community that cares and has faith that each child will find their own mask of hope and love.

I thank my family for giving me the strength to persevere and the courage to face my past. Behind everyone's journey lies troubled times. The question is how will your meet the challenges necessary to give you hope and strength for the future? Behind my smile resides a genuine, positive spirit. Behind my smile rests a person at peace with his past. My journey of self-discovery has made a major difference in my life. The secrets that hobbled forth from my forgotten region of pain, confusion, shame and ridicule have been recast. I am no longer a slave to my past; I am, in part, the architect of my own future. My mind is filled with clarity of purpose, honor, confidence and self - assurance. I pray each of you may be so richly blessed.

References

Norwegian Encyclopedia

1. "Cruel World: The Children of Europe in the Nazi Web" by Lynn H. Nicholas
2. "Norges Hjemmefrontmuseum: Norway's Resistance Museum
3. "Norway and World War II" by Tor Dagre (Ministry of Foreign Affairs)

Edwards Brothers, Inc.
Thorofare, NJ USA
November 18, 2011